C0-APE-899

355.0330536 Martin
M381u   The unstable Gulf

**Glendale College
Library**

The Unstable Gulf

DISCARD

The Unstable Gulf

Threats from Within

Lenore G. Martin
Emmanuel College

LexingtonBooks
D.C. Heath and Company
Lexington, Massachusetts
Toronto

355.0330536
M38121

Library of Congress Cataloging in Publication Data

Martin, Lenore G.
   The unstable Gulf.

   Bibliography: p.
   Includes index.
   1. Persian Gulf Region—National security.
2. Persian Gulf Region—Defenses. 3. United States—
Military policy. 4. Soviet Union—Military policy.
I. Title.
UA830.M36 1984   355'.033053'6   82–47681
   ISBN 0–669–05558–1 (alk. paper)

Copyright © 1984 by D.C. Heath and Company

All rights reserved. No part of this publication may be reproduced or
transmitted in any form or by any means, electronic or mechanical,
including photocopy, recording, or any information storage or retrieval
system, without permission in writing from the publisher.

Published simultaneously in Canada

Printed in the United States of America on acid-free paper

International Standard Book Number: 0–669–05558–1

Library of Congress Catalog Card Number: 82–47681

8/85

To my children and theirs . . .
for a world of peace and security

Contents

Contents

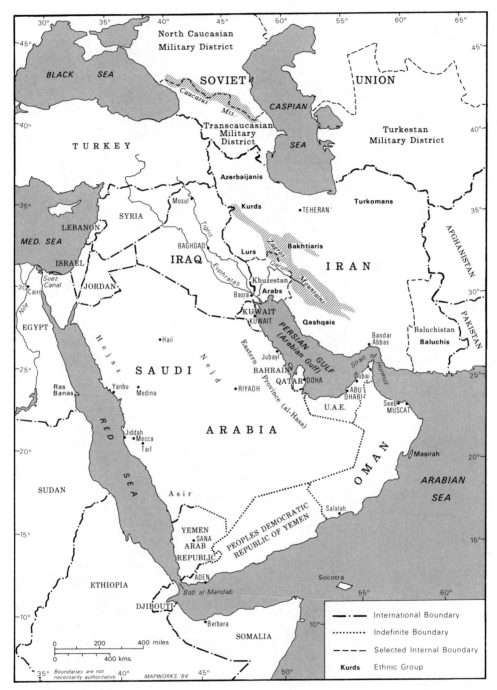

Map 1. The Gulf Region

Map 2. Iraq and Iran

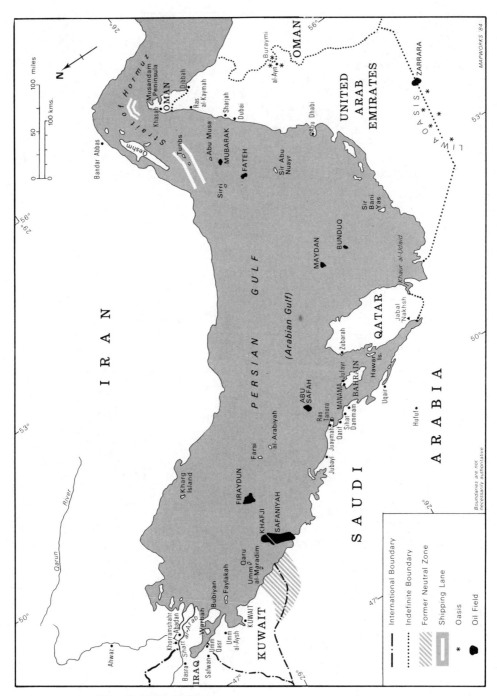

Map 3. The Gulf Sheikhdoms

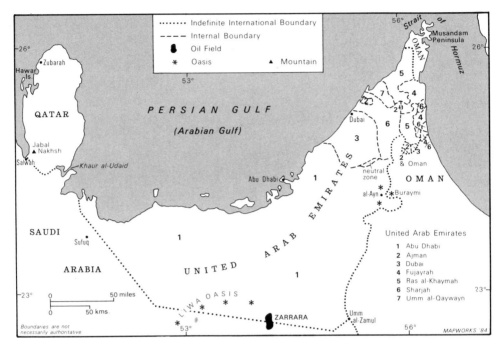

Map 4. The United Arab Emirates

Legend:
- ········· Indefinite International Boundary
- – – – Internal Boundary
- Oil Field
- ✳ Oasis
- ▲ Mountain

PERSIAN GULF
(Arabian Gulf)

QATAR

Zubarah

Hawar Is.

Jabal Nakhsh ▲

Salwah

Khaur al-Udaid

SAUDI

Sufuq

ARABIA

UNITED

ARAB

EMIRATES

Dubai

Abu Dhabi

neutral zone

al-Ayn ✳ Buraymi

OMAN

& Oman

LIWA OASIS

ZARRARA

Umm al-Zamul

United Arab Emirates
1 Abu Dhabi
2 Ajman
3 Dubai
4 Fujayrah
5 Ras al-Khaymah
6 Sharjah
7 Umm al-Qaywayn

Strait of Hormuz

Musandam Peninsula

0 50 miles
0 50 kms.

Boundaries are not necessarily authoritative

MAPWORKS '84

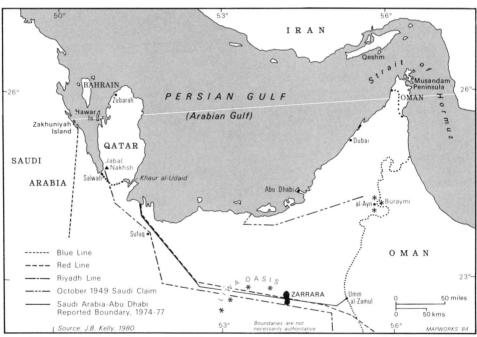

Map 5. The Saudi Arabian Eastern Boundary Claims

IRAN

Qeshm

BAHRAIN

Zubarah

Hawar Is.

Zakhuniyah Island

PERSIAN GULF
(Arabian Gulf)

SAUDI

ARABIA

QATAR

Jabal Nakhsh ▲

Salwah

Khaur al-Udaid

Dubai

Abu Dhabi

Musandam Peninsula

OMAN

Strait of Hormuz

al-Ayn ✳ Buraymi

Sufuq

OMAN

LIWA OASIS

ZARRARA

Umm al-Zamul

Legend:
- ----- Blue Line
- – – – Red Line
- –·–·– Riyadh Line
- –··–··– October 1949 Saudi Claim
- ——— Saudi Arabia-Abu Dhabi Reported Boundary, 1974-77

Source: J.B. Kelly, 1980

0 50 miles
0 50 kms.

Boundaries are not necessarily authoritative

MAPWORKS '84

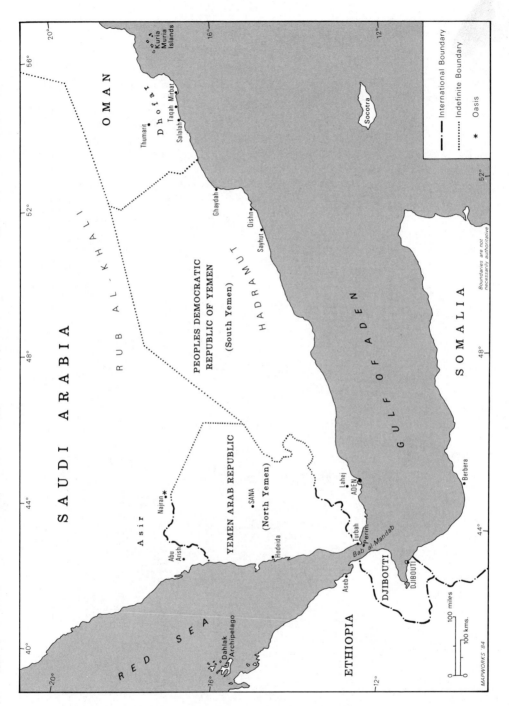

Map 6. The Yemens

Abbreviations

ANM	Arab Nationalist Movement
AWACS	Airborne Warning and Control System aircraft
CENTCOM	U.S. Central Command
FLOSY	Front for the Liberation of Occupied South Yemen
GCC	Gulf Cooperation Council
IEA	International Energy Agency
IKDP	Iranian Kurdish Democratic Party
IRP	Islamic Republican Party
KDPPC	Kurdish Democratic Party's Provisional Command
NDF	National Democratic Front
NDFLOAG	National Democratic Front for the Liberation of Oman and the Arabian Gulf
NLF	National Liberation Front
OAPEC	Organization of Arab Petroleum Exporting Countries
OECD	Organisation for Economic Cooperation and Development
OPEC	Organization of Petroleum Exporting Countries
PDRY	People's Democratic Republic of Yemen (South Yemen)
PFLO	Popular Front for the Liberation of Oman
PFLOAG	Popular Front for the Liberation of Oman and the Arabian Gulf; also known as the Popular Front for the Liberation of the Occupied Arabian Gulf
PFLP	Popular Front for the Liberation of Palestine
PUK	Patriotic Union of Kurdestan

RDF   Rapid Deployment Joint Task Force; predecessor
                   of CENTCOM; also the abbreviation for *rapid
                   deployment force* used in a general sense.

SAM   Surface-to-air missile

UAE   United Arab Emirates

YAR   Yemen Arab Republic (North Yemen)

YSP   Yemen Socialist Party

Preface

The Persian Gulf has become a frustrating area for the formulation of U.S. foreign policy. There is no doubt as to the significance of the region nor the risks of conflict it presents. Its oil resources are vital to the well-being of the West and it has become a potential arena of East–West confrontation. Yet policymakers have been unable to feel secure about U.S. relations with the Persian Gulf states, an insecurity often expressed on both these shores and those of the Gulf. To some extent this insecurity may be related to the dynamic changes of international politics in the Gulf from the early seventies to the early eighties. This hectic decade witnessed the Soviet build-up of Iraq, the Algiers Agreement between Iraq and Iran, the Iranian Revolution, the Iraqi invasion of Iran, and the formation of the Gulf Cooperation Council. The decade ahead confronts us with the possibility of equally dynamic changes in the international politics of the Gulf. Hence, this book is devoted to the examination of U.S. policy options for the achievement of security in the Gulf of the 1980s and beyond. It is offered to policymakers with sympathy for their responsibility of choice and to scholars with hope that that they will choose to respond.

There are a considerable number of people for whose help with this project I am deeply appreciative. I am most grateful to Emmanuel College for the 1981–82 Faculty Development Grant that provided research assistance and the ability to meet with scholars and policymakers of varying backgrounds and views concerning the Persian Gulf. To these scholars and policymakers I am indebted for their generosity of time and candor in our discussions. The research assistance of four Emmanuel College students was invaluable, and many thanks are due Mary Kaynor, Marigrace McNamara, Pat Neville, and Mary Beth Begley for their tenacity and care. My thanks are also due to the National Endowment for the Humanities for the opportunity to participate in the 1981 Summer Seminar at the Harvard Center for Middle Eastern Studies concerning Muslim Ethnic Minorities and obtain a valuable background for this project. I also benefited greatly from the help of Simon Samoeil of the Harvard College Library Middle East Department in transliterating the Arabic and Persian references used in this book. In addition, Herb Heidt and Eliza McClennan were particularly accommodating and careful in the drawing of the maps. Special thanks must also go to Julie Blattner of the Harvard College Library for her ever cheerful and invaluable help. And I am particularly grateful for the patience and assistance of the editorial staff of Lexington Books.

Some very personal thanks go to my parents, sister, and family for their unflagging encouragement and concern, and for those long and thought-provoking political conversations we have engaged in over these many years. Above all, I thank my political scientist–lawyer husband, Tony, with whom I was able to discuss and formulate ideas—and whose care in reading and editing this manuscript was truly an act of love.

Concerning the transliteration of Arabic and Persian names, the book has for the most part followed the Library of Congress cataloguing system stated in Bulletins 49 (for Arabic) of November 1958 and 92 (for Persian) of September 1970. Nonconforming transliterations have been provided, however, for names and geographical references for which no references in this system were available, or for which such commonly recognized popular transliterations, such as "ayatollah" or "sheikh" deviate from the system.

With respect to notes, in setting out, I determined that notes (at end of book) should be used as parsimoniously as possible so as to indicate sources for which there may be no consensus as to the fact or concept stated in the text. I also thought that in aid of this the bibliography would be as extensive as possible to enable verification of facts and concepts for which considerable consensus does exist. Unfortunately, there is very little consensus on at least current "facts" concerning Gulf affairs, and the notes became far more extensive than anticipated. I have in a number of instances attempted to spare the reader referring to the notes for every sentence by placing a single note reference at the end of a paragraph. The notes cited then support various facts provided in each of the sentences of such paragraph. I have, accordingly, been able to provide a more selective bibliography of the most useful works for this book without having to compile all works that might merely provide only additional support for various positions described or taken.

The maps have been prepared to display the location of various geographical features of the Gulf referenced in the text, including cities, towns, provinces, onshore boundaries, oil fields, oases, rivers, mountains, and ethnic areas.

1

United States Gulf Policy

The Policy Debates

The title of this book is a response to President Jimmy Carter's enunciation of what came to be known as the Carter Doctrine. In his State of the Union address of January 23, 1980, while Soviet troops were attempting to pacify Afghanistan and while Iranian revolutionaries were holding U.S. diplomats hostage, President Carter warned that "an attempt by any *outside* force to gain control of the Persian Gulf region will be regarded as an assault on the vital interests of the United States . . . [and] will be repelled by use of any means necessary, including armed force" (emphasis added). The response crafted by U.S. policymakers to potential Soviet military threats to the Persian Gulf region (henceforth, the Gulf)[1] was the development of a Rapid Deployment Joint Task Force (RDF). Eight months after the enunciation of the Carter Doctrine military forces were invading Iran. They were not the Soviet forces contemplated by the Carter Doctrine. They were Iraqi forces from *within* the Gulf.

President Reagan gave official recognition to such "threats from within" in his corollary to the Carter Doctrine. In October 1981 he stated, "Saudi Arabia we will not permit to be an Iran," and was understood to imply that the United States would be prepared to counter internal threats.[2] One year later it was announced that the RDF was to be reorganized, its forces almost doubled and its mission expanded. As of January 1, 1983 the RDF was renamed the U.S. Central Command (CENTCOM). CENTCOM's expanded mission was to respond to a broad range of threats to oil supplies in the Gulf, from Soviet invasion to internal revolt.[3]

The Carter Doctrine and the Reagan corollary together outline U.S. policy on the Gulf. It is a policy that seeks to protect Western supplies of Gulf oil by committing the United States to the defense of the region from external and internal threats. These are the threats from outside of the region by the Soviet Union and threats to Saudi Arabia and probably other Gulf sheikhdoms from within the region. The principal instrument to support these commitments is CENTCOM.

This strategy of dependence upon CENTCOM, however, subjects U.S. Gulf policy to criticism from two opposite sources. On the one hand are the critics who view the Gulf as highly unstable and CENTCOM's present posture as likely to be ineffective. On the other hand are the critics who view the Gulf as stable and CENTCOM as likely to be unnecessary. Such criticism engenders debates over the U.S. Gulf strategy in general and the stability or instability of the Gulf in particular. The debates, like this book, focus on the following questions.

1. What are the vital interests of the United States in the Gulf? There is little doubt that the definition of U.S. vital interests in the Gulf includes the security of the oil resources within Saudi Arabia in particular and the other Gulf states in general. Such definition would also include the security of the transmission of oil supplies through the potential chokepoints of the Strait of Hormuz and the Bab al-Mandab. The definition would also include America's interest in the Gulf as a marketplace for commerce. Questions arise, however, in times of an apparent glut in the supply of oil as to how vital it is to commit large-scale military resources to maintain these interests. Can the United States and its allies—the West—reduce their dependency on Gulf oil? Or will the oil glut reduce the incentives to maintain energy conservation measures?

If there is a lessening of concern for the maintenance of large-scale military resources to defend the Gulf, what are the implications for the global competition between the superpowers, the United States and the Soviet Union? As implied in the Carter Doctrine, the United States does consider as one of its vital interests the containment of the expansion of Soviet power and influence into the Gulf. But *is* containment vital, and if so, at what price?

2. What are the Soviet threats, both direct and indirect, to these U.S. vital interests in the Gulf? In times of an apparent lack of success of Soviet efforts to control Islamic freedom fighters in Afghanistan and apparent estrangement from Iraq, the Soviets' largest ally in the Gulf, the Soviet threats become less clear. Issues arise, accordingly, over interpretations of Soviet motives with respect to the Gulf and the adequacy of Soviet military capabilities for a projection of power into the region. Debate ensues between those who see Soviet motives as programmed to extend power and influence into the Gulf and those who see the Soviets as pragmatically concerned with the security of their Asian perimeter.

3. What are the threats to American vital interests that emanate from within the Gulf? And in particular, what are the threats to the security of Saudi Arabia? It is helpful to distinguish two kinds of threats that

are internal to the region. One emanates from the international politics of the Gulf and the fact that two Gulf states, Iran and Iraq, possess military forces superior to those of Saudi Arabia. The other emanates from the domestic politics of the Gulf and what is commonly viewed as the possibility of an overthrow of the Saudi system of government. Issues arise over the extent to which a radical regime in control of Saudi Arabia would constitute a threat to Western oil supplies. Debate ensues between those who view the possibility that such a radical regime, be it of the left or the right (such as an Islamic fundamentalist regime) would seek to disrupt oil supplies to the West for ideological reasons, and those who view even the most radical of Saudi regimes as needing to sell oil to the West to maintain oil revenues and economic development. How much would the West be threatened by a cutback in oil production or a cutoff of oil supplies? In times of an apparent glut in the supply of oil the answer is unclear. It is just as unclear in such times as to the possibility of threats from within the Gulf to cut back production or cut off oil supplies, pursuant to a price squeeze by the Organization of Petroleum Exporting Countries (OPEC) or to an Arab oil embargo, even without overturns of Gulf regimes. Should the United States be prepared to deploy military resources to seize Gulf oil facilities in response to such threats? Or, are alternative nonmilitary measures available to control supply and demand dislocations in the event of a disruption of oil supplies from the Gulf?

4. How should CENTCOM forces be prepared to safeguard these U.S. vital interests in the Gulf? The conventional answers are that, by blocking a direct Soviet invasion of Iran, CENTCOM will meet the external threat and, by aiding embattled regimes and securing Gulf oil fields and facilities, CENTCOM will meet the internal threats. In times of Iranian hostility to the United States and expressions by Saudi Arabia and other Gulf states of concern that U.S. forces be kept "over the horizon," these answers become too simple. It is by no means clear to what extent CENTCOM should be prepared to meet internal threats to Gulf sheikhdoms other than Saudi Arabia. The answer is clearer for threats to Oman because of the American build-up of Oman's military facilities to support CENTCOM operations. But what about Kuwait or Bahrain, Qatar and the United Arab Emirates? Issues arise, accordingly, over the extent to which the effectiveness of CENTCOM to meet direct and indirect threats to Gulf security depends on regional and local assistance and the extent to which Gulf states themselves can supply their own collective security through such organizations as the recently formed Gulf Cooperation Council (GCC). Debate ensues over the need for local bases for preparedness or pre-positioning of forces

and materiel and the supply of sophisticated weaponry and training to Gulf states.

Furthermore, what is the likelihood that the local regimes now willing to provide the cooperation needed for CENTCOM operations will still be in power in the event that CENTCOM deployment is necessary? What is the likelihood that the alignments the United States now has with Saudi Arabia, with Oman and other Gulf sheikhdoms, as well as their alignments with each other, will remain in place when CENTCOM deployment may be necessary? To these questions there seem to be no clear answers. Indeed, these questions lead to the fundamental issues addressed in this book: How stable are the Gulf states? How stable are their international relations? In sum, how unstable is the Gulf?

As with the other questions, the last also engenders debate. At one extreme are the policy advocates who view the Gulf and its constituent states as highly unstable. They advocate the continuing maintenance of large-scale U.S. military force commitments for the protection of oil supplies from the Gulf. The current oil glut may not last, they say, and dependency on Gulf oil may increase with the improvement of the global economy. Even if the allies of the United States, who generally have a greater dependency on Gulf oil supplies, refuse to recognize the need for military protection of those supplies, it is argued, U.S. policy should not be so shortsighted. The United States, according to this view, should be prepared to deploy forces rapidly into the Gulf for the maintenance of NATO and European security as well as that of Japan and the Pacific. Furthermore, from this viewpoint the United States has an equally vital interest in containing Soviet expansion. The USSR is viewed as having a programmatic interest in extending its power and influence into the Gulf by any means available, including direct invasion.

Because the projection of U.S. conventional forces into the Gulf region cannot rely on the highly unstable regimes, it is argued, the defense of the United States' vital interests must be based more securely on air and naval capabilities that can reach the region from secure bases in the Indian Ocean and outside of the Gulf, such as in Turkey. CENTCOM forces should be deployable as much as possible without reliance on unstable local regimes, hence dispensing with the need for local ground bases.

The other extreme of the debate over stability in the Gulf comes to some of the same conclusions but for very different reasons. This is a position most associated with the Gulf states themselves. This position denies any serious instability in the Gulf and views the location of

CENTCOM ground bases within the Gulf as contributing to such instability. For exponents of this position, direct U.S. intervention into the
Gulf carries with it the potential of U.S. intervention into local political
concerns. Worse still, CENTCOM could be used to secure oil facilities
against the will of local regimes in the event of oil supply disruptions.
The Gulf states that adopt this point of view also benefit from the
dependency of Western nations on Gulf oil.

The Soviet threat is viewed in this extreme position as pragmatically concerned with the security of the Soviet perimeter, but potentially more dangerous if the Soviets feel compelled to counter U.S.
intervention into the Gulf, thereby engaging in a risky competition of
superpowers. This position recognizes the need for international naval
deterrence of hostile seizure of the chokepoints of the Strait of Hormuz and the Bab al-Mandab. Anything more than over-the-horizon
deployment of Western or CENTCOM forces, it is argued, should be
avoided. Furthermore, such deterrent measures will become less necessary once pipelines are constructed to bypass the Strait of Hormuz.
(Saudi Arabia already has one bypassing the Bab al-Mandab.) Finally,
this position looks to the protection of Gulf security by regional military cooperation, particularly now with the GCC, as well as through
other local defense arrangements, such as Saudi Arabia's bilateral defense treaties with most of its neighbors. These states can obtain sophisticated military weapons and training in their use from the United
States and its allies without the complications of U.S. ground bases.

As with all extreme positions in debates over policy, these admit
to middle positions. One can maintain middle positions on the motives
of the Soviet Union in the Gulf. For example, it may be argued that
the Soviets will always need to maintain a pragmatic concern for the
security of their perimeter. Whether the Soviets can afford to realize
any long-term programmatic interest in seizing Gulf territory will depend on available opportunities and their assessment of the costs, risks,
and benefits of taking advantage of them. It may be that instability in
the Gulf will create opportunities for direct or indirect intervention by
the Soviet Union.

Middle positions on the use of CENTCOM to safeguard Gulf oil
supplies, however, are more complex. Local collective security efforts,
such as those of the GCC, may be effective against some kinds of
threats to the security of the constituents but ineffective for other kinds
of threats. Hence CENTCOM's deployment for some kinds of potential oil supply disruptions may be necessary, and for others not. When
CENTCOM may be needed in the Gulf, local cooperation will be
necessary. Instability within the Gulf will affect the availability of that
cooperation. Even with middle positions on the debate over U.S. Gulf

policy, therefore, the analysis returns to the need for an assessment of instability in the Gulf.

Instability in the Gulf

Instability in the international politics of the Gulf has two aspects: domestic political instability, which has international political implications, and international political instability itself. Domestic political instability with international political implications in turn has two meanings. The first entails a change of regimes. What is meant is not merely change of government or change of controlling party or leadership. What is meant is a change in basic form of government, a change in legitimating principles, such as from democracy to dictatorship, monarchy to republic. Such domestic political instability has international political implications because regime changes often herald changes in foreign policy and reorientation of international alignments. If the regime change is a radical one, it often carries a revolutionary fervor and interest in foreign adventure.

The meaning of domestic political stability as applied to the Gulf implies a continuation of monarchical forms of government among the six "Traditional states." These are the Kingdom of Saudi Arabia, the Sultanate of Oman, and the Gulf sheikhdoms of Kuwait, Bahrain, Qatar, and the United Arab Emirates (the UAE is a federation of seven "Trucial states"). It also implies a continuation of the form of regime of the four republican states of the Gulf, each of which has a different ideological bent. The four are: Iraq, currently a single-party Ba'thist regime; Iran, currently self-styled as a Shiite Islamic republic; the Yemen Arab Republic (North Yemen), a more or less military-dominated republican regime without a well-defined ideological slant; and the Peoples' Democratic Republic of Yemen (South Yemen), a clearly defined Marxist-Leninist regime. All ten states of the Gulf will be referred to collectively as the Gulf states, and any one individually as a state.

The second meaning of domestic political instability with international implications refers to changes to the integrity of the political community of a state. Such changes involve a fracturing of that political community by diverse ethnic or religious groups or other ideologically motivated political groups. Religious cleavages, ethnic group dissension, and ideological contests may seek to overturn regimes or may split political communities. Such strife may render the central regime incapable of external action. It may also render the country vulnerable to intervention by another state seeking to assist one or more opposition groups or merely to take advantage of the civil strife.

In order to better understand the concept of international political instability, it will be necessary to characterize "stability" in this context. International political behavior itself is composed of war, alliance, and diplomatic interaction. One construction of the concept of international political instability might be a change from peace to war, from alliance to neutrality, from diplomatic interaction to rupture of relations, and vice versa. For example, war is often referred to as "instability." But international political behavior appears to be continually changing. According to this construction, there is continuous instability in international affairs, and it is impossible to apply the concept of "international political stability". It would be better to seek stability in patterns of international political behavior rather than to look for it in individual international political situations. Instability in patterns of international political behavior then refers to changes in such patterns. For example, if there is a pattern of short-term alliances, a change to long-term alliances can be said to represent instability in the pattern. Such instability can then be identified by deviations from the norm or by erratic and unpredictable behavior. If such deviations themselves assume regularity and become predictable, new patterns may eventuate and behavior stabilize.

The investigation of international political stability and instability in the Gulf needs to be related to U.S. policy. Policymakers should take into account the stability and instability of the international politics of the region in defining their policy choices. For example, if U.S. policy in the Gulf intends to rely on the cooperation of certain Gulf states, it is important to know whether to expect alignments with such states to be of long or short duration, or indeed whether the patterns of alignment are so unstable that no expectation is possible either way.

There are, naturally, other considerations in policy choices for the United States, including domestic political concerns. Such concerns may include popular attitudes toward Gulf states and the budgetary process. This book will not try to assess U.S. domestic political concerns in the formulation of policy for the protection of U.S. interests in the Gulf. It will try to assess the basic strategic choices for U.S. Gulf policy. Similarly, in dealing with the Gulf states, there will be little if any consideration of any domestic political determinants of such behavior, such as the personalities of Gulf leaders, except as may be discussed in connection with domestic political instability with international political implications.

The Need for a New U.S. Strategy in the Gulf

Neither of the extreme positions of the debate concerning Gulf instability provides a firm foundation upon which to base an effective U.S. strategy in the Gulf. Both positions overlook the international political

developed through defense expenditures from the underlying gross national product and population of a state, or even the quality of its forces and the resolve of its population. Moreover, evaluation of these elements of power of a state is subject to distortion from professional and personal biases of the evaluators, be they diplomatic personnel, intelligence agents, or policymakers.

While measuring military capabilities is difficult enough, assessing motives is more difficult. Many states harbor territorial claims against their neighbors. These claims may blossom into boundary disputes or bids for wholesale takeovers. They may also be repressed or resolved. Many states profess ideological principles in competition with their neighbors'. These competitions can develop into acrid disputes or encourage subversion and intervention. They can also abate and coexist. In the absence of a sound method for determining international political motives, a prudent concern for the security of the state usually dictates that all doubts concerning potentially hostile motives be resolved in favor of increasing one's own military capabilities in relationship to other actors with superior capabilities. This prudent increase of capabilities can be accomplished by unilaterally increasing armaments and improvement of weapons. It can also be accomplished by seeking alliance partners so that the collective capabilities of the alliance can match or exceed those of potential opponents.

Strategic choices, accordingly, must take account of the number of actors in the system that may be available as potential alliance partners and the relative distribution of capabilities of other actors. Identifying which actors are within the system then becomes for the theorist a more or less empirical task requiring the observation of the frequency of interactions among contiguous states. Over a period of time it will be observed that alliances and wars occur among certain of these states. These states should correspond to those that the strategists themselves have identified as available alliance partners and as potential sources of conflict.

Having identified the elements of the international system, namely the numbers of actors and their relative capabilities, it is then possible to relate the structure to the international behavioral process. As changes occur in the underlying structure, changes should be evident in the patterns of international behavior. If the structure undergoes a radical change, a new structure should result, and one system will have been transformed into another.

How many transformations of international structures can there be? And which are of interest to the international politics of the Gulf? Theoretically a large number of types or models of international system structures can be derived from permutations and combinations of the two elements of the system. For example, one could start with two actors with relatively equal capabilities; two actors, but one with relatively superior capabilities; three actors with relatively equal capabilities, and so on. There are, however, only three such types or models of international systems with potential application to the Gulf.

These three can be identified as follows. (1) The *imperial system* is characterized by a single predominant actor with military capabilities superior to all combinations of the capabilities of the other actors. A modern example would be the USSR vis-à-vis the Warsaw Pact or so-called Communist bloc at the height of the cold war. An example from the Gulf would be the Ottoman Empire in the Gulf before World War I. (2) The *bipolar system* is characterized by two actors with military capabilities equal to each other's but superior to those of the other actors or of combinations of the other actors. A modern example would be the post–World War II contest between the United States and USSR and their respective blocs at the height of the cold war. An example from the Gulf would be the contest between the Ottoman Empire and British Empire before 1918 in the Gulf. (3) The *dynamic balance of power system* is characterized by a number of actors, usually three or more, with relatively equal military capabilities. The adjective *dynamic* is intended to avoid the common but static image of two relatively equal alliances and a major actor "holding the balance," as one would a pair of scales. A modern example would be a Middle East international system, whose major actors would be Egypt, Israel, Iraq, Syria, and possibly Jordan. There is still room to debate the relative equality of capabilities and the inclusion of other actors such as Saudi Arabia and Libya.[3] An example from the Gulf would be its current international politics. What patterns of international behavior are associated with each of the three different systems?

In the imperial system, wars within the empire are infrequent because the imperial power has an interest in maintaining order within the empire so that it can extend or defend its periphery. The pax Brittanica is an example. Wars by the imperial power in extending its empire are for unlimited control objectives. If wars within the empire are threatened, the imperial actor who possesses overwhelming military superiority seeks to prevent them. Alliances among the lesser powers within the empire do not exist. There would be concern that any such combinations would seek to break away from or overthrow the imperial power. The imperial power typically negotiates from strength with lesser actors within the empire. Hence the imperial power tends not to need or desire to make expedient deals. Imperial powers quite often are animated by ideological drives, hence negotiate with rigidity.

Wars within the bipolar system between the two polar powers, the superpowers, are fought for unlimited objectives. Unconditional surrender is an example. Hence wars between the superpowers are infrequent for two reasons. The first is that, if the superpowers have mutual and massive destruction capabilities, they will try to avoid major war and the risks of mutual destruction. The example here is post–World War II nuclear deterrence. Alliance changes within the bipolar system are infrequent. The superpowers seek to form more permanent alliances, called "blocs." Lesser actors join these blocs to obtain security from the superior military capabilities of one or the other superpowers. The infusion of ideological objectives into the system makes the bloc more cohesive. But it also creates rigidity in the diplomatic interchanges between the superpowers and their blocs. Such interchanges tend to turn into cold war.

International behavior within the dynamic balance of power system exhibits all the opposite characteristics from that of the bipolar system. Alliances and wars tend to be frequent and short-lived. Alliance switching makes conflict resolution easier, since actors can be induced to defect from even wartime alliances and conclude a separate peace. The defecting actor can choose to remain neutral or be available to join the opposing alliance. This could result in one or both of the combating alliances being weakened and therefore would create a preference for settlement of the conflict. In the absence of rigid ideological principles binding an alliance, opponents seek to encourage defections and switching by offering inducements, such as larger shares in the spoils of war. Actors accept whichever inducements appear to provide a larger increase in capabilities. With frequent bidding for alignments and easier settlement of conflicts, military objectives tend to be limited. Actors also seek to oppose potentially predominant actors or coalitions because these jeopardize the security of lesser actors or those outside of the coalition. Diplomacy is exceedingly flexible. Such flexibility is needed for the compromises required to resolve conflicts and reform alliances.

These three different types of systems with their distinct patterns of international political behavior also have different effects on strategic calculations. Expectations concerning behavior influence strategists perceptions of enemies and allies. For example, in an imperial system it can be expected that the imperial power will attempt to assert overwhelming force to crush any revolt. Potential rebels become very wary of who can be trusted to join a revolt. Those actors with binding ideological ties are more trustworthy. Unprincipled actors might defect and expose the rebels to obtain security or advantages. In a bipolar system it can be expected that members of the opposing bloc are perceived as enemies. Although détente may be possible, realignment with actors of the opposing bloc is less so. If there are nonaligned actors in the bipolar system, the superpowers will compete to bring them into their respective blocs. The nonaligneds, however, cannot be trusted or treated as either friends or enemies until they lose their nonaligned status and join a bloc. In a dynamic balance of power, no actor can be trusted to remain in an alliance or to refrain from joining an opponent. Hence every actor is perceived as a potential friend and a potential enemy.

These expectations, as we will observe later with respect to the Gulf, have ramifications concerning the peacetime deployment of military forces of the actors. In the imperial system, the imperial power would seek to deploy its forces by right throughout the empire. In particular these forces would be needed to reach quickly any troublespots from the core to the periphery of the empire, although most trouble would be expected at the periphery. In the bipolar system, the bloc partners would invite the deployment of the superpower's forces onto their territory so as to increase deterrence or enable defense against the perceived constant threat from the other bloc. In a dynamic balance of power, no forces would be invited into the territory of another actor except as part of allied combat. Actors would fear that the alliance could turn, making subsequent ejection of the then alien forces more difficult.

Reality, of course, never fits the ideal type or international model exactly. To the extent that the structure of the actual international system, such as that of the Gulf, varies from that of the model, variations from the typical patterns of behavior can also be expected. The introduction of variations from these patterns, hence deviations from the norm of expected behavior, also has an effect on the strategic calculations of each participant in the system. Additional uncertainties creep into the calculus as expectations concerning such patterns become unstable. As a result the system itself can be viewed as unstable. Instabilities may feed back upon and foster further instabilities. If such a pattern of feedback takes place, the totally destabilized system that develops will be transformed into a new system. Hence in observing the current reality of international politics in the Gulf, where signs of instability in the international system are detected we will consider possible transformations of the system in the future. For example, in a dynamic balance of power the introduction of conflicting ideological principles into the relations between the actors would be destabilizing. The diplomatic relations between the actors would become rigid and inhibit the formation of alliances. This instability might lead to the development of ideological blocs and transformation into a bipolar system.

Let us proceed first, however, to explore the relatively recent past international politics of the Gulf. To do so we will examine the changing structures and behavior patterns of the Gulf international system since the beginning of the twentieth century. That starting point is recommended because a number of current disputes among the Gulf states can better be understood from that historical perspective. The current Gulf states have not all been in existence since the turn of the century, and from time to time other, outside states have interacted with the states in the region. The international system in the Gulf has undergone five changes since 1900. Demarcating these changes by time periods is somewhat artificial, but is done for convenience. In reality, changes often appeared gradually, not abruptly, and older patterns of behavior disappeared only gradually in the period following introduction of the new patterns.[4]

1900–1918: A Bipolar System

During this period the Gulf international system resembled a bipolar system, the two superpowers of which were the Ottoman Empire (the *Porte,* or Turks) and the British Empire. Both empires had military capabilities superior to those of the local major actors. These included the sheikhs of Kuwait of the Āl al-Ṣabāḥ family, foremost of whom during this period was Mubārak; Sheikh 'Abd al-'Azīz ibn 'Abd al-Rahmān Āl Sa'ūd ("Ibn Saud"); the Imam of Yemen; and the shah of Persia. Other European actors, Germany and Russia, while possessing military capabilities superior to those of the local actors, still played minor roles in the system. Various tribes in the Arabian Peninsula also constituted lesser actors.

The driving force in the international politics in the Gulf during this period was the contest between the Ottoman Empire and the British Empire. The Ottoman Empire was entrenched in the Gulf from the Euphrates River and the head of the Gulf down the east coast of the Arabian Peninsula and was administered out of the *vilayat* (province) of Basra. The east coast was the Turkish province of al-Hasa (roughly equivalent geographically to what is now Saudi Arabia's oil-bearing Eastern Province). The Ottoman Empire also stretched down the west coast of the Arabian Peninsula through Yemen. The British

Empire sought to consolidate its control over the maritime passage through the Suez Canal to India by consolidation of its control over Aden and containment of Turkish expansion through the Aden–Yemen hinterland. At the same time, the British sought to contain the extension of influence over access to India by the Ottoman Empire and by other European powers.

The focal point for that contest was Kuwait. Kuwait developed strategic value at the turn of the century because it had been identified as the terminus for the projected rail system that became known as the Baghdad Railway.[5] By 1903 the Germans had obtained concessions from the Turks for the construction of railroad lines from Konya in central Turkey, which was already linked by rail with Smyrna on the Aegean and with Constantinople, to Baghdad and Basra. The Baghdad Railway was to be constructed by a European consortium dominated by German banks. For Germany the Baghdad Railway represented economic expansion; for the Porte increased mobility to a corner of the empire, hence additional military capability. This additional capability was needed to challenge British naval superiority in the Gulf, which jeopardized Ottoman control over its *vilayats* of Basra and al-Hasa and Ottoman expansion onto the Trucial coast.

Kuwait also became the focal point of the strategic competition between the British and Russian empires. The Russians were interested in Kuwait as a coaling station or naval base and as a possible terminus for a railroad from the Syrian coast.

The British had secured footholds on the Arabian Peninsula by the turn of the century through the conclusion of protectorate agreements with powerful tribal rulers around the Peninsula. The protectorate agreements pledged nonalienation of territory to foreign powers and acceded to British suzerainty. They had been entered into with the sheikhs of Bahrain, Qatar, and the Trucial sheikhdoms, as well as with the sultan of Qishn and Socotra on the Aden coast. The British had succeeded in concluding only a nonalienation agreement but not a suzerainty agreement with Oman. Oman's ruler wanted to preserve Omani independence and entertained the French interest in establishing a coaling station on the Gulf coast of Oman to counter the British.

The British contest for control over Kuwait was signaled in 1899 by the execution of a secret agreement with Kuwait. Without expressly so stating, the agreement had the effect of a protectorate treaty, notwithstanding Kuwait's status as a *qada,* or administrative district, within the Basra province of the Ottoman Empire. Thereafter the British landed forces in 1902 to deter a Turkish sponsored attack on Kuwait. The British deployment also warded off Russian advances, a Russian warship having landed at Kuwait in December 1901. Subsequently the

British concluded an agreement leasing land in perpetuity on Kuwait Bay for a naval base. The contest over Kuwait ended in 1913 as part of a comprehensive agreement between the British and Ottoman empires which settled a number of prior territorial contests. In these Constantinople Agreements the two empires worked out a curious compromise over Kuwait. The Turks recognized the status of Kuwait as a British protectorate, and the British recognized Kuwait as an "autonomous" *qada*.

Occurring simultaneously with their contest over Kuwait was the contest between the British and Ottoman empires over the Aden hinterland. British expansion into this hinterland from Aden threatened the Ottoman economic and communications lines from the southwest Arabian Peninsula and its Red Sea ports. Such expansion furthermore enabled arms to be smuggled to the rebel forces under the Imam of Yemen and diverted Turkish military capabilities into a distant corner of the empire.

Finally, on the northeastern flank of their empire, the Turks were threatened by encroachments from both the British and Russian empires. The Russians were for the most part interested in rail connections through northern Persia and also in northeastern Turkey to the Baghdad Railway. The British were interested in protecting their access to India and points east. In 1907 the British concluded a spheres of influence agreement with the Russians. This agreement gave the Russians paramount influence over northern Persia, the British over southern Persia from the Afghan border, and left a central Persian neutral zone. The Turks moved to consolidate their control over the Kurdish areas at their northeastern border with Persia in 1905. The Turks then moved farther into Persia in 1907 as the Persian regime succumbed to an internal crisis. Additional opportunities for imperial expansion were presented by the Persian civil war in 1909. Both the Turks and the Russians extended military control over parts of northwest Persia for their own gain and to contain each other's expansion.

From 1900 to 1914 the contest by the British and Ottoman empires over extension of influence in the Gulf region bipolarized the international politics of the region, but only loosely so, since the larger global international system in which these empires played major roles was itself not bipolarized. It was a dynamic balance of power. In the larger, dynamic balance of power system the Porte could not afford to alienate the British completely. It needed British cooperation to some extent with respect to the Baghdad Railway and it needed British mediation for conflicts with other European powers in other parts of the Ottoman Empire: the French and Spanish in Morocco, the Italians in Libya, the Russians in the Balkans. As a result of the loose bipolarization the Ottoman and British empires were able to reach agreements over their imperial boundaries at Yemen and Kuwait.

Further incentives to imperial settlements arose from the fact that Ottoman military forces were not concentrated enough to be able to dislodge the British from their entrées into the Gulf. Ottoman forces were dispersed into various parts of the empire to put down revolts such as that in Yemen, in Macedonia and in the Balkans. The British on the other hand exercised their naval superiority to good effect in the Gulf.

With the First World War, however, and the loose bipolarization of global international politics, the Gulf system became more distinctly bipolarized. The British concluded a series of anti-Ottoman alliances with Arab potentates. These included an agreement with Ibn Saud in 1915, in which he acceded to British suzerainty and agreed not to interfere with other Gulf coast suzerains in return for British recognition of Ibn Saud's control over al-Hasa. At the same time the British negotiated and in 1916 concluded an alliance with Ibn Saud's enemy, Husayn, the Ottoman-appointed sharīf of Mecca. Husayn with assistance from the legendary T.E. Lawrence ousted the Turks from the western province of the Hejaz. A similar alliance was concluded with the North Yemeni leader, Sayyid Idris, who controlled the Asir district and some Red Sea coastline. No alliance, however, was concluded with the Iman of Yemen and so British and Turkish troops had a stand off during World War I and did not attempt to dislodge each other from their respective garrisons in Aden and Lahej.

1918–1932: An Imperial System

During this period the international system in the Gulf resembled an imperial system. The collapse of the Ottoman empire in 1918, and the defeat of the Germans, plus the withdrawal of Bolshevik Russia from the war in 1917, left the British Empire as the paramount power in the Gulf region. Through its protectorate treaties and wartime alliances the British enjoyed suzerain control over the entire Arabian Peninsula except for the Yemen region at the hinterland of the Aden area. Britain also occupied and controlled the machinery of government of the three former Turkish *vilayats* that formed Iraq after the war and occupied and controlled less directly most of postwar Iran until 1921. Even with respect to Yemen, the British occupied the key port of Hodeida and with support of the Idrisi forces in North Yemen maintained some pressure on the Imam of Yemen, who remained independent of British control. Indeed, the one war involving the imperial

power in this period was a protracted border war with the Imam of
Yemen, a war that was not settled until the Imam became more concerned about the potential Saudi threat in 1934.

The British imperial system in the Gulf was one with loose political
controls, since the British exerted very little military control over the
core of the Arabian Peninsula. As a result Ibn Saud was for the most
part unimpeded in his pursuit of control over much of the Peninsula
north of Yemen. In 1926 Ibn Saud succeeded in wresting the Hejaz
from Husayn. In 1927 Britain formally recognized Saud's independence by terminating suzerainty in the Treaty of Jiddah, and obtained
Ibn Saud's pledge to maintain friendly relations with the other Gulf
states with which Britain had suzerainty agreements.

In Iraq the British had established imperial control through its
wartime military occupation and postwar League of Nations Mandate.
The British installed Faisal, son of Sharīf Husayn, as king of Iraq after
an abortive attempt to install him as king of Syria. A series of insur-
rections against British rule induced the British to loosen their hold on
Iraq. They withdrew their ground forces in 1921 leaving air forces
stationed west of Baghdad. In 1922 an Anglo–Iraqi Treaty was concluded still incorporating the terms of the mandate but conceding limited Iraqi controls over foreign and domestic affairs.

The one area in which the extension of the British imperium was
severely checked was in Persia. In a secretly negotiated postwar 1919
Anglo–Iranian Agreement, the British obtained suzerainty in return
for development assistance. The Soviet Union reacted by sending forces
into northern Persia and supporting secessionist efforts in Azerbaijan
and the establishment of a Soviet Socialist Republic of Gilan, at the
Iranian shore of the Caspian Sea. The coup of 1921 by Reza Khan,
later Reza Shah, abrogated the Anglo–Iranian Treaty and concluded
a Treaty of Friendship with the Soviet Union, which, among other
things, obtained the removal of the Red army from Gilan in return for
guaranteeing that Persian territory would not be used for attacks on
the Soviet Union.

Britain's hold over the Gulf, as loose as it was, loosened even
further with the termination in 1932 of the British mandate over Iraq.
This had been preceded by the Anglo–Iraqi Treaty of 1930, which
pledged mutual defense assistance and granted Britain rights to air
bases and to move troops across the country. In 1931 the British withdrew their remaining British air forces.

Thus by 1932 Britain was left with alliance relationships with only
two major Arab actors, Ibn Saud, whose territory was proclaimed the
Kingdom of Saudi Arabia in that year, and Iraq. Britain maintained
suzerain relationships with coastal but minor potentates around the

perimeter of the Arabian Peninsula from Aden to Kuwait. But Britain had no formal alliance with Iran.

This gradual loosening of the British hold on the Gulf occurred in the absence of any major challenges to the British imperium from the larger global international system. The only Gulf state with an interest in outside assistance was Yemen, whose Imam negotiated a Treaty of Amity and Commerce with Mussolini's governor of Eritrea across the Bab al-Mandab. The British blunted this move with a hands-off agreement with Italy requiring mutual consultation before any intervention into their respective spheres of influence. Thereafter in 1928 the Imam concluded a Treaty of Friendship and Commerce with the Soviet Union, but without gaining any materiel or military assistance.

Although no global major actor had sufficient interest or military capability to challenge the British in the Gulf, it is also the case that Britain did not attempt to incorporate Yemen into the Empire. British moderation toward Yemen is probably explainable by Britain's concern to play a moderating role in global international politics during this post–World War I period. In particular the British wished to demonstrate support of the League of Nations, which legitimized the mandate system. This system provided ostensible legitimacy for British imperial control over the northern tier of Arab states. A British attempt to absorb Yemen would have been viewed as illegitimate, as was Mussolini's attempt in 1935 to absorb Ethiopia. Britain also supported the League's efforts to resolve the Mosul dispute between Turkey and Iraq to resist Turkey's reclamation of its former *vilayat*. Furthermore, it is unlikely that Yemen represented a sufficiently valuable acquisition to the British Empire to justify the expenditure of forces for its conquest.

1933–1945: An Emerging Dynamic Balance of Power

During this period the British Empire continued to loosen its hold over the Gulf and the international politics of the region began to exhibit more and more characteristics of a dynamic balance of power. British military capabilities were still superior to those of the regional powers. On the Arabian Peninsula, Saudi Arabia did not possess the military capability to challenge the British and did not switch allegiance during the Second World War. On the other hand Ibn Saud did raise claims to parts of the al-Hasa province that had been considered as belonging to Abu Dhabi, which was under British suzerainty, and did engage in protracted negotiations with the British over these territorial claims rather than concede to their military advantage.

In the southwestern region of the Arabian Peninsula Ibn Saud was not inhibited by British military forces in Aden. The British were themselves engaged in protracted warfare against the Imam of Yemen. Ibn Saud took advantage of the British preoccupation with Yemen to pursue a military campaign against the Imam himself. The British, in dynamic balance of power style, offered to permit military assistance to the Imam in return for settlement of their disputes and negotiated a status quo agreement in early 1934. At the same time Ibn Saud invaded Yemen and, also in dynamic balance of power style, halted his forces before capturing the capital city. Ibn Saud thus compelled negotiations over limited objectives rather than engaging in an overthrow of the Yemeni regime or a potentially protracted struggle. The British at this time also sent warships into Yemen's major port of Hodeida, possibly to check Italian warships there and possibly to deter any Saudi takeover. Ultimately Britain and Italy in 1938 entered into another hands-off agreement recognizing their mutual spheres of influence: Italy recognized British interests in the Arabian Peninsula, while Britain pledged to respect the independence and territorial integrity of Saudi Arabia and Yemen.

Dynamic balance of power behavior was also evident in the Iran and Iraq sector of the Gulf. There the British imperium had receded completely and the Soviet Union reasserted its interests. Iraq, notwithstanding its alliance with Britain, joined in 1935 with Iran, Afghanistan, and Turkey in initialing a collective security pact that became in 1937 the Sa'dabad Pact. In effect Iraq withdrew from the British alliance and joined the other regional powers who shared a concern over potential Soviet aggression and Italian expansion. There had been an evident failure of any effective European response, particularly British to the Italians' Ethiopian campaign. In the summer of 1941 Iraq actually switched its alignment to oppose Britain by joining the Axis powers. In response British invasionary forces took Basra, then advanced on Baghdad. The leaders of the pro-Axis coup fled, and the restored regime reasserted its adherance to the 1930 alliance with Britain, declaring war on the Axis powers in 1943. Iraq permitted British forces access to bases in Iraq, which assisted with the British occupation of Iran and the Levant during the war.

Iran, which did not have an alliance arrangement with Britain, attempted to maintain neutrality at the onset of World War II. This Iranian neutrality became viewed as an obstacle after the Soviet Union joined the Allies and the Allies needed access through Iran to provide military assistance to the Soviet Union. In August 1941 Britain and the Soviet Union invaded Iran and occupied it, thereby obtaining a supply route to the Soviet Union. Reza Shah abdicated in favor of his son,

Muḥammad Reza Pahlevi, and Iran joined the Allies in 1943. At the subsequent Teheran Conference of 1943, the United States, Britain, and the Soviet Union agreed to respect the independence and territorial integrity of Iran, and ultimately to withdraw foreign forces from Iran after the war.

1945–1971: A Subordinated Dynamic Balance of Power

Transformation to a dynamic balance of power system in the Gulf continued as Britain emerged from World War II with grossly diminished military capabilities. As its empire was gradually dismembered, Britain's forces and suzerainty were gradually withdrawn from the Gulf. During this period Britain granted independence successively to Kuwait in 1961, then Aden, which became South Yemen in 1967, and finally the Trucial states in 1971. As the British as well as other European powers, particularly France, withdrew, new independent states emerged in the larger Middle East system: Egypt, Israel, Syria, Jordan, Lebanon. At the same time the already independent Gulf states of Iran, Iraq, and Saudi Arabia gradually increased their military capabilities. These increases were made possible by gradually increasing oil revenues and by the competing military assistance programs of the superpowers in the larger global system. That larger global system after World War II had bipolarized. But it never succeeded in bipolarizing either the Middle East system or the Gulf system. The international interactions of the Gulf states, their alignments and confrontations, were worked out during this postwar period, through interactions within the larger Middle East system.

Thus, many of the hallmarks of the dynamic balance of power were evident in the alliances among the Gulf states and major actors of the Middle East system during this period. For example, in 1951 the attempts by Britain and the United States to create a Middle East Treaty Organization, to supplant diminishing British capabilities and shore up Britain's faltering position in Egypt, were resisted by the Egyptians. Egypt rejected the joint British–French–U.S.–Turkey proposal for a Middle East Command with headquarters in Cairo. A collective security organization did succeed in 1955, however, with the conclusion of a Turko–Iraqi agreement on mutual security. This formed the nucleus of the Baghdad Pact, which thereafter gained the adherence of Britain, Pakistan, and Iran in the same year.

Egypt, which had been denied American aid after an Israeli raid in Gaza in 1955, concluded a major arms deal with the Soviet Union.

Egypt also countered the Baghdad Pact with the formation of a series of security pacts with Middle East and Gulf states in 1955–56. Egypt formed a Joint Command with Saudi Arabia, Yemen, and Syria; a separate Defense Treaty with Saudi Arabia; a Unified Frontier Plan with Saudi Arabia, Jordan, and Syria; and a Five-Year Defense Pact with these states plus Yemen in April 1956. None of these alliance arrangements, however, held up in the face of the Anglo–French–Israeli Suez crisis in October and November 1956. Nor did the United States support its British and French allies in their Egyptian invasion.

Alignments among Gulf and Middle East actors continued to switch in the ensuing years in dynamic balance of power style. The 1958 coup in Iraq, which overthrew the monarchy, brought Qāsim to power. Iraq turned toward the Soviet Union and abrogated the Baghdad Pact. Iraq also engaged in rivalries with Nasser's Egypt and the Syrians, both of whom in 1958 formed the United Arab Republic. The union lasted until 1961. Even after the Syrian rupture with Nasser, Syria remained willing to support Egypt and the Arab League forces against Iraq. These forces had been organized by the Arab League to oppose Qāsim's threat to take over all of Kuwait after the British withdrawal in 1961.

During this period, the alignment of Egypt and Saudi Arabia turned into opposition as each backed different sides in the Yemeni civil war, which began in 1962. Egypt and Saudi Arabia agreed on a Yemeni settlement at Jiddah in 1965. The Yemeni factions, however, did not accept this agreement, and Egyptian and Saudi troop withdrawals from Yemen did not take place until after the 1967 Israeli–Arab war and resulting Egyptian losses.

Iran's foreign policy during this period remained acutely sensitive to potential pressures from the Soviet superpower on its northern border. This pressure intensified for a while following World War II when Soviet forces refused to withdraw on schedule simultaneously with withdrawing British forces in 1946. Furthermore, the Soviets assisted with the Iranian Communist party's involvement in an independent Azerbaijan, catalyzing one of the first cold war crises with the United States and Britain. Soviet troop withdrawal was ultimately engineered by the negotiation of oil concessions, and Iranian forces recovered Azerbaijan.

After Iraq withdrew from the Baghdad Pact, the remaining allies renamed it the Central Treaty Organization (CENTO) and obtained the pledge of U.S. military assistance. Although Iran remained a member of CENTO, the shah retained some flexibility in his relations with the United States. In 1962 he refused to permit U.S. missiles on Iranian soil, and in 1966 concluded an arms deal with the Soviet Union. Iran proceeded to build up its military capabilities, and in particular its naval forces. As the British withdrew from the Gulf, the shah promoted Iran as the policeman of the Gulf. Limiting Iranian objectives in dynamic balance of power style, the shah refrained from attempting to press the Iranian territorial claim to Bahrain. The shah did, however, move to take over the strategically located Gulf islands of Abu Musa and the Tunbs. The former was gained by agreement with its owner, Sharjah; the latter by military occupation against the will of Ras al-Khaymah.[6]

1972–1983: The Dynamic Balance of Power System

The British withdrawal from the Trucial states in late 1971 left as major actors within the system Iran, Iraq, and Saudi Arabia. The Gulf international system emerged as a dynamic balance of power with interactions by its actors directly with each other and not primarily as participants in the larger Middle East system. All three major actors have vastly increased their military capabilities during this period. The increases are due primarily to substantial increases in financial capabilities from oil revenues, particularly as a result of precipitous price hikes by OPEC in 1973 and 1979.

Both the Soviet Union and the United States have become active participants in the international politics of the region. The Soviet Union participates primarily through major arms sales to Iraq and military assistance to North Yemen, as well as to South Yemen, with which the Soviets have an ideological connection. The Soviet Union has obtained the use of military facilities from these states varying from access to ports to control over base facilities. The Soviet Union has also supplied some military assistance to Kuwait and maintains diplomatic relations with Kuwait, but with none of the other Traditional states. The United States participates primarily through major arms sales such as those to Iran before the Iranian Revolution as well as to Saudi Arabia and the other Traditional states. With respect to Oman and Bahrain the United States obtains the use of certain military facilities.

The Gulf System before the Iranian Revolution

From 1972 to the Iranian Revolution of 1978–79, dynamic balance of power behavior continued to be evident in the Gulf region. As Iran increased its military capabilities it became more confident in its reassertion of rights to navigation of the Shatt al-Arab, which had been

denied by Iraq. At the same time Iran increased pressure on Iraq by
subsidizing anti-Iraq Kurds and engaging in a series of border incidents
in the 1972–74 period. These activities culminated in the negotiation
of a boundary settlement and general agreement between Iran and
Iraq mediated with OPEC assistance in Algiers in 1975. The settlement
resolved a number of border issues and accorded Iran equal navigational rights to the Shatt. It also had dynamic balance of power benefits
to both sides. From Iraq's point of view the Algiers settlement dis-
rupted the Iranian–Kurdish alliance. From Iran's point of view the
settlement forestalled the possibility of Iraqi invitation of larger Soviet
presence, particularly naval, in the Gulf. Iran was sensitive to any use
of Iraq's Gulf ports of Basra and Umm Qasr by the Soviets. Both sides
agreed to end their propaganda campaigns against each other. Both
sides looked to the settlement as providing opportunities to repair relationships with the Traditional states. In particular Iran's relationship
with the lesser Gulf actors had broken down after its seizure of the
Gulf islands in 1971. Iran took the opportunity of improved relations
to offer a collective security arrangement. The other Gulf states, however, rejected Iran's invitation as they did Iraq's.

The Gulf System after the Iranian Revolution

The Iranian Revolution overthrew the dynastic regime of the shah and
brought Ayatollah Khomeini to power in 1979 with his own brand of
radical Shiite ideological fervor. This ideological force introduced the
possibility of changes in the patterns of international political behavior
in the Gulf that could lead to the polarization of the Gulf international
system. These behavioral changes, attributable to Iran's ideological
fervor, have been evident in the conduct of the protracted Iraq–Iran
war and the formation of the Gulf Cooperation Council, or GCC.
Nevertheless, the Iranian Revolution has not introduced radical changes
to the underlying structure of the Gulf international system. The same
major actors with the same relative distribution of military capabilities
continue. Dynamic balance of power behavior continues to be evident
in the tentative alignment between the GCC states and Iraq. (Some
hallmarks of dynamic balance of power behavior in the relationships
between the superpowers and the Gulf states are examined in more
detail in chapter 5.)

Nonetheless the Iranian Revolution did introduce elements of instability into the balance of power in the Gulf, principal evidence of
which can be found in the prosecution of the Iraq–Iran war. It is not
clear whether Iraqi objectives in initiating the war were merely limited

to the capture of border areas. The possibility of capturing Khuzestan, the heart of Iranian oil production, was a more ambiguous goal. Khuzestan could have served as one of the spoils of war to be exchanged for an ultimate agreement to legitimize Iraq's retention of its other border area gains. On the other hand, the Iraqi invasion may have been motivated by more political objectives. For some period before the war Iraq had been chafing at the potential subversion against the Iraqi regime that could be created by Khomeini's revolutionary appeals to Iraqi Shiites, who constitute a majority of the Iraqi population. Iraq was aware of the turmoil in other ethnic areas of Iran caused by the Khomeini revolution. A successful capture of Khuzestan, therefore, might have been calculated upon by Ṣaddām Ḥusayn of Iraq as the entry point of a wedge with which to lever the overthrow of the Khomeini regime. Moreover, the Traditional states were also concerned about potential Shiite subversion. Under Saudi Arabian leadership the Traditional states heavily financed Iraqi war efforts in fall 1980.

When the war turned against Iraq, however, the Iranian regime did not stop at the former Iraqi border but reiterated that its war objective was the overthrow of Ḥusayn's regime. Notwithstanding multiple opportunities to negotiate a settlement of the conflict on withdrawal of Iraqi forces and return of the status quo, Iran has insisted on the removal of Ṣaddām Ḥusayn and heavy war raparations as additional conditions for peace.[7] Such unlimited objectives, obviously ideologically inspired, are destabilizing the dynamic balance of power.

The second sign of instability in the dynamic balance of power following the Iranian Revolution has been the formation of the GCC. In a stable dynamic balance of power, alignments are expected to be flexible and short-lived and all actors are expected to be available alliance partners. Before the Iranian Revolution the potential predominance in the Gulf of Iran or Iraq could be opposed by a coalition of the other Gulf states with whichever of the rivals appeared as the underdog. After the introduction of Iranian revolutionary ideological principles into the international politics of the Gulf, coalitions by the Traditional states with Iran became difficult. This created a dilemma for the Traditional states, who would not wish to increase the risk of either Iraqi predominance by an overt coalition to assist in the potential dismemberment of Iran or Iranian predominance if the Iraqi invasion failed. Their resolution of this dilemma has been the creation of a more cohesive alliance among themselves, which is intended to increase their collective security.

The GCC was not an automatic reaction to the revolutionary Iranian state. Various collective security arrangements had been discussed among the Gulf states after the Iranian Revolution. For example, after the new Iranian regime engaged in naval exercises in 1979, Oman reacted by proposing an international Western force to operate sophisticated surveillance equipment to counter superior Iranian naval forces, as well as a coordinated Gulf states ground force to respond to potential Iranian threats. Both Iraq and Saudi Arabia rejected the Omani proposal. Iraq proposed instead a collective security force with a joint military command composed of Gulf states (excluding Iran). The Saudis also responded by pressuring Oman to avoid inviting American and British forces into the Gulf and by conducting talks with South Yemen, Oman's enemy. Saudi Arabia also offered Oman financial assistance for weapons purchases.[8]

After Iraq became embroiled in the war with Iran, Saudi Arabia proposed the formation of the GCC in the January 1981 meetings of the Third Islamic Conference. The GCC was announced at a Gulf foreign ministers' meeting in February and its inaugural session took place in May 1981. It is not clear what subjects and priorities were privately discussed among the GCC states at these initial sessions. It has been reported that their topics included coordinating security efforts for oil fields and installations, as well as collective efforts against subversion.[9] These topics indicate some concern for security measures against the spread of Iranian revolutionary Shiism. Conceivably there was also concern over potential Iranian retaliation for massive financial assistance by the Traditional states to Iraq in its war against Iran. In its initial public posture, however, the GCC stressed matters of economic cooperation, safe topics that belied the lack of consensus on matters of collective security.

This inability to achieve an initial consensus on collective security was manifest in the polar positions on this issue taken by Kuwait and Oman. Kuwait, whose foreign minister made a point of visiting the Soviet Union prior to the inaugural meeting, strongly opposed the Omani proposal to coordinate Gulf defenses with U.S. assistance.[10] The Saudis through most of 1981 were sympathetic to the Kuwaiti objections. In fact the Saudis were reported to have offered substantial economic and military assistance, up to $1.2 billion, to induce Oman to deny the United States access to military facilities in Oman.[11] The Saudis underscored their own desire to maintain distance from the U.S. involvement in the Gulf by seeking during this same period to purchase enhanced air power and the AWACS (Airborne Warning and Control System aircraft) that the United States was operating from Saudi Arabia during the Iraq–Iran war. Outright purchase meant greater control over these sophisticated weapons and greater independence from the United States.

GCC positions on the institution of collective security measures softened by the end of 1981, however. Kuwait felt pressures during 1981 by both Iraq and Iran. Iraq wanted Kuwaiti concessions of a long-term lease over the disputed islands of Bubiyan and Warbah. And Kuwaiti oil installations were the target of a number of Iranian aerial bombing raids, including a damaging one in October 1981 on installations at Umm al-Aysh. Movement toward open collective security arrangements accelerated after the December 1981 Shiite plot to overthrow the Bahraini regime. At the January 1982 meeting of the defense ministers of the GCC states it was reported that an informal mutual defense pact was agreed upon. In addition, discussions were held on coordination of arms procurement, establishment of a local arms industry, coordination of armed forces, and integration of air defenses.[12] No formal mutual defense agreement among the GCC states has been reported, although Saudi Arabia proceeded in 1982 to conclude a series of bilateral mutual defense pacts with each of the GCC members except Kuwait.[13] Kuwait's reluctance to lessen its flexibility in dealing with Saudi Arabia by the conclusion of such a pact appears to have impeded the conclusions of a formal collective security agreement for the GCC at this time.

The absence of a formal consensus on a collective security agreement among all the GCC states has not impeded continuing efforts at economic integration as well as military coordination. A GCC Unified Economic Agreement of March 1, 1983 was reported as setting the grounds for interstate business regulation, free movement of vehicles, unified customs levies, labor regulations, foreign ownership regulations, and other common market concepts.[14] Furthermore, joint military maneuvers with ground and air forces of all six GCC states took place in October 1983.[15] Some other joint economic efforts, such as the twenty-mile causeway linking Saudi Arabia and Bahrain scheduled for completion in 1985, may also have military uses.[16]

Notwithstanding the destabilizing effects of the Iranian Revolution, the international political system of the Gulf retains its essential structure as a dynamic balance of power. The formation of the GCC itself demonstrates the continuing interest of the Traditional states to maintain flexibility in their relations with the United States, notwithstanding their continuing need for U.S. military assistance.

The Soviet Union has similarly been subjected to dynamic balance of power flexibility in its alignments with Gulf states. Iraq, despite its 1972 Treaty of Friendship with Moscow, distanced itself from the Soviet Union during the latter part of the seventies, when it persecuted Iraqi Communists and criticized the Soviet invasion of Afghanistan. The estrangement has continued for much of the Iraq–Iran war. Iraq substituted France for the Soviet Union as a major source for its weaponry, thus weakening Moscow's connection. Moscow's strongest link to the Gulf is with the Marxist-Leninist regime of South Yemen. Still it is not clear how much suzerain control the Soviet Union has over South Yemeni foreign relations. Saudi Arabia has made overtures toward South Yemen indicating its willingness and more recently GCC willingness to offer financial assistance. A pact among South Yemen, Ethiopia (which is a Soviet ally), and Libya (which is not necessarily a Soviet ally) was concluded in August 1981. The pact afforded South Yemen economic assistance from Libya, possibly as a counter to South Yemen's accepting the Saudi offer. The pact may also have been formed in reaction to a fear of an increased threat to South Yemen posed by the GCC.

Moscow has not created alignments in the Gulf between its allies Iraq and South Yemen. And it has not concerted the unification of South Yemen with North Yemen, with which Moscow has also attempted to form a close relationship. Iraq and South Yemen had broken off diplomatic relations after incidents involving South Yemen's harboring Iraqi Communists and Iraq harboring South Yemeni dissidents in 1979–80. Relations were resumed in 1982, but the South Yemeni regime declined to support Iraq's war efforts against Iran.[17]

North Yemen's relations with its neighbors also exhibits the flexibility of a dynamic balance of power player. North Yemen has long felt threatened by the radical Marxist regime in South Yemen, which has sponsored tribal border incidents and subversive groups operating in North Yemen, particularly the National Democratic Front. On the other hand, the two regimes have attempted to resolve their potential disputes by unification agreements. The Saudis have attempted to maintain their influence over North Yemen with significant amounts of foreign aid by way of both subsidies to the regime and direct sponsorship of community projects. Nonetheless, the Saudis even with additional U.S. military assistance for the North Yemen regime were unsuccessful in 1979 in warding off Soviet advances. The North Yemen regime accepted Soviet offers of a large military assistance package. To induce the North Yemen regime to relinquish the Soviet military connection, the Saudis threatened in vain to withdraw assistance to the North Yemen regime.[18] The Saudis simultaneously maintain other pressure on the North Yemen regime by providing certain tribal groups in North Yemen with subsidies and military assistance. These groups could also serve as a separatist force in the event of any unification of the Yemens. Although the GCC has spoken out in favor of unification efforts between North and South Yemen, it is doubtful that the Traditional states would welcome such a new state if it professed Marxist-Leninist principles. Hence, GCC discussion of a possible invitation for

North Yemen to join have also been reported. And it has also been reported that the Soviet Union has encouraged the repair of relations between Oman and South Yemen, possibly to counter these moves.[19]

It remains to be seen how this current international system in the Gulf will develop. If Iranian revolutionary fervor continues to bipolarize the other Gulf states ideologically, then the destabilizing effects on the system will probably continue. If the revolutionary fervor subsides, for example after Khomeini, possibly Iran will become a more acceptable alliance partner and greater flexibility will return to the dynamic balance of power alignment patterns. These, however, are only two of a large number of possible outcomes of the present instability of the Gulf international system. The others will be explored in the next chapters.

Conclusions

The foregoing examination of the international politics of the Gulf by investigation of the structure of its international system and the patterns of international political behavior demonstrates considerable changes to those international politics since the turn of the century. The current international politics, a dynamic balance of power, may change, just as prior systems changed from a loosely bipolar contest between the Ottoman and British empires, to an imperial system under British hegemony, to the present system. Even the dynamic balance of power system changed from pre–World War II to the current version according to changes in the number of major actors and distribution of their capabilities.

U.S. policy in the Gulf will need to be attuned to the possibility of changes to the current international system in the region. The likely sources of such changes are two: contests over territorial claims; and cleavages within political communities in the Gulf that create religious, ethnic, and ideological contests seeking to overthrow regimes or fracture their political communities.

3 Gulf Territorial Disputes

Conflicting territorial claims are conventionally viewed as sources of instability in international politics. In the Gulf such claims abound. Furthermore, Gulf territorial claims can involve valuable oil resources. Threats by a major actor such as Iraq against the territory of a lesser actor, particularly one with valuable oil reserves and installations such as Kuwait, are viewed as even more potentially destabilizing. They represent precisely the kinds of threats from within that may endanger Western oil supplies and evoke U.S. military reactions.

From the perspective of international political systems, however, territorial contests are an integral part of the international political process. They are another form of the unending concern for national security and the competition over capabilities that ensues. Territorial contests may or may not be destabilizing for any particular type of system. From the international systems perspective, therefore, the questions become: Can we distinguish patterns or types of contests over territory? How are these types of territorial contests related to the different patterns of international political behavior in each system? Can we therefore distinguish those patterns that may be destabilizing for each system, and in particular, the current dynamic balance of power system in the Gulf?

In a bipolar system contests over territory between the rival blocs are protracted. There are few incentives to resolve territorial disputes in order to bargain for alignments with the rival bloc. In the imperial system the imperial power is expected to impose quick settlements of potential territorial problems within the empire. At the periphery of the empire there is little incentive to resolve territorial disputes. In the dynamic balance of power system there are general expectations that territorial contests can be quickly settled. Actors need to preserve their flexibility of alignment, hence limit their objectives and avoid rigid diplomatic interactions. Territorial claims in a dynamic balance of power are advanced to increase capabilities but are repressed or retracted in order to satisfy the need for alignments.

The kinds of territorial disputes that are destabilizing for the international politics of the Gulf can therefore be identified as those that vary from the expected patterns. In the dynamic balance of power in the Gulf, principally one kind of territorial dispute is destabilizing:

contests involving claims not limited to border regions. Such disputes
are destabilizing for two reasons. One is that they risk creating revanchism, the kind of obsessional rivalry that interferes with flexible
alignments. An example of revanchism was the contest between France
and Germany between 1870 and 1918 over Alsace Lorraine. Second,
there is the risk in territorial contests not limited to border regions that
success may eliminate a major actor or cripple its capabilities. Hence
the other actors in the system risk losing an available or effective alliance partner and risk a bid for predominance by the victor of the
territorial contest.

The foregoing analysis raises a question of theoretical interest with
respect to the Gulf. Why should territorial contests not limited to border regions be destabilizing in the Gulf dynamic balance of power if
they involve contests between a major and a lesser actor? The risk
here is that the major actor will seek a wholesale takeover and will
eliminate the lesser actor. The risk of destabilization is illustrated by
the domino theory. According to the theory, once an aggressor has
whetted its appetite for conquest it will not stop at the borders of its
latest victim. Having measurably increased its capabilities, the aggressor will knock down the neighboring lesser actors until it has dominated
the region.

In the Gulf there has not yet been any international example of
the domino theory. There is a potential application of the theory and
hence the concern over wholesale elimination of lesser states. We have
identified two potentially predominant major actors with relatively superior capabilities to the others, Iran and Iraq. The lesser Gulf sheikhdoms have formed the GCC around Saudi Arabia for collective security
against predominance by either or both Iraq and Iran. Saudi Arabia,
although considered a major actor, could not unilaterally match the
military capabilities of either Iraq or Iran; nor could the collective
resources of the GCC. Hence, elimination of even lesser Gulf actors
by either Iraq or Iran would worsen the plight of the remaining Traditional states.

Would the same consideration apply if it were Saudi Arabia that
eliminated the lesser Gulf actors? Theoretically not, since the dynamic
balance of power in the Gulf could continue with the three major actors
of Iran, Iraq, and greater Saudi Arabia. As a practical matter, there
are a number of serious constraints on an expansionist Saudi Arabia
that make such actions unlikely. First, the current Saudi regime (unlike
that of Ibn Saud) is not ideologically expansionist. One would have to
imagine a radical regime taking over and pursuing expansionist objectives. The United States has declared its interest under the Reagan
corollary to the Carter Doctrine in preventing a radical takeover of

Saudi Arabia. This may have some deterrent effects. Even assuming a successful radical takeover, the Gulf sheikhdoms themselves might seek protection from Iraq and/or Iran. Some, such as Oman, would seek protection from the United States. Others, such as Kuwait, might seek protection from the Soviet Union. These alignments by the Gulf sheikhdoms would also have some deterrent effects. Finally, even if all deterrence failed, the result of conflict by an expansionist radical Saudi Arabia and the potential intervention into the region by the United States or the Soviet Union, may have its own effects on the dynamic balance of power system. As will be explored in chapter 6, such a system may not survive.

The Scope of the Review

Let us proceed to examine systematically the relations between each of the Gulf states and its neighbors for potentially destabilizing territorial claims and disputes. There are currently twenty-one such territorial relationships, represented by the twenty-one on-shore and off-shore boundaries between the ten Gulf states. We will not examine the territorial relations between Gulf states and other countries outside of the Gulf international system. Furthermore, the United Arab Emirates will be treated as a single state. The territorial relations (represented by twenty-three boundaries, including twelve small enclaves) between its seven constituent Trucial sheikhdoms will be excluded from this review. (See map 4 for UAE internal boundaries.)

Why examine all twenty-one relationships if some territorial disputes and boundaries may have been settled? The problem rests with the definition of "settlement." Some boundary settlements may indeed permanently withdraw a boundary from dispute; others may not. In the latter category falls the recent notable example of Iraq's abrogation on the eve of its invasion of Iran in 1980 of the Algiers Agreement of 1975, which had purportedly settled their boundary. Moreover, the absence of any recent claim does not necessarily preclude the future advancement of a territorial claim. This seems particularly a risk with a radical change of regime, as for example after the overthrow of the Iraqi monarchy in 1958 and the assertion of Iraq's claim to Kuwait in 1961 or after the overthrow of the shah of Iran in 1979 and the apparent revival of Iran's claim to Bahrain.

Furthermore, it is difficult to talk of the settlement of boundaries that have never been defined. Five of the twenty-one boundaries of the Gulf fit that category. In particular the boundaries at the periphery of the Rub al-Khali (Arabic for 'empty quarter') remain undefined.

Thus all of Oman's boundaries remain undefined except possibly part of its boundary with the UAE. Similarly Saudi Arabia's boundary with South Yemen has yet to be defined and there are only partially defined boundaries for the Yemens. Nor have all of the sixteen defined boundaries been substantially demarcated. This is of some significance because disputes over actual demarcation of boundaries already defined by agreement occasionally provide pretexts for disputes.[1]

Finally, the assertion or revival of any "settled" claim does not seem to lack for cause or pretext. In particular ample pretexts are available in the Gulf for ideological rejection of imperial definitions of Gulf boundaries. Most of the Gulf boundaries were the product of negotiations with at least one imperial power. Conversely, pretexts for territorial claims can also be found in acceptance of imperial definitions. Iraq, for example, has advanced territorial claims over Kuwait and Khuzestan based upon Iraq's succession to the imperial Ottoman boundaries and claims. Furthermore other kinds of pretexts also exist, as will be demonstrated in the review that follows of the territorial relations between each set of contiguous Gulf states.

Territorial Relations between Major Gulf Actors

Iraq and Iran

Pre-Twentieth-Century Conflicts and Settlements. The current conflict between Iraq and Iran over their border areas has its historical roots in conflicts between the Turks and the Persians over their imperial boundaries for more than three centuries. In 1639 the Turks and Persians drew the forerunner of the current Iraq–Iran frontiers in their Treaty of Zohab. This agreement divided the Kurdish tribes of the mountainous areas east and northeast of Baghdad. The frontiers continued to be battlegrounds, but the Treaty of Zohab was reaffirmed in a series of peace treaties marking conclusions of conflicts for the next two hundred years. These treaties also made provision for the safe passage of Persian Shiite pilgrims to Shiite shrines under Ottoman control in the three *vilayats* of Mosul, Baghdad, and Basra (all three of which comprise modern Iraq). The first Treaty of Erzerum in 1823 provided seasonal grazing rights across the border for frontier tribes, as well as payment of customary tributes and rents for pasture. No precise demarcation of the boundary, however, occurred until a mixed boundary commission of Turkish, Persian, British, and Russian members produced the basis for the 1847 Treaty of Erzerum. It took the commission another twelve years, from 1857 to 1869, to produce a

more detailed survey, and it took Turkey and Iran until 1875 to ratify
it. Even then religious and ethnic problems continued to recur at the
border regions.

The religious problems resulted from the animosities between the
Sunni Turks and Shiite Persians. The Turks were fearful of Shiite dissension and agitation. The Persians complained of the exploitation of
Shiite pilgrims to the now Iraqi shrines of Karbala, Kazimiyah, Sa-
marra, and Najaf. (Najaf is also considered a holy city for the burial
of Shiites.) The ethnic problems involved Kurdish dissension. In the
1880s Kurdish forces with Ottoman assistance raided Persia seeking to
unite Persian Kurds into a pro-Turkish state.

Territorial Conflicts at the Turn of the Century. A major territorial
conflict in 1905 was sparked by the alleged murder of the son of a
Persian Kurdish chieftain at the palace of the governor of the Persian
province of Azerbaijan. The chieftain switched his allegiance to the
Turks. This gave the Turks a pretext to invade and to reclaim northeastern Persian territory ceded to Persia in the Treaty of Erzerum. The
Turkish attack was contained by 1906 and negotiations were commenced through the good offices of the Germans. The Turks then took
advantage of a constitutional crisis in Persia to advance farther. The
Russian and British Empires had in the meantime been negotiating
their respective spheres of influence within Iran. In the Russian–British Convention of 1907 they agreed upon a Russian sphere in the north,
a British sphere in the southeast, and a neutral zone between them.
Under Russian and British pressure the Turks were then forced to
renounce their Persian territorial gains by troop withdrawals.

Another constitutional crisis in Persia in 1909 provided opportunities for further Turkish advances into northwestern Persia. The Russians also invaded. A second border area was put in dispute by Turkish
assistance to Persian Kurds in the central mountains. The Kurds were
supporting the efforts of the brother of the deposed shah to regain the
throne that had been lost during the constitutional crisis. The smaller
scale Turkish invasion in 1909 petered out into raids into Persia over
the next five years.

Yet a third border area, in the southern region, was put into dispute in 1910–11 when the Turks revived claims to the Hawiza district,
an area within the control of the semiautonomous sheikh of Mohammera. The district includes parts of the present day Iranian province
of Khuzestan. (Hawiza is now referred to by the Iraqis as "al-Ahwaz"
and Mohammera has been renamed by the Iranians as Khorramshahr.)
The Ottoman territorial claims affected British interests in the oil of
Hawiza, which had in 1909 been discovered by the British banker Wil-

liam Knox D'Arcy. British plans for the commercial exploitation of this Persian oil included a proposed pipeline through Hawiza to the refinery to be built on Abadan Island.

Territorial Settlements 1913–14. Intermittent negotiations over their Gulf boundaries occurred between the Ottoman and British empires between 1911 and 1913. The Turks were interested in establishing the terminus of the Baghdad Railway in Kuwait. The British were interested in containing Ottoman expansion by establishing Kuwait's boundaries and Ottoman territorial limits in Hawiza and the Turkish province south of Kuwait known as al-Hasa (which now forms part of the Saudi Arabian Eastern Province).

Agreements on all of these territorial issues, which form the basis of modern Gulf boundaries, were reached by the Ottoman, British, and Russian imperial powers, as well as Persia, over a period of extended negotiations between 1911 and 1914. The first agreement was a Protocol of Teheran between the Turks and Persians over procedures for establishing their common boundary. This was followed by a joint British–Turkish declaration of July 29, 1913. The declaration was never ratified by the Turks. Finally an agreement was reached in Constantinople in November 1913 by all powers, establishing a boundary commission with Turkish, Persian, British, and Russian members for the demarcation of the entire Turkish–Persian boundary from Mohammera to Mount Ararat. (These extended agreements will collectively be referred to as the Constantinople Agreements.)

The international boundary commission established by the Constantinople Agreements completed its work on the eve of World War I. The result of their work was to require Turkish withdrawal from invaded territory except for one strip in the Khanaqin–Mandali area and another north of the Sirwan River. These areas have proven to be problematic in subsequent border disputes including the current Iraq–Iran war. First, within these areas lies the westernmost projection of the Iranian boundary. From this projection the Iranian border is less than one hundred miles from Baghdad without significant obstacles to any Iranian invasionary force presented by the terrain between the border and the Iraqi capital.[2] Second, Khanaqin is within an oil-bearing region, part of a subterranean basin that includes the Nafte-Shah and Khaneh oil fields on the Iranian side. Cooperation of both sides is required for extraction of oil resources of this basin for their mutual benefit. Finally Iran's failure to have returned approximately 200–300 square kilometers of territory in this region as promised as a result of the Algiers Agreement of 1975 has been attributed as one of the causes of the current conflict.[3]

The other major border area whose resolution in the Constantinople Agreements has been the subject of enduring dispute involves the Shatt al-Arab. The 1847 Treaty of Erzerum had given Turkey control over the Shatt and gave Persia access to it at the town of Mohammera (Khorramshahr) at the confluence of the Qarun River. Persia was given navigation rights to that confluence from the head of the Gulf. Iran was also given the land on the eastern boundary of the Shatt, including the islands and waterways between the islands. Because of the increase of navigation at the turn of the century the British and Russians were inconvenienced by having to submit to Turkish inspection and unloading cargoes before reaching Mohammera. The international boundary commission of 1913–14 deferred to British and Russian pressure. It established the border one mile below the Qarun River, thus allowing free access to the port of Mohammera.

Disputes and Settlements, 1918–1975. The Constantinople Agreements represented territorial concessions made as part of general realignment negotiations among three imperial powers, the British, Ottoman, and Russian empires. Nonetheless, they have formed the bases for the two subsequent major settlements of 1937 and 1975, between the independent states of Iraq and Iran. Both of these settlements were also occasioned by dynamic balance of power needs for realignment.

After World War I during the period of British imperial predominance in the Gulf there were two recurring problems at the Iraq–Persian border. One was a problem of tribal raiding across the borders in the central Khanaqin and Qasr-i-Shirin areas and the Kurdish areas to the north. The other was a problem over navigation rights on the Shatt. Most of the tribal raiding problems were resolved by local frontier authorities. More major problems, such as the attempts by the brother of the deposed shah to instigate a Kurdish uprising against the Teheran regime in 1924–25 were dealt with by cooperation at the national level. Navigational disputes on the Shatt, however, proved more intractable because of the international interest.

The British had controlled the Shatt during the First World War through a Basra Port Directorate, which was turned over to Iraq after the war and renamed the Basra Port Authority. Iran claimed that Iraq's control over the Shatt through the Basra Port Authority and its collection of revenues from all but local ships using the Shatt violated the Constantinople Agreements. Iran construed those agreements as locating the international boundary in the middle of the Shatt. Disputes ensued over Iran's use of its own pilots and navigational signals, supported by the small Iranian navy, in disregard of the Basra Port Authority. Iran did not possess the military capability, however, to force the issue. Bilateral negotiations began in 1929 and dragged through to 1934, before Iran submitted the issue to the League of Nations. No settlement was reached until 1937, however.

During the mid-1930s concern by Iran, Iraq, Turkey, and Afghanistan over potential Soviet aggression and the absence of any credible British deterrent gelled the need for a collective security agreement. In 1937 this arrangement became known as the Sa'dabad Pact. A byproduct of this realignment was the 1937 Iraq–Iran border agreement called the "1937 Agreement." It recognized the land boundaries of the Constantinople Agreements but set the thalweg of the Shatt as the riverine boundary for 6 kilometers opposite the port of Abadan. The thalweg is the line of greatest depth or fastest current, hence the most navigable channel of a navigable waterway. This gave Iran freer access to Abadan but still allowed Iraq to control most of the Shatt. The 1937 Agreement also called for a joint commission to regulate navigation, but the operation of the commission soon broke down over its powers. Iraq maintained they were consultative; Iran maintained that they were executive. The 1937 Agreement otherwise required the use of Iraqi pilots on all of the 120 miles of the Shatt. It reaffirmed Iraqi control of the Shatt by designating the low-water mark at the east bank as the international boundary, other than the thalweg area.

Disputes over Iraq's navigational control of the Shatt flared up from time to time after the 1937 Agreement. One flare-up occurred in 1954 when Iran protested the revenue allocation of the Basra Port Authority. Iran claimed that 70 percent of the shipping on the Shatt used Iranian ports but the Authority spent only 40 percent of its revenues on maintenance of the Shatt and 60 percent on improving Iraqi ports. The dispute was quieted when both states joined the Baghdad Pact in 1955. Iraq left the Baghdad Pact in 1959 after Qāsim's overthrow of the Iraqi monarchy, and the Shatt dispute revived between 1959 and 1960 as well as in 1961. Iraq reasserted the prerogatives of the Authority and interfered with Iranian shipping. Iran questioned the validity of the 1937 Agreement and claimed sovereignty to the thalweg of the entire Shatt. Qāsim reclaimed the small thalweg area opposite Abadan. Iran in early 1961 then used Iranian pilots at Iranian ports. Iraq retaliated with a strike of Iraqi pilots that shut down Abadan for nine weeks. Iranian pilots were withdrawn, but no further settlement was reached. After the Ba'thist regime took power in Iraq in 1968, it revived the Shatt issue by declaring its intensions to reassert sovereignty over the entire Shatt in April 1969. Iran responded by unilaterally abrogating the 1937 accords and escorting a freighter up the Shatt with gunboats and jet fighters. Thereafter Iraq neither interfered with Iranian navigation nor conceded the Iranian claim to the middle of the entire thalweg riverine boundary. This concession was not made until the 1975 Algiers Agreement between the two states, which resolved all boundary issues.

The 1975 Settlement. The Algiers Agreement of 1975 had been preceded by a series of border incidents in 1972 in the central border area of Khanaqin and Qasr-i-Shirin in the north to Badrah and Mehran in the south. The incidents were interrupted by the common front during the October War against Israel in 1973, then resumed in later 1973 and in 1974. As the border fighting escalated, Iraq sought United Nations mediation. The United Nations arranged a cease fire in March 1974 and made recommendations for resolution of the demarcation problems of the 130-mile central border area. Notwithstanding UN mediation efforts, border incidents increased in the fall of 1974 with a recrudescence of the Kurdish rebellion against Iraq. Iran increased its military assistance to the Kurds with sophisticated weaponry. In the early part of 1975 Soviet military assistance to Iraq under their 1972 Treaty of Friendship increased and a major escalation of border hostilities was anticipated in the spring of 1975. Hostilities, however, were abated through the mediation efforts of the Algerian premier at the OPEC conference at Algiers. This mediation led to the March 6, 1975 agreement between the combatants known as the Algiers Agreement.

The Algiers Agreement compromised all of the outstanding issues between the parties. Iraq conceded equal control over the Shatt by recognizing sovereignty of both Iraq and Iran up to the thalweg along the entire waterway. Both sides agreed to a joint commission to demarcate their central border. Iran agreed to halt its military assistance to the Kurds. The work of the joint commission was agreed upon in June 1975 by the Treaty of Baghdad. The Treaty of Baghdad also attempted to settle grievances created over Iraqi persecution of Shiites. Iraq had expelled some 65,000 Shiites in retaliation for Iran's reassertion of rights to the Shatt in 1969 and seizure of the Gulf islands of the Tunbs, as well as occupation of the island of Abu Musa, in 1971. The Treaty of Baghdad established a commission to consider compensation to the expelled Shiites, as well as another commission to assist with the resettlement of Kurdish refugees from Iraq in Iran.[4]

The Algiers Agreement can be viewed as a dynamic balance of power settlement for a number of reasons. Both sides settled for limited gains without preserving the interests of their respective allies. Both sides were facing the possibility of escalation into a major conflict. From the Iranian point of view, whatever the balance of their military capabilities with Iraq, Iraq's need for continuing and increasing Soviet weaponry would have only entrenched Soviet influence in the Gulf.

From the Iraqi point of view, they would be facing both Iranian and Kurdish forces. It is not clear that the interests of the USSR were adverse to those of Iraq. It is clear, however, that Iran's separate peace with Iraq was so surprising to the Kurds that their revolt collapsed within two weeks of the Algiers Agreement.[5]

Furthermore, the context of the settlement at the OPEC meeting suggests that an alliance of Iran and Iraq on OPEC issues may have been a further incentive. Besides, Iraq was facing an acrid dispute with Syria over Syria's damming of the Euphrates during the 1974–75 drought. Iraq welcomed the respite on its eastern flank to deal with potential hostilities on its western flank. Settlement with Iraq had additional benefits from Iran's point of view. Iran anticipated reviving its efforts to improve relations in the Gulf after the Gulf island takeovers of 1971. Iraqi sponsored efforts to "liberate Arabestan" (Khuzestan) as well as to maintain anti-Iranian propaganda in retaliation for the island takeovers had interfered with Iran's potential Gulf state alignments.[6] Settlement with Iraq offered the possibility of abatement of Iraqi propaganda and subversion. Iraq also was provided with the opportunity to solidify its relationships with the other Gulf states after settling with Iran. Iraq's need for increased Soviet weaponry and the implicit close Soviet connection had contributed to its alienation from the Traditional states. With increased oil revenues and decreased military commitments, Iraq was able to diminish its dependency on Soviet arms.

The Iraq–Iran War, 1979–Mid-1983. In 1979 there was a change of government in both Iran and Iraq. The Khomeini regime came to power in Iran, and Ṣaddām Ḥusayn in Iraq, although the latter brought about no radical change of orientation in Iraq's Ba'thist regime. An ideological struggle ensued. Khomeini championed Shiism in Iraq, causing agitation among Iraqi Shiites, and calling Ḥusayn an infidel. Ḥusayn championed autonomy for the Arabs of Khuzestan, supporting the Al-Ahwaz Liberation Front, and calling for return of the Gulf islands occupied by Iran since 1971. Ḥusayn, who had assisted with the negotiation of the Algiers Agreement, considered it a humiliation and expressed desires for recognition of Iraqi sovereignty over the Shatt and for border readjustments. Some border incidents were reported in 1979 but were associated with efforts by both sides to suppress Kurdish dissidence.[7] As the tensions in the ideological war increased in 1980, particularly in the late summer, so did the frequency of border incidents in the central border region. Then on September 10, 1980 Iraq seized strips of territory around Musian that Iraq claimed should have been returned pursuant to the Algiers Agreement. One week later,

Iraq officially abrogated the Algiers Agreement and five days afterward launched a full-scale invasion at four points along the border.

Iraqi war aims appeared to be greater than mere border readjustments and were most likely the capture of Khuzestan. Securing Khuzestan would have been necessary, among other things, to support Husayn's reassertion of Iraqi sovereignty over the entire Shatt and to compel a favorable settlement of other claims including a withdrawal of Iran from the Gulf islands. Iraqi military strategy appeared to aim for a fait accompli by capturing the key oil facility areas of Khuzestan before any military campaign would bog down in the November rainy season. Iraqi targets included Abadan, which contained key refining facilities, Khorramshahr, which had significant terminal facilities, and Dezful and al-Ahwaz, where critical pipeline junctures were located.[8]

Iraq's strategy for advancement of its territorial claim on Khuzestan appeared to take advantage of Iran's postrevolutionary political predicament. Within Iran itself Husayn may have overcalculated the degree of popular support among Khuzestani Arabs for his campaign to "liberate" them. However, Iraq believed it was generally advantaged by the new Iranian regime's problems with dissident minorities, particularly the Kurds, and with demoralization in the Iranian armed forces. Fear of the export of Khomeini's revolution had alienated Iran from potential Gulf state support and conversely encouraged significant financial contribution to Husayn's campaign from Saudi Arabia, Kuwait, and to a lesser extent from the UAE. In the larger Middle East system Iraq may not have counted upon Syria's alignment with Iran, but it did gain important logistical assistance from Jordan. The Jordanian alignment was critical to Husayn's campaign because it permitted Iraq to import vital supplies across its western border in the face of the superior Iranian naval capabilities that could block supplies coming through Iraq's Gulf ports.

In the global international system Iraq probably counted correctly on the neutrality of the United States and at least the neutrality if not the assistance of the Soviet Union. The Soviet Union, although an official ally of Iraq, had been estranged by Iraqi persecution of Communists and substitution of France as a significant source of military supplies. In any event the Soviet Union was preoccupied with its own problems in pacifying Afghanistan. The United States was embroiled with the Khomeini regime over its holding of U.S. diplomats and others as hostages. Moreover, Iran's alienation from the United States deprived Iran of the opportunity of obtaining U.S. parts, supplies, and maintenance for much of the sophisticated weaponry in the Iranian armed force, particularly its air force.

The Iraqi strategy failed. Iran had by the time of this writing re-

pelled the Iraqi forces and had declared its own war aims of the overthrow of Ḥusayn, large-scale war reparations, and territorial settlement
(possibly, but not clearly a return to the status quo of the Algiers
Agreement).[9] Iran's alignment with Syria had proved disastrous for
Iraq because the Syrians prevented the transit of Iraqi oil through the
pipeline to the Mediterranean and Iran had cut off all other Iraqi oil
exports except through the pipeline through Turkey.[10] Iraq's failure to
eliminate Iran's capability of exporting oil and its inability to maintain
significant financial support from Iraq's Gulf state allies has locked
Iraq into a defensive war of attrition with Iran. Iraq now appears committed to seeking a settlement of the war, and Iran just as committed
to prosecuting it in Iraqi territory.

Iraq and Saudi Arabia

The Iraq–Saudi border was created by the British in negotiations with
Ibn Saud during the heyday of the British imperium in the Gulf. After
World War I, the British, who controlled Iraqi affairs through a League
of Nations mandate, became concerned over the territorial definition
of their mandate as Ibn Saud expanded his control north and west of
Nejd. By the end of 1921 Ibn Saud had taken the key town of Hail
and was in a position to exert control over the various tribes that
engaged in spring raiding and counterraiding into Iraq. Following such
tribal contests in the spring of 1922, the British high commissioner in
Iraq invited Saudi representatives to Baghdad to settle the border. The
Treaty of Mohammera, concluded in May 1922 subject to Ibn Saud's
ratification, drew a straight line through the tribal region, assigning
certain tribes to each side of the border and setting up a commission
to define the ownership of border wells. It also established agreements
on prevention of raiding and the protection of pilgrims. Ibn Saud refused to ratify the treaty.
    Direct negotiations between the British high commissioner and Ibn
Saud reconvened at Uqair at the end of November 1922. Ibn Saud
objected to the straight line boundary as interfering with the annual
tribal migrations to the Euphrates and proposed a tribal boundary
based upon ownership of desert wells, with commonly owned wells to
be declared neutral. The British high commissioner reacted by drawing
a straight line boundary from the Gulf to a point close to the Iraqi–
Transjordan frontier, and to compensate Ibn Saud, the commissioner
drew a new boundary with Kuwait and gave Ibn Saud a large chunk

of Kuwaiti territory. Out of the straight line boundaries the commissioner drew two Neutral Zones to assure tribal migration into both Iraq and Kuwait. It was also agreed that no forts would be built close to either side of the border or in the Iraqi Neutral Zone. The parties also ratified other provisions of the Treaty of Mohammera concerning raiding and pilgrims, referring to their agreements as the Protocol of Uqair.

The 1922 agreements concerning the Saudi–Iraqi boundary have withstood the test of time with very few adjustments despite their potentially ideological offensiveness to a nationalist Iraq because of their imperialist genesis. Adjustments occurred principally as a result of tribal raiding and over the need for joint administration in the Neutral Zone. Tribal raiding, which Ibn Saud failed to control, compelled the British to erect border forts in violation of the Treaty of Mohammera. The issue was settled without the British in the Treaty of Bon Voisinage, Friendship, and Extradition of 1931 signed by Ibn Saud with Iraq.

Agreements over the administration of the Neutral Zone have not necessarily been easy to achieve. Consistent with dynamic balance of power expectations, they have been concluded only during periods of closer alignment between Iraq and Saudi Arabia. In 1936 King Ghāzī of Iraq concluded a Treaty of Alliance with Saudi Arabia. The alignment overcame the dynastic feud that had been created between Ibn Saud and Ghāzī's Hashemite family, which resented the earlier defeat of the Hashemite ruler of the Hejaz by Ibn Saud. The need for alignment with Ibn Saud was probably occasioned by Iraq's need to neutralize potential Saudi objections to King Ghāzī's pretentions to Kuwait. In 1936 King Ghāzī had founded an Association of Arabs of the Gulf and was directing propaganda into Kuwait seeking to convince the population of the need for union with Iraq.[11] During this same period Iraq joined the Sa'dabad Pact for collective security reasons. Iraq was just as interested in maintaining friendly relations with Saudi Arabia. Thus in 1938 the two states concluded an agreement providing for joint administration of the Neutral Zone.

After Qāsim's overthrow of the Iraqi monarchy in 1958 and subsequently the Ba'thist entrenchment of power in Iraq in 1968 relations with Saudi Arabia became estranged, notwithstanding their occasional collective opposition to Israel. A Ba'thist propaganda campaign against Saudi Arabia, as well as the Iraqi regime's development of close relations with the Soviet Union after 1972 heightened this estrangement.[12] In 1975 after the Algiers Agreement with Iran, Iraq sought a similar dynamic balance of power realignment with Saudi Arabia. Iraq

needed to repair its relations with Saudi Arabia to obtain Saudi neutrality in the confrontation with Syria over the Euphrates water flow.
In July 1975 it was reported that Saudi Arabia and Iraq had concluded
an agreement dividing the Neutral Zone by a line of demarcation as
straight as possible to the existing border.[13]

The Iranian Revolution occasioned another period of Iraqi–Saudi
cooperation in the face of potential Iranian subversion against both
states. Thus in September 1979 Iraq and Saudi Arabia concluded a
security agreement. This agreement reportedly included provisions for
intelligence coordination and extradition. The Shiite coup attempt in
Bahrain in December 1981 possibly indicated that greater cooperation
between Saudi Arabia and Iraq was necessary, notwithstanding Saudi
Arabia's development with the GCC of a collective security organization. Further agreement between Iraq and Saudi Arabia over the
Neutral Zone was announced by both states in December 1981 and
was followed by the announcement of two protocols over tribal movements and border administration in February 1982.[14]

Iran and Saudi Arabia

Iran and Saudi Arabia share no boundary except that involving their
respective continental shelves. Each state has taken different approaches to the measurement of this boundary in order to maximize
the amount of continental shelf that could be claimed and within which
oil exploration concessions could be granted. Iran has a steep coastline
and few islands. Hence in dealing with a division of the continental
shelf by drawing a median line from opposite Gulf coasts Iran prefers
to measure from the high-water line, rather than the conventional low-
water line, which favors the shallower coastlines of the Arab states.
Iran also prefers to disregard islands in determining baselines for the
division, except for the Iranian island of Kharg.

Both Saudi Arabia and Iran had granted overlapping oil exploration concessions, as a result of their differing conceptions of the continental shelf baselines. Agreement over a common boundary became
necessary after the discovery of oil at the Firaydun-Marjun oil field,
which overlaps the median line of their continental shelf division. The
international political conditions for a boundary agreement matured
with the prospect of British withdrawal from the Gulf and the potential
hostility of the Ba'thist regime, which took power in Iraq in 1968. Both
Saudi Arabia and Iran probably wanted to remove the obstacle of a
potential territorial dispute from the path of their mutual need for
alignment in the face of potential Iraqi threats.

In the continental shelf agreement of 1968 that resulted, Saudi Arabia, which has few islands in the Gulf, agreed to give Kharg Island a special status. Kharg Island was given a "half effect," halfway between ignoring it and treating it as part of the mainland. This enabled the parties to adjust the median line to reflect their economic solution to the Firaydun-Marjun oil field to enable each side to obtain a half share in the oil from that field. The agreement also compromised a potential dispute over the Gulf islands of Farsi and al-Arabiyah. It gave Farsi to Iran and al-Arabiyah to Saudi Arabia, as well as recognizing a twelve-mile territorial limit for each of the parties.[15]

Territorial Relations between Major Actors and Lesser Actors

Iraq and Kuwait

The shape of the Kuwaiti boundary with Iraq originates with British imperial decisions at the beginning of the century and remains a source of dispute between the two states. In establishing their de facto protectorate over Kuwait during the period of 1902–1904 British agents reported what support they could find for the legitimacy of Sheikh Mubārak's claims to areas north of Kuwait Bay that were under occupation by Ottoman troops. From these reports, as well as from concerns over the amount and nature of the military capabilities they would need to commit to maintain a defense of the Kuwaiti area, the British determined they could not support all of Mubārak's claims. The sheikh's claims to the northernmost town of Safwan they rejected, but they accepted his claims to Bubiyan Island. Bubiyan and the neighboring island of Warbah command the access to the channel close to the coast on which the port of Umm Qasr is located. The Turks had maintained a garrison of forces at Umm Qasr.

The ultimate resolution of these imperial boundary disputes was reached during the negotiation of the Constantinople Agreements of 1913. The imperial powers gave Umm Qasr to the Turks, gave the Islands of Bubiyan and Warbah to Kuwait, and drew an almost semi-circular perimeter for the northern boundary which conceded Safwan to the Turks. After the British relinquished their post–World War I mandate over Iraq, Iraq and Kuwait acknowledged their boundary in an exchange of letters in 1932 between the prime minister and ruler of the respective parties.

Subsequently Iraq has attempted to incorporate Kuwait into Iraq on at least two occasions. The first occurred in the 1930s when an attempt was made by King Ghāzī of Iraq to induce a union between Iraq and Kuwait. Iraqi propaganda succeeded in getting the advisory council to the Kuwaiti ruler to advocate such a union, emphasizing the economic advantages. The British pressured the sheikh of Kuwait to dismiss the council and disown the resolutions. The British also deterred Ghāzī's proposed intervention in Kuwait after riots ensued.[16] The second attempt to incorporate Kuwait occurred after the British withdrew from Kuwait and its independence was announced in 1961. Qāsim, the dictator of Iraq, proclaimed that Kuwait should be considered part of Iraq on the basis of its status as a *qada* within the Ottoman *vilayat* of Basra. It is not clear, however, that Qāsim was prepared to support his proclamation militarily. Iraq was embroiled at that time in a struggle with the Kurds and maintained only a small garrison force at its southern border with Kuwait.[17] In any event the sheikh of Kuwait invoked his defense treaty with Britain and the British returned with a contingent of forces. Attempts to resolve the dispute at the United Nations were blocked by the Soviets. Kuwait was then admitted to the Arab League over Iraqi objections and a joint contingent of Saudi, Egyptian, Jordanian, and Syrian forces replaced the British contingent.

Since the overthrow of Qāsim, successive Iraqi regimes appear to have repressed any interest in the incorporation of Kuwait and have limited their territorial objectives to portions of Kuwait that affect their free access to Umm Qasr. The short-lived Ba'thist regime, which overthrew Qāsim, sought to improve Iraq's relations with other Arab states. It concluded an agreement in October 1963 with Kuwait recognizing Kuwait's independence within the frontiers that had been confirmed in 1932 and established a joint commission for a final delimitation of the boundary. Kuwait in return agreed to provide economic assistance to Iraq and undertook to renounce its defense agreement with the British at an opportune time.[18]

The Ba'thist regime that took power in Iraq in 1968 revived Iraqi interest in Kuwaiti territory. The British had earlier in 1968 announced their intention of withdrawing all forces from the Gulf within four years. Without a credible British deterrent in the Gulf, Kuwait chose to align with Iraq to protect its security interests, and in May 1968 Kuwait terminated its defense agreement with Britain. As the new Iraqi regime confronted Iran in 1969 over the Shatt, Kuwait, which aligned with Iraq over the issue, was pressured to permit Iraqi forces to be stationed over the border to protect Umm Qasr.

Additional reasons for Iraqi acquisition of Kuwaiti territory became clearer as Iraq developed its oil production and Soviet connection in 1972. The deep water off Bubiyan Island became attractive as an oil terminal that could be serviced by pipelines from the Iraqi mainland. Furthermore, incorporating the Kuwaiti islands of Bubiyan and Warbah would extend the Iraqi Gulf coastline and with it Iraqi claims for additional continental shelf at the head of the Gulf. The Soviet Union, which was assisting with Iraq's oil and military development, also looked to Umm Qasr's potential as a naval base that would be made available to the Soviet navy.

Iraq began to pressure Kuwait for concessions late in 1972 and after Kuwaiti rejection of a proposed agreement embodying Iraqi demands, Iraq attacked two Kuwaiti border posts in March 1973. Saudi mobilization at the border with Iraq and Arab League diplomatic intercession, as well as a possible financial inducements, appear to have obtained an Iraqi pullback of forces from the area of the border. Iraqi forces did not, however, pull back from the coastal strip south of Umm Qasr, on the grounds of needing to protect Iraq's Gulf port from Iranian threats.

After the resolution of the Shatt dispute by the 1975 Algiers Agreement between Iran and Iraq, the maintenance of Iraqi forces on the coastal strip south of Umm Qasr could no longer be justified. The troops were not withdrawn, however, until 1977 in the wake of Iraq's general concern to mend its relations with the Gulf states.

After the Iraqi attack on Iran in September 1980, Iraq revived its efforts to obtain the use of Bubiyan and Warbah to protect Umm Qasr and began to pressure Kuwait into conceding a long-term lease of these islands. The pressure was applied through the Kuwaiti National Assembly and possibly by promotion of sabotage.[19]

Iran and Bahrain

Iran within this century has asserted two kinds of territorial claims over Bahrain. The one that preceded the Iranian Revolution was purely dynastic. The other, which followed the revolution, stemmed from Khomeini-inspired religious fervor and looked to an additional common Shiite connection. The dynastic claim stemmed from Persian control over the island prior to its seizure in 1783 by the Āl Khalīfah sheikhs and 'Utaybī Arabs. This claim was maintained by Reza Shah in the form of various diplomatic protests and offers to Britain. For example, Reza Shah offered to sell Britain the Iranian claim to Bahrain for concessions during the negotiations of the 1929 Anglo–Iranian treaty. Furthermore, Iran protested the oil concessions to Standard Oil on Bahrain and the naval base built by the British at Jufayr in 1934. Reza Shah also kept alive Iran's claim to Bahrain by listing the island as a Persian province in official publications. This practice was followed by the Shah's son and successor, Muḥammad Reza Shah, who in 1957–58 included Bahrain within a list of places covered by a new administrative province.[20]

As Muḥammad Reza Shah perceived the need for Gulf state alignments in the 1960s to counter Nasserite propaganda as well as potential Gulf state hostility to the shah's pretensions to becoming policeman of the Gulf, the Iranian claims against Bahrain were repressed. This Iranian policy was directly challenged after the British announcement in early 1968 of its withdrawal from the Gulf. The shah's naval build-up would have provided the capability of a military takeover of Bahrain after the British left. Iran's reassertion of its claims to Bahrain, particularly in opposition to the proposed federation of Trucial states with Bahrain, would have completely alienated other Gulf states.

The shah opted to maintain his relationships with the Gulf states and announced in early 1969 that Iran would allow Bahrainis to choose their own fate. The UN secretary general was invited to appoint a commission of enquiry, which reported in May 1970 that almost all Bahrainis wanted independence. (Independence was gained in August 1971.) In June 1971, just prior to independence the shah and Bahrain reached agreement over their continental shelf boundary. The agreement drew a median line of approximately twenty-nine nautical miles, essentially equidistant from both shores but wedged between other continental shelf boundaries of Iran with Saudi Arabia and with Qatar.

After Khomeini took power in Iran in early 1979, Iranian claims to Bahrain were revived. An unofficial but nevertheless widely reported statement of Ayatollah Sādiq Rūhānī, a revolutionary leader, in February 1979 claimed Bahrain as Iran's "fourteenth province." Official disavowal of that position notwithstanding, Iranian appeals were made to instigate revolution among the substantial Shiite population of Bahrain. Iran also promoted subversion against the Bahraini regime, most notably in the December 1981 Shiite coup attempt. And Iran reportedly maintains an Islamic Front for the Liberation of Bahrain.[21]

Iran and the UAE

Iran occupied three Gulf islands, Abu Musa and the Greater and Lesser Tunbs, on the eve of the British withdrawal from the Gulf in November 1971. Although the occupation of Abu Musa was with the agreement of its owner, Sharjah, the takeover of the Tunbs Islands was opposed by Ras al-Khaymah, their former owner. Moreover, Iran's rights to these Gulf islands have been disputed by Iraq, which proclaimed their recovery as one of its war aims in 1980.

Iran's claims to these Gulf islands were dynastic and based upon tribute occasionally paid to the Persians in the eighteenth and nineteenth centuries by the Qawasim sheikhs who controlled Sharjah and Ras al-Khaymah. The shah had asserted such dynastic claims during negotiations with the British over Bahrain and the status of the Trucial sheikhdoms after the British announcement of its proposed withdrawal from the Gulf. The British bargained for Iranian recognition of the proposed federation of the Trucial sheikhdoms into the UAE in return for not opposing the shah's dealings with Sharjah over Abu Musa.[22] No negotiations were possible over the Tunbs since Iran and Ras al-Khaymah refused to deal with each other.

The shah's real interest in these islands appears to have been economic and strategic. Their economic value results from the additional baselines they provide from which to measure Iran's continental shelf within the Gulf. These extensions of the Iranian coastline support claims to potential oil deposits. The strategic value of the islands is somewhat symbolic. The navigational channels after the Strait of Hormuz pass between the Tunbs and Abu Musa (outbound) and on the other side of the Tunbs (inbound). It is conceivable, however, that other navigational channels could be found, as could other strategic locations that may command them. Iran already possesses a number of islands for that purpose, including Qeshm and Sirrī, as well as the coastline opposite the Strait of Hormuz. The Tunbs are in effect desolate rocks, and Abu Musa does not appear suitable for an air field, although it has a small port and is large enough to support a military base.

Iran reached an agreement with Sharjah in November 1971 over joint sovereignty of Abu Musa that permitted the stationing of Iranian troops and shared revenues from oil deposits. The agreement also provided Iranian financial assistance to Sharjah until its oil revenues reached approximately $7 million annually. Both sides also recognized a twelve-mile limit of territorial waters around the island. At the end of November 1971 Ras al-Khaymah was in no position to oppose Iran's forcible takeover of the Tunbs. It had chosen to remain outside of the UAE and with the withdrawal of British forces lost its source of protection.

The Khomeini regime, which has renounced the shah's pretensions to become the policeman of the Gulf, has not renounced Iranian occupation of the disputed islands. Nor has the new regime renounced its claims to other smaller Gulf islands disputed with constituents of the UAE. These include Sir Bani Yas, disputed with Abu Dhabi, and Abu Nuayr, disputed with Sharjah, as well as the island of Sirri still claimed by Sharjah notwithstanding Iranian occupation.[23]

Iran and Kuwait

The boundary between Iran and Kuwait is a continental shelf boundary like that between Iran and Saudi Arabia. Unlike the Saudi Arabian boundary, however, the Kuwaiti boundary is a casualty of the rivalry between Iraq and Iran. Agreement was reached between Iran and Kuwait in January 1968 that gave both parties full effect to the Iranian island of Kharg and the Kuwaiti island of Faylakah. Iraq denounced the agreement as prejudicial to its own continental shelf claims. Hence there has been no ratification of the Kuwait–Iran agreement.

Iran and Oman

The only boundary between Iran and Oman is the continental shelf boundary of approximately 125 nautical miles established by the agreement of July 1974 between the parties. The definition of the end point of the continental shelf within the Gulf was left open pending a resolution of the dispute between Oman and Ras al-Khaymah. The median line stretches for about 15 nautical miles at their overlapping territorial waters in the Strait of Hormuz.

It is doubtful that Iran has any viable claim to the Musandam Peninsula. Any latent historical claim has a long period of quiescence to overcome. The Āl Bū Saʿīd dynasty, whose sultan currently rules Oman, has been in power since 1749.[24]

Iran and Qatar

Iran and Qatar also share a boundary that divides their continental shelf. An agreement over such division was concluded in 1969. The median line is generally equidistant from both shores. Unlike the Iranian continental shelf division with Oman, which gives effect to some offshore islands in some areas, the Iranian division with Qatar completely disregards all islands in the Gulf. Furthermore, one section of the division is undetermined because of the dispute between Bahrain and Qatar.

Saudi Arabia's Eastern Boundaries
(with the UAE, Qatar, Oman)

The original eastern boundary agreed to by Ibn Saud was set by the Constantinople Agreements. These drew a so-called Blue Line directly south of the island of Zakhuniyah to the west of Qatar. A Violet Line was drawn at a 45 degree angle from the end point of the 1905 agreement between the imperial powers over the Yemen–Aden boundary to intersect with the Blue Line at the twentieth parallel.

There have been a number of challenges to that boundary by Ibn Saud and later Saudi Arabia in the sixty years that followed the Constantinople Agreements. (See map 5.) An incomplete resolution of the boundary was achieved in an agreement of 1974 between Saudi Arabia and Abu Dhabi (in effect the UAE). The Saudi challenges to that boundary have raised three issues. The first involved tribal loyalties claimed by the Saudis and used as a basis for demands to extend the frontier northeastward to the Buraymi oasis and north through the Liwa oasis. The second issue involved strategic access to the Khaur al-Udaid and coast south of the Qatar peninsula. And the third issue involved competition for oil concessions and resources at the eastern projection of the boundary.

In the period of 1925–1927 Saudi forces penetrated to the Buraymi oasis and began collecting *zakat* (tithes), symbols of allegiance and dominion, from the Abu Dhabi tribes at the oasis. This penetration was based upon historic grounds. During the nineteenth century until their expulsion in 1869 Wahhabi forces from Nejd, the Saudi stronghold, had intermittently garrisoned Buraymi. Buraymi was at that time strategically located for the purpose of raiding or threatening the Trucial coast to the north or the Omani interior to the south.[25] To forestall Saudi assistance to a pretender to the sultanate, the ruler of Abu Dhabi agreed in the late 1920s to permit regular *zakat* collectors to enter Buraymi. In 1930, the sultan protested and local tribes resisted similar *zakat* collection efforts at the Liwa oasis.

In 1933 Ibn Saud granted an oil concession to Standard Oil of California to the easternmost boundaries of the Kingdom. The oil company's request for clarification from the British as to the location of such boundaries precipitated the next phase of the Saudi claims. The British affirmed the Blue Line, and after some negotiation, the Saudis proposed the Red Line in 1935. The Red Line gave the Kingdom the Khaur al-Udaid, a series of wells through Sufuq and Jabal Nakhsh, and very little of the Liwa oasis, but laid no claim to Buraymi. The British proposed a compromise from the Blue Line, which was named the Green Line and after some adjustment the Riyadh Line, but refused to concede the Khaur, the Sufuq and Jabal Nakhsh line of wells, or any of the Liwa oasis. Negotiations continued but stalemated, since Saudi Arabia was in no position to challenge Britain militarily over the issue.

The third Saudi challenge to its British-imposed eastern boundary occurred as oil explorations by the Arabian American Oil Company (Aramco, jointly owned by Standard Oil of California, the Texas Oil Company, Standard Oil of New Jersey, and Socony Vacuum–Mobil Oil) ventured into the disputed territory under Saudi armed escort in March 1949. Protests and negotiations ensued; then in October 1949 Saudi Arabia proposed a new boundary starting at the Abu Dhabi coast sixty miles west of Abu Dhabi town running approximately east to the Buraymi oasis. The Saudis thereby claimed about four-fifths of Abu Dhabi and part of Oman. Negotiations followed with intermittent arbitration and mediation efforts including those of the United Nations and the United States, unable to resolve the impasse, which continued into the sixties. The Saudis were still unable to force the issue militarily. A small Saudi force that had entered one of the Buraymi villages in 1952 was ousted by the British officered Trucial Oman Levies in 1955.

The proposed federation of the Trucial states with Bahrain and Qatar after the British withdrawal gave the Saudis another opportunity to put forward their claims over their eastern boundary. At about the same time in early 1970 Aramco and its British counterpart discovered a large oil field at the frontier region, known as the Zarrara field. It took four more years of negotiations before a bilateral agreement was reached in July 1974. During this period and particularly after the British withdrawal Abu Dhabi and the UAE were vulnerable to Saudi pressures, which included the withholding of Saudi Arabian recognition of the UAE. Additional pressure was created by the arms build-up during this same period by Iraq and Iran and the need by the UAE for alignment with Saudi Arabia for its own security.

The Saudi Arabian–Abu Dhabi agreement of 1974, while not publicly available, appears to have given the Saudis access to the Khaur al-Udaid plus a small coastal strip south of Qatar, the line of wells through Sufuq, some of the Liwa oasis, and much of the Zarrara oil field, plus Abu Dhabi's agreement not to exploit the Zarrara field on its side of the border. In exchange for all this Saudi Arabia agreed to renounce its Buraymi claims and to recognize the UAE. It is not clear, however, to what extent both sides have demarcated this boundary. Some agreement on demarcation was reported as having been reached in 1975. Further negotiations were required in 1976–77 and a UAE oil concessions map of 1977 indicates a settlement of the demarcation problem.[26]

It is not apparent whether either Qatar or Oman harbor any objections or resentments over the 1974 Saudi–Abu Dhabi agreement or to what extent it impacts on their own boundaries with Saudi Arabia. In 1965 Qatar and Saudi Arabia concluded a boundary agreement that was protested by the British, who had not resolved their more comprehensive dispute with Saudi Arabia over the Saudi boundaries with Abu Dhabi and Oman. Although not published, the 1965 agreement conceded the Khaur al-Udaid to Saudi Arabia in exchange for additional territory for Qatar at the base of its peninsula. The agreement also delimited the continental shelf boundary on the western side of Qatar in the Bay of Salwa. There has been no formal agreement, however, between Saudi Arabia and Oman over their boundary.

Saudi Arabia and Kuwait

Saudi Arabia's land boundaries with Kuwait were the product of the British negotiations with Ibn Saud at Uqair in 1922 over the Iraqi boundary. Prior to this agreement Kuwait had been threatened by contingents of Ibn Saud's fanatical Wahhabi warriors known as the *Ikhwān* (from the Arabic for 'brotherhood'). The 1922 agreement, it may be recalled, created the Kuwaiti–Saudi Neutral Zone and provided that oil revenues from the zone would be shared equally.

After the British withdrew, the Saudis and Kuwaitis in 1963 commenced negotiations over the partition of their Neutral Zone, but did not reach agreement over the actual partition until the end of 1969. While maintaining the economic agreements over oil sharing and grazing, the partition agreement was not able to resolve the offshore boundaries between the two states. Both Kuwait and Saudi Arabia dispute the ownership of two offshore islands, Qaru and Umm al-Maradim. Resolution of the dispute affects each side's claims concerning partition of their continental shelf. Kuwait claims sole sovereignty; Saudi Arabia joint sovereignty. There have been conflicting reports as to how this dispute has affected oil exploration offshore. On the one hand it has been reported that both sides have recognized de facto an offshore boundary line that continues the partition and runs through two oil fields. On the other hand it has also been reported that Saudi protests halted operations of the Kuwaiti concessionaire in the area.[27]

In June 1977 Saudi Arabia appears to have forced the issue by occupying both islands. The move may have been part of Saudi pressure to keep Soviet advisors out of Kuwait as a consequence of Kuwait's military assistance deal with the Soviet Union, which had been concluded in 1976. Kuwait had commenced trade relations with the

communist bloc in 1964 and concluded an earlier arms deal with the
Soviet Union in April 1974. The 1976 arms agreement had reportedly
included Soviet advisors for training local Kuwaiti forces in the use of
the sophisticated equipment in the $400 million arms package. This
equipment included advanced artillery and tanks, antipersonnel weapons and air-to-air and air-to-ground missiles. Possibly as a result of
Saudi pressure final agreement was reached with the Soviets on only
air-to-ground missiles and Egyptian trainers. Curiously, the Kuwaiti
defense minister denied the existence of any arms deal with Moscow
in 1977. This was the same minister who denied Saudi seizure of the
offshore islands as well.[28]

Saudi Arabia and Bahrain

The Saudi Arabian boundary with Bahrain divides their continental
shelf. Dispute over the offshore region of Fasht Abu Safah, northwest
of the Saudi port of Ras Tanura, prevented any offshore boundary
agreement as well as any oil exploration by the Bahraini concessionaire. After oil was discovered in the disputed area, an offshore boundary agreement was concluded in 1958. Bahrain renounced its claims to
sovereignty in return for half of the Abu Safah revenues, and the
approximately 99 nautical mile long continental shelf boundary was
demarcated along a series of equidistant points between mainland land-
marks. This agreement was negotiated and concluded while Bahrain
was under British suzerainty and during the period of intense Saudi
concern over the spread of Nasserite propaganda and subversion in
the Gulf. There had been considerable republican and nationalist protest stirred up in Bahrain during the 1950s. From the Bahraini point
of view, the prospect of additional oil revenues in the light of Bahrain's
diminishing oil reserves was a substantial inducement to agreement.[29]

Saudi Arabia and North Yemen

The partially defined border between Saudi Arabia and North Yemen
resulted from a contest between Ibn Saud and Imam Yahya of Yemen
in the early 1930s over control of the buffer area of Asir. In 1926 Ibn
Saud had extended his rule to the Yemen frontier after conquering the
Hejaz and concluding an agreement with the Idrisi of Asir. On the
other side of Asir in Yemen, the Imam after 1928 had reached a stale-
mate in his contest with the British over control of their frontier at the
Aden hinterland. While engaged in negotiations with the British in

1931 over this issue, the Imam turned his attention to his northern border.

In early 1931 the Imam sent forces into the Abu Arish highlands of the Asir region and northeast of them to take the Najran oasis, approximately 200 miles from the Red Sea coast. Frontier clashes with Saudi forces ensued. The contest was not limited to the Asir region, however. The Saudis simultaneously engaged in an ideological contest with the Imam over conversion of tribes in the Hadramut area northwest of Aden. Wahhabi successes in this frontier region had frustrated the Imam's own contest with the British for control over the Hadramut. In 1932 the Saudis succeeded in dislodging the Yemenis from Najran but not from Abu Arish. Ibn Saud chose to negotiate the issue, and negotiations dragged on for two years while intermittent border clashes continued.

Ibn Saud decided to force the issue in the spring of 1934 by sending armies to two major Yemeni cities. One force was sent down the coast to take the key port city of Hodeida, and the other was sent from the Najran area south to threaten the capital city of Sana. Facing a cutoff of his supply of arms through Hodeida, the Imam quickly concluded a status quo agreement with the British over their border dispute, so as to obtain arms through southern Yemen. British, French, and Italian warships were also sent into Hodeida on various pretexts, possibly to contain one another's intervention and/or restrain the Saudis from keeping Hodeida. In dynamic balance of power fashion, however, Ibn Saud halted his forces, called for a truce, and negotiated a settlement with the Imam, known as the Treaty of Taif. The treaty established a boundary commission, which in 1936 finished demarcating the border with a five-kilometer demilitarized zone on each side of the border, commencing at Najran and following a mountain ridge in the Abu Arish region to the coast. No attempt was made, however, to demarcate a border in the desert areas southeast of Najran.

The next major Saudi involvement with the North Yemeni border arose as a result of the republican coup against the Imamate in September 1962. Civil war ensued, with the republican forces obtaining military assistance, including a contingent of forces, from Egypt and the Imam rallying the northern tribes and obtaining Saudi support. During the civil war the Saudis were unable to contain North Yemeni republican forces at the Saudi frontier. Concern over the build-up of Egyptian forces and the ideological threat of Nasserism led the Saudis to negotiate mutual withdrawal terms with the Egyptians by agreement at Jiddah in August 1965. As a result of the agreement Egypt radically reduced its troops from Yemen and pulled back from the northern border areas with Saudi Arabia.

The partisans in the Yemeni civil war, however, refused to settle the struggle, and Nasser refused to remove all Egyptian forces. Indeed Nasser recognized a new opportunity to influence the fate of South Yemen after the British announced in early 1966 their plans to withdraw from the Aden in 1968. Faced with the lack of British support for the containment of Egypt and Nasserism, Saudi Arabia then sought military assistance in Iran. Any need for active Iranian assistance, however, was obviated by Egypt's need to obtain Saudi and other Arab aid at the time of the Six Day War with Israel in 1967. After its defeat in that war Egypt agreed to withdrawal of all forces from the Yemen in return for Saudi economic assistance.[30]

This Egyptian–Saudi realignment was consistent with dynamic balance of power politics but did not succeed in removing all ideological threats from the Saudi border. After the British withdrew from Aden toward the end of 1967, a radical Marxist regime was established as the People's Democratic Republic of Yemen in South Yemen under the National Liberation Front (NLF). The new regime had consolidated power by 1969 and became perceived by Saudi Arabia as a greater ideological threat than the republican regime in North Yemen, which the Saudis had opposed. The Saudis therefore realizing the greater need for Northern Yemeni assistance to contain the Marxist South Yemen, stopped aiding the royalist partisans in North Yemen in 1969. In dynamic balance of power fashion the Saudis switched their alignment and reached a modus vivendi with the new Yemen Arab Republic (North Yemen) that was established in 1970.[31]

Saudi policy toward North Yemen has been to maintain an alignment by means of military assistance to the regime and to maintain pressure on the regime by military assistance to tribal federations in the north and frontier regions that could threaten to bring down the regime or revive the civil strife. The northern tribes constitute approximately one-third of Yemen's population of approximately six million. It has been estimated that Saudi subsidies to the northern tribes have approached $300 million annually, whereas Saudi subsidies to the North Yemen regime have approached $400 million. The Saudis have also directly subsidized economic development projects within North Yemen at an estimated rate of approximately $300 million annually.[32] Saudi subsidies have been intended to create considerable economic dependency by the regime in North Yemen in order to counter North Yemen's interest in obtaining military assistance from the Soviet Union and in pursuing unification negotiations with South Yemen.

This Saudi policy received a severe challenge in 1979 after border clashes with South Yemen induced the North Yemenis to seek additional military assistance. The Carter regime responded with a large

$390 million arms package underwritten by the Saudis. When the fighting subsided, the Saudis held up delivery of the additional arms and North Yemen obtained an even larger $700 million package from the Soviet Union, including Soviet military advisors. Late in 1979 the Saudis pressured the North Yemen regime in an attempt to get the North to relinquish its Soviet connection by cutting Saudi aid to Sana. This move was followed in early 1980 by clashes at the Saudi border with North Yemen. Other border clashes were reported at the end of 1980 ostensibly over possible discovery of oil at the border region. The Saudis have also evidenced concern over North Yemeni revanchism arising from Ibn Saud's annexation of the Asir region in 1934.[33]

Saudi Arabia and South Yemen

The frontier between Saudi Arabia and South Yemen has not been defined. This lack of definition has not deterred border conflict, nor has it, in contrast to the undefined Omani frontier with Saudi Arabia, encouraged negotiations over drawing a boundary line. The boundary conflicts occurred primarily during the period of the Dhofar rebellion in Oman, during which South Yemen and Saudi Arabia were on opposite sides. After the radical Marxist regime had consolidated its own power within South Yemen by 1969, it turned to increasing its assistance to the Popular Front for the Liberation of Oman and the Arabian Gulf (PFLOAG), which led the Dhofar rebellion. South Yemen also received increased military assistance from both the Soviet Union and the People's Republic of China for the benefit of PFLOAG. In 1969 South Yemeni attacks on Saudi border outposts were reported. These were possibly in response to an abortive attempt by Saudi Arabia to extend control over the Hadramut and establish that region as a buffer zone. Another clash at the frontier was reported in 1973.[34]

Following a series of military setbacks the Dhofar rebels reorganized as the Popular Front for the Liberation of Oman (PFLO) in 1974. The Soviet Union then became the main source of military assistance to both South Yemen and the rebels. Saudi strategy, accordingly, turned to weaning South Yemen away from its Soviet connection and its support of the rebels.[35] In March 1976 Saudi Arabia and South Yemen established diplomatic relations, but no mention was made of any negotiation or agreement over their boundary.

Relations between the two states worsened when South Yemen suspected Saudi Arabia of complicity in the assassination of the North Yemen president in 1977 as he was departing to discuss unification with South Yemen; ambassadors were withdrawn; and border clashes were again reported in early 1978. Opportunities to apply pressure to either side by border incidents continue. As with North Yemen, there may also be greater economic harm to South Yemen threatened by such border pressures because of the possibility of oil at the frontier.[36]

Territorial Relations between Lesser Actors

North Yemen and South Yemen

The partially defined boundary between North and South Yemen originated at the turn of the century with the contest between the British and Ottoman empires for the loyalty of the tribes at the hinterland of the British protectorate of Aden. After a number of victories by tribes supported by the British in buffer areas negotiations between the British and Turks to settle their boundary began in 1901. The negotiations spanned four years, during which both sides jockeyed for advantage. The Turks, however, were hampered by rebellion against Ottoman rule in northern Yemen. Agreement on the line that snaked northeast following tribal territories from the southwest corner of the Arabian Peninsula opposite the Bab al-Mandab was finally concluded in 1905. This agreement was followed by another in the Constantinople Agreements. The Violet Line was drawn at a 45-degree angle from the northeast terminal point of the 1905 agreement, thus completing the imperial division of the Arabian Peninsula.

After World War I, the Imam of Yemen refused to recognize these boundaries and engaged in a protracted struggle with the British at the frontier areas to expel them from the Aden hinterland. By 1934 the Imam's efforts in the Hadramut had borne no fruit, and a status quo agreement was reached with the British, to give the Imam the ability to defend his northern frontier from Ibn Saud.

The border remained quiet, except for a reported clash in a remote area during 1938, until 1950.[37] The Imam's son and successor engaged in further border clashes to force further determinations over the boundary. Negotiations brought no agreement and sporadic border incursions continued. British attempts after 1957 to consolidate the government of the Aden hinterland by the formation of a Federation of South Arabian Amirates were similarly greeted with border incidents created by the Imam. North Yemen, however, failed to prevent the federation. Further border fighting occurred during the North Yemen civil war after the British announced in 1966 their intention to withdraw from Aden in 1968. Indeed, even after the British withdrew from Aden earlier than expected in 1967, border clashes continued to occur into 1968.

After the radical Marxist regime consolidated its hold in the South in 1969, the regimes on both sides of the border gave haven to dissidents from the other side and supported subversion attempts. In 1972 hostilities at the frontier escalated until the Arab League mediated a ceasefire. One result of this mediation was the conclusion of an agreement at the end of November 1972 in which both sides pledged to work toward unification of their states.

Unification negotiations subsequently broke down and subversive activities revived. Mutual suspicions led to escalating border hostilities in the latter half of 1978, leading to the attempts at mediation by the Arab League. In February 1979 North Yemen complained of larger scale attacks by South Yemen across their border, and a ceasefire was mediated by the Arab League in March. That same month an agreement was concluded between North and South Yemen pledging both sides to the goal of unification of the Yemens.

It is unknown whether this goal of unification is attainable. There were reports of continuing agreements between the two Yemens through 1982 concerning economic cooperation, notwithstanding delay with actual merger. According to these reports it was agreed to remove trade barriers and draw up plans for jointly manned guardposts. There were also agreements reported on the development of oil resources in both countries. It may be harder, however, to obtain agreement on the political-economic issues of private versus state ownership of the resources of the state.[38] On ther other hand, South Yemen sponsors the dissident National Democratic Front (NDF), which has operated across the border in North Yemen since 1976. The NDF, which also obtains Syrian and Libyan support, has been reported to have over 5,000 combatants, with a mixture of ideological backgrounds and disaffected tribesmen.[39] Saudi Arabia sponsors two major federations of northern tribes, which can field combatants and bring counterpressures against the North Yemen regime to block unification. The Soviet Union, which is the mainstay for military assistance to South Yemen, also provides substantial military assistance to North Yemen. In fact, it has been reported that of the twelve North Yemen army brigades, the Soviet Union trains eleven and Saudi Arabia, one.[40] The North may be looking to the Soviet Union to restrain the South. On the other hand, the Soviet Union may be merely acting as a counterweight to the Saudis. It may not be willing to protect North Yemen from South Yemen, its protégé. It is not clear generally what the Soviet Union's commitments to this unification process may be.

South Yemen and Oman

No boundary has yet been defined by South Yemen and Oman. During their administration of the Aden Protectorate the British drew a boundary for administrative purposes to demarcate the extent of their administration at the easternmost edge of the Hadramut. Its terminal point was the juncture with the so-called Riyadh Line of November 1935, which had been drawn by the British during negotiations with Saudi Arabia over its eastern boundaries. Any other settlement of the boundary area between Oman and South Yemen has received little publicity. It is known, however, that the British did resolve a potential dispute with Oman over the offshore Kuria Muria islands before the British withdrew from Aden. After the British withdrew at the end of November 1967, the new South Yemeni government protested this settlement, which recognized Omani sovereignty over these islands.[41]

Following the British withdrawal the border region became embroiled in the promotion by South Yemen of the Dhofar rebellion in Oman. During the highpoint of rebel military activity in 1972 there were major clashes at the frontier and in May 1972 the Omani air force bombed South Yemeni artillery positions across the border. The war in Dhofar turned after the failure of the rebels to penetrate the coastal towns in July 1972 and the introduction of Iranian contingents on the side of the Omani government in 1973. By the end of 1975 the sultan had declared the rebellion as suppressed, and South Yemeni support for rebel activity diminished after the normalization of relations between South Yemen and Saudi Arabia in March 1976. It has been reported that this diminution was the result of South Yemen's agreement with the Saudis to curtail rebel movements across the frontier into Dhofar.[42]

The termination of the Dhofar rebellion did not, however, restore normal relations between South Yemen and Oman. Tensions continued. The sultan continued to engage in mopping up operations in the Dhofar mountains. The South Yemenis discontinued rebel training in 1977 but permitted 500 or so rebels to remain at their training camp in South Yemen across the border. In addition, border incidents were reported during 1981, possibly over some revived insurgency activity and/or South Yemeni oil surveys in the border area.[43] Tensions were maintained also with the introduction of numbers of Soviet bloc personnel into South Yemen. Reportedly some 16,000 Cubans and East

Germans, as well as 5,000 Soviets, have been serving as advisors and, among other things, assisted in the construction of a military air base in South Yemen at al-Ghaydah, less than sixty miles from the border.[44]

GCC mediation efforts by both Kuwait and the UAE have attempted to decrease tensions between South Yemen and Oman. These efforts succeeded in bringing about the October 1982 agreement between South Yemen and Oman on the principles for the normalization of their relations, including an agreement to establish a multilateral committee with Kuwaiti and UAE representatives, to discuss border problems.[45]

Oman and the UAE

There has been no publicly available formal definition of the two boundaries separating Oman and the UAE. One boundary stakes Oman's control over the tip of the Musandam Peninsula, the other starts at the eastern base of that Peninsula and cuts through the Buraymi oasis southward. In medieval times Oman controlled the entire Peninsula and as far west as the western frontier of Abu Dhabi. In more recent times the British administration of the affairs of the Trucial states led to the need to demarcate areas of tribal control as well as the rights of the seven Trucial sheikhdoms to dispense oil concessions in the 1950s.[46] Both the Musandam and the western boundaries have been subject to disputes.

The western boundary of Oman with Abu Dhabi was victim to Saudi Arabian claims that included the Buraymi oasis from 1949 to 1974. Saudi forces were ejected from Buraymi in 1955 by British officered Trucial Oman Scouts and the British-led negotiations with Saudi Arabia thereafter resulted in an impasse. During this impasse Abu Dhabi and Oman in 1966 confirmed their own jurisdictional division of the oasis. Oman was given jurisdiction over three villages adjacent to the town of al-Ayn that it needed for the maintenance of sources of fresh water in the mountains surrounding al-Ayn. This jurisdictional division was not disturbed by the subsequent settlement in 1974 by Abu Dhabi and Saudi Arabia of their border. This 1974 agreement withdrew the Saudi claim to Buraymi and left in place the Abu Dhabi–Omani de facto agreement of 1966.

During the Dhofar rebellion Oman's need for UAE financial assistance overrode any latent Omani concerns over its Musandam boundary. After the suppression of the rebellion Oman's claims to territory disputed by Ras al-Khaymah were revived. The issue arose in 1977 over the discovery of oil offshore at the frontier of Oman's

Musandam boundary with Ras al-Khaymah on the west coast of the Peninsula. Ras al-Khaymah had begun oil exploration and Oman sent troops five kilometers into the disputed sixteen kilometers of coastline and a warship into the area to compel suspension of the oil exploration. Omani personnel serving in the Ras al-Khaymah armed forces also created unrest during this incident.[47]

The dispute continued into 1978 with an escalation of tensions, notwithstanding various mediation efforts by the UAE, Saudi Arabia, and Kuwait. Oman threatened to expand its claims to include larger amounts of the Musandam as historically part of Greater Oman. Oman also threatened to revive its claims over Buraymi. The federal administration of the UAE did not wish to escalate the dispute and threatened to cut off its financial subventions for Ras al-Khaymah. Ras al-Khaymah resisted these pressures by obtaining support for its position from the Soviet Union as well as Kuwaiti financial assistance for an oil refinery with a view to establishing financial independence. Pressures for a resolution of the dispute increased as the Iranian Revolution in early 1979 created a new need for Omani–UAE alignment. There are reports that the GCC has succeeded in resolving the dispute.[48]

Another boundary issue arose on the other side of the Musandam Peninsula over the tribal loyalties of the Shihuh and Habus tribes in the village of Dibbah. Dibbah is located at the juncture of the boundaries of Oman with Fujayrah and Sharjah. There is no report as to the outcome of this specific dispute.[49]

Qatar and Bahrain

Qatar and Bahrain have two long-standing territorial disputes. One concerns the former Bahraini settlement of Zubarah on the northwest coast of Qatar. The other involves the Hawar islands located less than 1 kilometer off the same coast but to the south. The Zubarah dispute has historical origins in the dynastic contest over control of the Qatar Peninsula between the Āl Khalīfah ruling sheikhs of Bahrain and the Āl Thāni ruling sheikhs of Qatar. By aligning with the Ottomans in 1871 the Āl Thāni liberated Qatar from Āl Khalīfah domination and in 1878 razed Zubarah. Āl Thāni sovereignty was asserted over the Zubarah area in 1937 despite the protest of Bahrain, which maintained its rights to the area on the basis of the fealty of a local Qatari tribe, the Āl Nu'aym.[50]

Qatar, however, did not succeed in ejecting Bahraini forces from the Hawar islands. The dispute over their ownership remains economically significant, especially for Bahrain, which has diminishing oil reserves. The islands represent a significant extension of Bahrain's potential continental shelf, and with it a claim to any additional oil resources that may be discovered off the Qatar coast. There have been numerous attempts, particularly by Saudi Arabia, to mediate the Qatar–Bahrain disputes, but as yet no reported solution.[51]

Qatar and the UAE (Abu Dhabi)

Prior to the Saudi Arabian agreement of 1974 with Abu Dhabi, in which Abu Dhabi withdrew its claim to territory at the base of the Qatar peninsula, there had been dynastic disputes between the ruling family of Qatar and the Bani Yas tribe of Abu Dhabi over that territory. Abu Dhabi concessions to Saudi Arabia in 1974 as well as the earlier Qatari concessions to Saudi Arabia in 1965, mooted these historical disputes between Qatar and Abu Dhabi over their land boundary.

The offshore boundary between Qatar and Abu Dhabi was resolved by an agreement concluded in March 1969, thereby ending prior disputes over a number of offshore islands and exploitation of the offshore Bunduq oil field. The agreement was impelled by the discovery of oil at the field and probably the impending withdrawal of British administration of the Trucial states, which had been announced in 1968. The agreement deviated the otherwise relatively equidistant boundary so as to run it through the Bunduq oil field, but permitted the Abu Dhabi concessionaire to exploit the field in return for sharing oil revenues equally between Qatar and Abu Dhabi.[52]

UAE (Internal Boundaries)

The United Arab Emirates was formed in December 1971 upon the withdrawal by the British from the Trucial sheikhdoms. (See map 4.) This confederation of Trucial sheikhdoms developed from the proposed Federation of the Arab Amirates that had been promoted by the British after they had announced their intention to withdraw from the Gulf in 1968. The original proposal for the federation had included Bahrain and Qatar. The territorial disputes between these two states, as well as between Qatar and Abu Dhabi, led both Bahrain and Qatar to remain outside of the ultimate federal entity. Ras al-Khaymah also briefly remained outside of the UAE as it was established in December 1971. After the seizure of Ras al-Khaymah's islands of the Tunbs by Iran, Ras al-Khaymah was persuaded to join the UAE in February 1972. The federation remains a loose one with Abu Dhabi, the largest of the constituents, providing its main centripetal force. It is still burdened with the rivalry between the Āl Niyahan sheikhs of the Bani Yas tribe, who constitute the ruling family in Abu Dhabi and two other major tribal groups, the Āl Makhtūm sheikhs, who rule Dubai, and the Qāsimī sheikhs, who rule Ras al-Khaymah and Sharjah.[53]

The British attempted to resolve internal boundary problems of the Trucial sheikhdoms prior to the British withdrawal. As oil concessions were being distributed after the Second World War during the British tenure in the Trucial states, the need to obviate boundary disputes and establish concession limits impelled the British demarcation of boundaries among the seven Trucial states. In 1958 the British political agent made recommendations for the demarcation of the thirty-six border areas within the Trucial states and was unable to make recommendations for nine cases. The map that resulted reflected a mosaic of irregularly shaped boundaries and enclaves on the southeast coast, representing tribal allegiances.[54]

After the British announcement in 1968 of their proposed withdrawal from the Gulf within four years, Abu Dhabi and Dubai, the largest of the Trucial states and the key members of the proposed federation of the United Arab Emirates, resolved their long-standing boundary dispute. Fighting over their common border had broken out during the 1945–1947 period over their conflicting claims to a twenty-five mile strip along their coastal boundary. The fighting ended after British mediation but without any resolution to these claims. Further British mediation in 1965 had concerted a settlement of their offshore boundaries. The settlement was put into dispute after oil was discovered. Another agreement in 1968 between Abu Dhabi and Dubai resolved both their territorial and offshore boundaries by creating a neutral zone out of the disputed internal section of the boundary and conceded Dubai's sovereignty over the disputed Fateh offshore oil field.

Since the British withdrawal from the Trucial sheikhdoms no other internal boundary settlements have been reported and a number of actual and potential disputes may still exist among the UAE constituents, including disputes over all of their offshore boundaries, other than those of Abu Dhabi and Dubai, as well as the following onshore disputes: Dubai and Sharjah over their coastal boundary; Fujayrah, Sharjah, and Ras al-Khaymah over Dibbah. There are recently reported settlements of UAE disputes, without any details, however.[55]

Territorial Disputes and Gulf International Instability

Settled and Inactive Disputes

Having reviewed the twenty-one territorial relations of the ten Gulf states, what can we now conclude concerning the potential for the territorial disputes of the Gulf for destabilizing the international politics of the region? Of the twenty-one, six relations may be considered as settled, or without evidence of any recent attempt to disturb agreements negotiated over their boundary lines. These six include two relationships between major actors: Saudi Arabia and Iran, and Saudi Arabia and Iraq; and three relations between a major and a lesser actor: Iran and Oman, Saudi Arabia and the UAE, and Saudi Arabia and Bahrain. There is also the lesser actor relationship between Qatar and the UAE that can be considered settled.

There are also eleven other territorial relations in which the boundary between the actors has not been settled but no evidence exists of any actively pursued dispute. These are relationships in which the potential territorial claims have been repressed for international political reasons. The quiescence of these relations should not be credited to the absence of any grounds for advancing territorial claims. As we have observed, there is no lack of bases for territorial contests in the Gulf. These range from interests in oil and its transmission, particularly through the potential chokepoints of the Strait of Hormuz and the Bab al-Mandab, to local concerns over tribal fealty, grazing rights (dirah), and oases. Nor is there any lack of ideological underpinnings for the articulation of any such interests. These range from renunciation of the imperial imposition of a boundary (for example, Saudi Arabian objections to the British–Turkish delimitation of Ibn Saud's eastern boundaries) to reassertion of an imperial boundary (for example, Iraq's claims to Kuwait and to Khuzestan).

The reasons for the repression of these potential territorial claims, or indeed for the unwillingness to overturn the six settled relationships, can be found in the current dynamic balance of power system of international politics in the Gulf. Claims for territorial extension might be viewed not only as a future economic or strategic resource but generally as part of the currency of the international politics of the Gulf. They represent bargaining chips in the negotiation of the alignment of actors and the settlement of conflicts. The long-standing nature of some territorial disputes is testimony to the great reluctance with which the international actors renounce these claims—or cash in their chips, to extend the metaphor. Such renunciations may occur in exchange for a favorable alignment; though even here claims may also be revived when the advantage of the alignment is lost. Iran under the shah, for example, renounced its claims to Bahrain in order to increase the chances of alignment with the Traditional states. Iran under Khomeini has apparently revived the claims to Bahrain since the chances for alignment with the Traditional states have for ideological reasons decreased.

The dynamic balance of power system, however, creates a preferred strategy of repression of territorial claims over the strategy of renunciation and revival. Where international political alignments remain fluid as in the dynamic balance of power it is better to repress a territorial claim if no firm alignment can be bought for its renunciation. The threat of prosecution of a territorial claim can then be used to restrain a switch in alignment. Saudi Arabia, for example, has generally repressed its territorial dispute with Kuwait over their offshore islands. When Kuwait turned to the Soviet Union, the Saudis revived their claims and occupied the islands.

Potentially Destabilizing Disputes

We have also viewed four territorial relations in the Gulf that involve recurrent disputes and can be considered potentially destabilizing for the international politics of the Gulf. These are the territorial disputes between Iraq and Iran; the Iraqi claims over Kuwait or the Kuwaiti islands of Bubiyan and Warbah; the Iranian claims over Bahrain; and the South Yemeni attempts at 'unification' with North Yemen.

The Iraq–Iran dispute is potentially destabilizing for the Gulf because a victor in the contest could become a predominant actor in the Gulf. A predominant actor would constitute a potential threat to the security of the other actors and lead to a transformation of the international system. This potential transformation will be considered in greater detail in chapter 6. At this point, suffice it to say that the predominance of either Iraq or Iran would constitute the ultimately destabilizing threat from within the Gulf.

What is the likelihood of either an Iraqi or Iranian victory in their recurring territorial disputes? Or, alternatively, what is the likelihood of the settlement of their recurrent disputes? Within the twentieth century there have been three major settlements of the Iraq–Iran border: the Constantinople Agreements of 1913–14, the 1937 Agreement, and the Algiers Agreement of 1975. Each of the settlements was based upon the principles contained in prior agreements. There is no reason to believe the next settlement will diverge from this pattern and not use as its foundation the 1975 accords. Both sides have considerable mutual interest in the settlement of the three areas of their frontier that have always occasioned dispute: the Kurdish areas in the north, the Shatt in the south, and the central promontory of the border in the Khanaqin and Qasr-i-Shirin area. The two states have a mutual interest in controlling their respective Kurdish populations and inhibiting cross-border Kurdish nationalism. They share a mutual interest in commercial navigation on the Shatt al-Arab. The Shatt is the only maritime access to Basra for Iraq and Abadan and Khorramshahr for

Iran. Both sides have an interest in the regulated extraction of oil from the Khanaqin area.

On the other hand, it is also the case that each of the three major settlements between Iraq and Iran in the twentieth century was concluded when both sides needed to realign and obtain the cooperation of the other. The introduction of ideological issues into the present territorial conflict, the formulation of war aims and settlement demands, has slimmed the chances for achieving cooperation and realignment. Hence dynamic balance of power expectations are destabilized for both sides and settlement is inhibited. Even were settlement possible, there would remain the possibility of recurrent conflict.

The Iraqi claim over Kuwait or parts of it is potentially destabilizing to the international politics of the Gulf because of concern by the other Gulf states that the Iraqi claim would lead to further Iraqi conquests. This Kuwaiti claim would be actively pursued in the event of Iraqi predominance. Similarly, the Iranian claim over Bahrain represents a measure of Iranian predominance within the Gulf. The claim would be actively pursued if such predominance were achieved.

The possibility of the unification of South Yemen and North Yemen raises a different kind of risk of destabilization. The South Yemeni regime has a strong ideological kinship with the Soviet Union. It is highly likely that the Soviets would be relied upon for security assistance. The new state would then pose a threat to Saudi Arabia, particularly the west coast of the Peninsula.

Future Disputes

Our consideration of the potentially destabilizing territorial contests of the Gulf has assumed the continuation in power of the current regimes in the Gulf. We have already observed that a radical change in regime can lead to the creation of disputes or revival of repressed territorial claims. For example Qāsim asserted Iraqi claims to Kuwait after the overthrow of the monarchy in 1958; the Iranian Revolution revived Iranian claims on Bahrain. In order for us to assess the likelihood of such changes and their effects on future territorial disputes within the Gulf we need to consider what are the possibilities of such radical changes in regimes. This will be examined in further detail in the next chapter.

Territorial Disputes over Gulf Oil

Having identified the territorial disputes of the Gulf that are most destabilizing to its international politics, we may still be concerned that other territorial disputes may yet be dangerous for U.S. interests in the Gulf. These interests have been declared as the protection of Gulf oil supplies and the resulting commerce. The question therefore arises: Why are not all territorial contests in the Gulf involving oil-bearing areas of concern to the United States, even if they involve only border regions and not destabilizing territorial claims not limited to these regions? The question invites closer examination of the value of the Gulf's oil resources and the ease or difficulty of resolving territorial disputes involving them.

How Valuable Are Gulf Oil Resources?

Estimations of "published proved" crude oil reserves as at the end of 1982 show the Gulf states as possessing a little over one-half of the world's oil reserves. These are estimates of the volume of crude oil remaining in the ground that current geological and engineering information indicates with reasonable certainty to be recoverable under current economic conditions.[56] Appendix A shows the percentages of such global reserves possessed by the six Gulf states with significant amounts of reserves.

How valuable are those oil resources? Calculation of the value involves such variables as the available technology and the economic calculus of production and pricing. It is generally assumed that with currently available technology the cost to the producing nation of each barrel of crude oil recovered is approximately $1 to $2 per barrel.[57] The revenue effects, therefore, at the prices set by OPEC in 1983 at $29 per barrel for "benchmark crude" are tremendous. OPEC's prices are government selling prices. Benchmark crude is one of the grades of crude oil known as Arabian light crude. Other crude oil, which is graded according to specific gravity, fetches different prices. Various prices may be obtained on the spot market for short-term supplies of oil. Various prices are also obtained for refined oil, the four main products of which are gasoline, kerosine, heating oil, and heavy fuel oil. OPEC's benchmark crude prices have climbed from approximately $3 per barrel in 1973 just before the Arab oil embargo of 1973–74 to $34 per barrel in 1981. The increase has not been a steady one. There were two well-known jumps in prices, the one during the embargo, the other during 1979 at the time of the Iranian Revolution.[58]

Production and pricing decisions, however, are a function of global demand for crude oil and to a great extent OPEC's responses. To what extent OPEC prices can remain high enough to sustain the tremendous revenues for most of the Gulf states is itself the function of a number of variables. These variables include the following: (1) global economic growth rates; (2) the utilization efficiency of energy; (3) the availability and efficiency of alternative forms of energy other than petroleum products with known costs of recovery, such as the other "primary energy" products: natural gas, coal, nuclear power, and hydropower; (4) the availability and efficiency of other energy products without as yet efficient recovery rates, such as synthetic fuels, solar power, fusion; (5) conservation measures; and (6) energy product stockpiling.

There are also international political variables that affect the cartel power of OPEC or other producers. Not all Gulf oil exporters are members of OPEC: Oman and Bahrain are not. Neither of these states has significant oil exports, and both most likely follow OPEC's pricing and production decisions. Bahrain, however, is a member of the Organization of Arab Petroleum Exporting Countries (OAPEC), whereas Oman is not; nor is Iran. OPEC itself includes six of the Gulf states: four GCC members, Saudi Arabia, Kuwait, UAE, and Qatar, as well as Iran and Iraq. OPEC, however, also includes two other Arab states, Algeria and Libya; two African states, Nigeria and Gabon; two Latin American states, Venezuela and Ecuador; and one Asian state, Indonesia.

OPEC's pricing and production limitation decisions are themselves affected by the divergent interests of the price hawks and moderates. The hawks are composed primarily of those non-Arab members with large populations and small reserves who need to accelerate the generation of oil revenues for domestic political development. This they propose to do by obtaining the highest prices before depletion of their reserves.[59] The moderates, and OPEC generally, are led by Saudi Arabia. Saudi leadership derives not merely from its superior reserves, approximately 38 percent of OPEC's, but from its "swing capacity." Saudi Arabia has a substantially greater capability to increase or reduce its oil production than do other OPEC members. Saudi Arabia can vary its oil production possibly as much as from 4 million barrels per day (mbd) to 12–13 mbd. The Saudis have conventionally produced approximately one-third of all OPEC's output. The moderates within OPEC strive to control prices sufficiently to limit the incentives of the West to develop alternative energy sources to crude oil.[60]

The problem of divergent interests within OPEC is exacerbated by its lack of true cartel power to enforce its pricing and production quota decisions. OPEC's members occasionally suspect each other of cheating.[61] Were the cartel to disband, however, it would still remain possible for the Gulf state members of OPEC to form their own pricing and production group. Indeed the GCC has established its own petroleum committee and could easily form the nucleus for a new cartel.

Given the large number of variables involved in the calculation of the likely levels of prices and production of OPEC oil, it is not surprising that there is little expert consensus on the long-term prospects for sustained high prices and production.[62] There is, accordingly, no certainty to the continuation of large-scale revenues from oil production by the Gulf states. Nonetheless, for some reasonably foreseeable near future period, one can expect the oil resources of the Gulf states to represent a valuable source of governmental revenues and a substantial component of their overall capabilities. Moreover, even though the current global decrease in demand for oil, and its concomitant oil glut, depresses the value of Gulf oil reserves, the steady depletion of these reserves by some Gulf states will in the future enhance the attractiveness of the huge reserves of other Gulf states, such as Saudi Arabia and Kuwait. Finally, it has often been noted that concentrated oil installations, such as terminal platforms and pumping stations make attractive military targets. These installations are considered vulnerable to destruction from both large-scale military attack such as naval and aerial bombardment as well as sabotage and scorched earth defensive maneuvers. (See chapter 6.) Military engagements between actors that result in the destruction of their oil facilities may make the oil facilities of other actors even more valuable. Hence contests over oil-bearing territory will remain for the near future more significant than the mere claim over territory would otherwise appear. Even so, does the presence of oil in contested territory increase the likelihood of a military contest and decrease the likelihood of resolving Gulf territorial disputes?

Oil Resources and Gulf Territorial Disputes

Two kinds of territorial disputes have been distinguished. One is a contest over a significantly large territorial area, including an entire state. The other is a contest over a relatively limited boundary area, more commonly termed a "boundary dispute." Gulf statistics on currently recognized territorial disputes do not clearly support the proposition that the presence of oil exacerbates such disputes or renders them more difficult to resolve than would be the case in the absence of oil resources.

There are currently four large-scale territorial disputes in the Gulf. The most active of these has been Iraq's claim at the outset of the current Iraq–Iran war over the Iranian oil-bearing province of Khuzestan. Iraq has in the past also claimed the whole of Kuwait. While this claim may be latent, Iraq does from time to time pursue a claim to Kuwait's large offshore islands of Bubiyan and Warbah as well as some Kuwaiti coastline contiguous to the Iraqi Gulf port of Umm Qasr. In the recent past Iran has claimed the entire island of Bahrain. Bahrain currently has diminishing oil reserves. The fourth territorial dispute does not involve states with measurable oil resources: North and South Yemen. South Yemen in particular has been pursuing unification with North Yemen. Thus only two of the four current territorial disputes (Khuzestan and Kuwait) involve substantial oil resources. This does not, of course, eliminate the possibility of future territorial disputes involving oil-bearing areas. Some consideration of those future possibilities will be entertained in chapter 6.

With respect to Gulf boundary disputes, problems arise from drawing boundaries through an oil-bearing region, since one side can deprive the other of the benefit of an apparent division of the resources by extraction methods that deplete the other side's reserves.[63] Hence we should examine more closely those territorial boundaries in areas of actual or suspected oil deposits. It would be helpful here to distinguish between onshore and offshore areas. Of twelve onshore or land boundaries, only one, that between North and South Yemen, does not appear at this time to involve any potential oil-bearing area. Of the eleven remaining boundaries, only three have active oil extraction at the boundary area: Saudi Arabia and the UAE (Abu Dhabi), Saudi Arabia and Kuwait, and a portion of the Iran–Iraq border. Only at the Iran–Iraq border, where a large oil field stretches across the border from Khanaqin on the Iraqi side to Nafte-Shah and Khaneh on the Iranian side, has there been a recent active dispute. There had been an agreement by Iran and Iraq in 1963 over sharing of the oil resources of this border region. This agreement was abrogated by the current Iraq–Iran war.

Of the other two boundaries areas in which oil extraction occurs, disputes over the oil resources have been resolved by agreement. In the Saudi Arabia–Kuwait Neutral Zone there is a sharing arrangement by which each country is permitted to extract no more than 50 percent of the oil. Gauging this percentage is by no means troublefree. There is a report of a 1983 suit by the Saudi concessionaire, Getty Oil Company, complaining that the Kuwaiti Oil Company breached this agreement by extracting in excess of 50 percent since 1977.[64] But at least the dispute is removed from that of an international contest. In the 1974 settlement between Saudi Arabia and Abu Dhabi of their common border (hence of Saudi Arabia's border with the UAE), there was no sharing agreement over the oil resources of the Zarrara oil field astride the border. Saudi Arabia compelled Abu Dhabi to relinquish any rights to exploit that oil field.[65] Although boundaries between constituents of the UAE have not been treated here as international boundaries, it might also be noted that there was an oil-sharing arrangement instituted by the settlement under British aegis of the Abu Dhabi–Dubai border. A neutral zone was created, and both sides were to share oil revenues equally. With respect to the other oil-bearing land boundary regions there are neither active disputes, nor are there reports of active oil extraction. Border incidents involving South Yemeni oil survey teams and Omani forces have been reported in 1981, however.[66]

The offshore boundaries of the Gulf states are susceptible to more dispute over oil resources. A substantial number of oil fields have been discovered in offshore Gulf waters. Under the prevailing definition of *continental shelf* as used in the United Nations Convention on the Continental Shelf of 1958, the entire Gulf constitutes a continental shelf subject to claims by all bordering Gulf states. Only one of the Gulf states, Iran, actually signed that convention, but Iran never ratified it. Nonetheless sovereignty over the natural resources of the subsoil and seabed contiguous to the mainland can be extended by states claiming rights in the continental shelf to a depth of 200 meters under the UN convention. The Gulf rarely has depths over 100 meters.[67] Hence it is important to establish all continental shelf boundaries in the Gulf in order to delimit oil exploration in this potentially oil-bearing region.

Not all of the fourteen offshore boundaries of the Gulf have been demarcated, however, and six or seven could be considered as subject to dispute: Iran and Iraq; Iraq and Kuwait; Saudi Arabia and Kuwait; Iran and the UAE; Bahrain and Qatar; Oman and the UAE; and possibly Saudi Arabia and Qatar. The seven remaining offshore boundaries that have been settled by agreement are: Iran's boundaries with each of Saudi Arabia, Kuwait (somewhat subject to any Iran–Iraq and Iraq–Kuwait offshore boundary settlement), Bahrain, Qatar, and Oman (subject at one end to any offshore boundary settlement of Oman with the UAE). Five of these settlements have included sharing arrangements over the oil resources at the common border. Each of these arrangements has been different, but all are testimony to the variety of opportunities available to settle potential disputes over oil resources.

The first such sharing arrangement was instituted to settle a long-standing offshore territorial dispute over the Abu Safah region between Saudi Arabia and Bahrain in 1958. Under the agreement Bahrain conceded sovereignty in return for Saudi Arabia's agreement to pay Bahrain one-half of the Abu Safah oil field's net revenues. A variation of this sharing arrangement was instituted in the 1969 settlement of the offshore boundary dispute between Qatar and Abu Dhabi.

The boundary line was drawn through the Bunduq oil field, thereby avoiding any concessions of sovereignty, but the Abu Dhabi concessionaire was to give each side an equal share of fees, profits, and revenues. A third variation occurred in the demarcation of the offshore boundary between Saudi Arabia and Iran in 1968. At the Firaydun-Marjan oil field the median line between the respective shores was zigzagged according to the estimated reserves of the oil field in order to apportion them equally, thereby avoiding both concessions of sovereignty and one side's relinquishment of control over a concessionaire.[68] A fourth variation is found in the agreement of November 1971 between the shah of Iran and Sharjah over the island of Abu Musa. Sharjah had previously disputed the Mubarak oil field 9 miles off that island with Umm al-Qaywayn and had asserted a 12-mile territorial limit around the island in support of its claim. The shah and Sharjah agreed to share equally the oil revenues from oil extraction and both recognized the 12-mile limit. It has been reported that the parties also agreed to let Umm al-Qaywayn share 15 percent of these revenues, out of Sharjah's share.[69]

The particular problem of offshore boundary settlements involving oil resources can be appreciated by the anomaly in the boundary between Saudi Arabia and Kuwait. Although both sides have agreed upon sharing arrangements in their onshore Neutral Zone, they have failed to reach agreement on sharing offshore resources. Their offshore boundary remains disputed. Kuwait claims full sovereignty over the tiny islands of Umm al-Maradim and Qaru, 16 and 25 miles, respectively, off the coast of the Neutral Zone. Saudi Arabia claims joint sovereignty under the Neutral Zone status. In 1965 Kuwait and Saudi Arabia agreed in principle to partition the Neutral Zone while maintaining the equal sharing arrangement over its oil resources. The demarcation of the partition was not agreed upon until 1969. Saudi Arabia took forceful possession of the disputed islands in June 1977. It is reported that part of the offshore boundary passing through the Safaniyah and Khafji oil fields has been recognized de facto, but oil operations by Kuwait's concessionaire, Aminoil, have been halted.[70]

In sum, although oil resources have been involved in territorial disputes in the Gulf, they have not necessarily proved to be such a complicating factor as to prevent resolution of a number of disputes over oil-bearing border areas.

4

The International Political Implications of Religious Cleavages, Ethnic Dissension, and Ideological Contests in the Gulf

The analysis, in the preceding chapters, of the international politics in the Gulf has proceeded on the assumption that the Gulf states are unified, integrated actors. That assumption will be examined more closely in this chapter. We will explore the impact that domestic political divisions may have on the ability of the Gulf states to act in the international arena. Those divisions include religious, ethnic, and ideological cleavages within the political communities of the Gulf states. Each of the states is to some extent beset by some of these cleavages in the form of religious minorities or nonruling majorities, indigenous ethnic groups and foreign workers, or ideological opponents to the ruling regime. "Ideological" refers to political value systems other than may be contained in religious systems or ethnic group loyalties. The questions we pose are, first, to what extent do these sociopolitical divisions produce religious divisions, ethnic dissension, and ideological contests that may destabilize a Gulf state's regime? And what are the international political implications of such instability?

Let us consider first the potential international implications of Gulf states that are subject to these divisions, and hence may be deemed not fully integrated. These implications will vary according to the degree of political disintegration occurring within the state. A highly disintegrated situation, a recent example of which would be Lebanon in 1982–83, implies the absence of any viable central regime and the inability to maintain any centralized armed forces. Other states may easily intervene directly with military forces to restore order or support one or more factions contending for power or for autonomy.

Less disintegration implies the diversion of centralized armed forces to restore order and maintain internal security. Opposition groups seek alignments with foreign states to obtain military assistance for their struggle against the central regime. Such indirect intervention may assist in the overthrow of the central regime. The result may be a radically different regime, with a change in alignments and reorientation of foreign policy.

In general the fostering of internal dissension by outside states is inconsistent with a dynamic balance of power system. The system expects each of the actors to be readily available to join alliances and to switch from alliances. Fostering the disintegration of an actor therefore may eliminate a potential alliance partner. Similarly, contributing to the overthrow of another regime so as to install an ideologically friendly regime may inhibit the flexible alliance relationship of that new regime with others.

How susceptible are the political communities of the Gulf states to fragmentation from religious cleavages and ethnic dissension? And how vulnerable are their regimes to being overturned by ideological contestants? The answer to these questions will be sought on a state-by-state basis. It should be borne in mind, however, that the central regimes in each of these states maintain their own programs for counteracting the disintegrating potential of such cleavages. Those programs will also be identified. They involve both positive and punitive incentives for the integration of their respective states. The positive incentives include social, educational, and political measures to increase loyalty to and reliance upon the central regimes and development of nationalism and socioeconomic integration. The punitive incentives include suppression of dissent, counterintelligence against subversion, relocation of minorities, and purge or exile of opposition leadership.

It should also be noted that this examination of the potential for internal disintegration within the various Gulf states is not intended to be a detailed examination of their internal politics and socioeconomic development or a catalogue of the religious, ethnic, and ideological minorities and majorities of each state. It is intended to highlight the most significant of the religious, ethnic, and ideological cleavages, in terms of their potential impact on the international politics of the region. Let us turn first, therefore, to the significant religious cleavages in the Gulf.

Religious Cleavages

Religion, specifically Islam, has a particular significance in the Gulf. Religious authority provides the basis of the potential legitimacy for the monarchical regimes and Iran as well as the potential for disruption in the republican regimes. Recent examples include the disruption within Saudi Arabia caused by the seizure of the Great Mosque in 1979 and the revolution in Iran, which overthrew the shah in 1978–79. Therefore, divisions within Islam at once threaten not only the religious and social order, but also the political order. Religious groups within the

Gulf possess leadership and organizational capabilities that can be mobilized by or against central regimes. They also transcend many state
boundaries. Islam itself has many theological variations, each of which
has spawned factions and sects whose members adhere keenly to their
own version of the true religion. The most significant Islamic cleavage,
however, is that between Sunni and Shiite. The Sunni are the religious
majority within the community of Islam. Within the Gulf, however,
Shiites, who are generally a substantial minority in Islam, are, significantly, the religious majority in the two major actors of the Gulf, Iran
and Iraq.

The Sunni–Shiite Split

The Shiites' doctrinal differences with the Sunni are deeply ingrained.
These differences stem from historical attitudes toward the successors
of the Islamic Prophet Muhammad. Shiites believe in 'Alī, Muhammad's cousin and only son-in-law. Indeed, the word "Shiite" comes
from the Arabic, "Shi'at 'Alī," meaning "partisans of 'Alī." 'Alī was
assassinated by followers of a rival caliph (meaning 'successor' to Muhammad). Shiites believe that 'Alī and his line of eldest male descendants are the only legitimate successors to Muhammad. These
descendants, who are known as the Imams ('leaders of the congrega-
tion'), were cloaked with infallibility and endowed with divine rights
to rule in both religious and political spheres.[1]

Gulf Shiites are themselves split in accordance with their beliefs
concerning the descendency from 'Alī. The majority of Shiite adher-
ants in the Gulf are in Iran and Iraq. They are "Twelvers," who derive
their name from the belief in the Twelfth and last of the Imams,
Muhammad al-Muntazar (the 'awaited'). The Twelfth Imam is believed
to be in hiding and expected to return as a *Mahdī* ('messiah'). In the
absence of an Iman the Twelvers devolve the performance of his religious
functions upon the Shiite clergy, *'ulamā'* (the 'learned'), who are entitled
to make interpretations of Islamic doctrine and act as intermediaries
with Allāh. Of the *'ulmanā,'* the highest order is the *mujtahid*, the
authoritative interpreters. In Iran the leading ranks of *mujtahids* are
called "Ayatollah," an honorific title denoting great learning and personal integrity. The lowest order of Iranian clergy is that of the *mullah*.

Another, smaller, Shiite sect in the Gulf is known as the Fivers,
or Zaidites, most of whom reside in North Yemen. The Zaidites believe in the legitimacy of Zayd, a grandson of Husayn, son of 'Alī, as
the Fifth Imam. They do not share the Iranian and Iraqi Shiite belief
in a hidden Imam. They trace their Imams from Zaidite succession and
do not endow their Imams with any supernatural qualities. There is

one other important Shiite group, although not prevalent in the Gulf, known as Seveners or Ismailites. Their name derives from their dispute over the succession to the Sixth Imam. The Ismailites have their principal following in India and East Africa and their own mystical offshoots such as the Druze in Lebanon.[2]

The Sunni, who are the orthodox, derive their name from the teachings and life of the Prophet known as the *Sunna* ('Customs'—of the Islamic community). In contrast to the Shiites, the Sunni believe that the caliph must be elected by a consensus rather than succeed by lineage. They also believe that the faithful need no intermediary like the Shiite *'ulamā'* and that all dutiful believers have equal access to Allāh. The *'ulamā'* for Sunnis are the leaders of prayers and are not inspired with the same charismatic qualities as are ascribed to them by Shiites.

Sunnism also has its movements, the most notable of which in the Gulf is that of Wahhabism in Saudi Arabia and Qatar. Wahhabis follow the puritanical teachings of Muḥammad ibn 'Abd al-Wahhab. Wahhab in 1744 had sought refuge in the village of Muḥammad ibn Saud. The two concluded a pact pledging themselves to spread Wahhab's interpretation of Islam, with Wahhab in charge of religious matters and Saud in charge of political and military decisions. Wahhabism opposes any innovation to the rigid interpretation of the Koran and *Hadith,* 'statement' or traditions based upon the words and deeds of the Prophet. The fundamentalism of Wahhabism, and similar puritanical movements such as the *Ikhwān al-Muslimīn* ('Moslem Brotherhood'), has been ascribed to a common thread of protest against the corruption and laxness of modern Islam and the call for purification and spiritual revolution.[3]

There is one other Islamic sect, which has broken with the traditions of both Sunnis and Shiites and become rooted in the Gulf—the Ibadites of Oman.[4] These are the descendents of followers of 'Abd Allāh ibn 'Ibād, one of the Kharijite ('seceders') leaders who broke with 'Alī over his willingness to have his legitimacy as caliph subjected to arbitration. Ibadites are described as puritans, without the Kharijite fanaticism, who believe in the Imamate but by election, and in the absence of any candidate, its vacancy.

The Impact of the Sunni–Shiite Schism on the Gulf

The Iranian Revolution of 1978–79 and the creation of an avowedly Shiite regime in Iran under the leadership of Ayatollah Khomeini suddenly created challenges to the loyalty of the Sunni within Iran to the new regime and to the stability of other Gulf states with significant

Shiite populations. Many Gulf states with significant Shiite sections of their population evidenced great concern over Khomeini's power to export the Iranian Revolution and influence their Shiite populations. The two states most affected were those with majority Shiite populations: Iraq and Bahrain. Let us examine each of these for the effects of the Iranian Shiite revival on the stability of their regimes.

Iraq

In Iraq the government is dominated by Sunnis, who compose an estimated forty percent of the population.[5] The political underrepresentation of Iraqi Shiites has been exacerbated by their economically underprivileged position. This situation, no doubt, creates fertile ground for the sowing of Shiite revolution. There are numerous reports of Khomeini's appeals to Iraqi Shiites to revolt.[6] The question remains as to why they have not? Three types of answers may be suggested. One looks at the ineffectiveness of Khomeini's appeals; the second at the ineffectiveness of the Shiite opposition to the Husayn regime; and the third at the effectiveness of the regime's suppression of dissent.

General rejection of Khomeini's appeals, even by Iraqi Shiites, has been attributed to their highly nationalistic or Persian chauvinistic content or implications. In addition, the excesses of the Iranian Revolution have caused rejection by some, particularly by economically advantaged classes.[7] These rejections have also been encouraged by Iraqi propaganda. This propaganda has attempted to stir Arab opposition to Khomeini's Persian chauvinism and Iraqi Shiite opposition to Khomeini as a charlatan who denies the sacredness of 'Alī's burial place in Iraq.[8]

On the other hand, potential Shiite opposition to Husayn in Iraq preceded the Iranian Revolution. Shiite opposition has been fragmented along the political spectrum, from conservative religious groups to radical leftist organizations. The conservative religious groups have a well-developed system of religious institutions and leadership. Through major seminaries in the Iraqi cities of Karbala, Najaf, and Kazimiyah, the religious groups have been effective in reaching Shiites both inside and outside of Iraq.[9] Led by *mujtahids,* the religious groups have had considerable influence and have been identified with three political action groups opposed to the central regime. The most long-standing of these is the *al-Da'wah al-Islāmīyah* (the 'Islamic call'), which was formed in the late 1960s. The group was believed to have had indirect connections with the late shah and sprung from clerical concern over the weakening of Shiism in the Iraqi secular state. Two more recently formed religious opposition groups are the *al-Mujāhidīn* (the Muslim Warriors) and the *Munazzamat al-'Amal al-Islāmī* (Organization of Islamic Action). The *Mujāhidīn,* who became known in 1979, are led by graduates of secular schools who preserve their religious leanings but do not believe that Iraq should become a theocracy.

Both the *al-Da'wah* and the *Mujāhidīn* have been guided by the philosophy of the Iraqi Ayatollah Muḥammad Bāqir al-Ṣadr who envisioned an Islamic polity in Iraq similar to Khomeini's Iran. The *Mujāhidīn,* however, have extracted the economic tenets of that philosophy, which denies economic exploitation for the few and promises material comforts for all. They have rejected its theocracy.[10] After the execution of Muḥammad Bāqir al-Ṣadr in 1980 the *Munazzamat* group split off from the *al-Da'wah* in opposition to the "adventurism" of the latter, proposing to build their strength quietly.[11]

The onset of the Iranian Revolution created ferment among the Iraqi Shiites. There was rioting in the Shiite centers of Najaf and Karbala as well as within Baghdad in February 1979 and early 1980.[12] In addition the *al-Da'wah* and *Mujāhidīn* engaged in guerrilla attacks on government officials and Ba'th party targets, killing perhaps twenty officials and wounding Iraq's Deputy Prime Minister Tariq 'Aziz in an assassination attempt in April 1980.[13]

The Iraqi regime reacted strongly, especially to the April 1980 bombings, by making membership in the *al-Da'wah* punishable by death, by executing Muḥammad Bāqir al-Ṣadr as well as hundreds of his followers, by expelling many thousands of Shiites of Iranian origin, and by making it a capital offense for anyone in the armed forces, or anyone who had served in them since 1968, to be a member of any party other than the Ba'th.[14]

Notwithstanding the ideological tension in Iraq between Ba'thism as a proponent of a secular and pan-Arab state and Shiism as dedicated to theocracy by the majority of the population, Ḥusayn cannot afford to alienate Iraqi Shiism. The regime maintains the Shiite clergy by its control over the corporate revenues and finances of the Shiite establishment.[15] Ḥusayn has visited and maintained Shiite shrines and has declared the birthday of 'Alī a legal holiday.[16]

The result of this compromise with Shiism appears to be the continued loyalty of substantial numbers of Iraqi Shiites under the test of the Iraq–Iran war. There is no clear evidence of significant Shiite resistance to participation in the Iraqi military or rallying to Khomeini after the turn of the war in 1982 and resultant Iranian attacks on Iraq.

Bahrain

Bahrain is similar to Iraq in the split between the religious affiliation of its regime and the majority of its population. The ruling family of

Bahrain, the Āl Khalīfa, are Sunni; the majority of Bahrainis are Shiite. Exactly how much of a majority is Shiite is subject to differing statistics, with estimates varying from 55 to 75 percent, with the larger percentage including Iranian Shiites who have been long-time residents of Bahrain.[17] The Sunni minority compose a class of gentry within Bahrain as well as immigrant merchants from other Gulf states. The Shiite majority compose the bulk of Bahrain's working class and small retailers in the capital city of Manama, but a number of Shiite families have also become financially successful, and Shiites have obtained government positions including cabinet ministries.[18]

Traditionally the Bahraini Shiites have looked to religious centers in both Iraq and Iran for leadership. Until his execution they had looked to Muḥammad Bāqir al-Ṣadr of Iraq for guidance. Currently they look to the Ayatollah Khomeini. His return to Iran in 1979 brought with it considerable foment among the Shiite population, including two days of rioting. Iranian ayatollahs called for an uprising against the Āl Khalīfa ruling family and one, Ayatollah Sādiq Rūhānī, claimed Bahrain as Iran's fourteenth province.[19] The leading Shiite clergyman in Bahrain, Sheikh Muḥammad ad Akr, responded by calling for the proclamation of Bahrain as an Islamic state, as well as for the prohibition of alcohol and for measures to combat unemployment. He visited Iran, where he conferred with Ayatollah Rūhānī and publicly declared his support for Iran's revolution. Upon his return, Sheikh ad Akr was arrested and more Shiite rioting ignited.[20]

The Bahraini regime is more vulnerable than the Iraqi regime to the fervor emanating from the Iranian Revolution for a number of reasons. The legitimacy of the Āl Khalīfa rule is dynastic but also supported by Islamic principles, unlike the secular Ba'thism of Iraq.[21] Bahrain has a pro-Western orientation and has cultivated its commercial attractiveness to Western business. In so doing it has compromised Islamic prohibitions concerning alcohol, dress, and dancing, particularly around Manama to accommodate Westerners. Bahrain has also maintained its U.S. security connection by extending the use by the United States of naval facilities at Jufayr.

As a result, Bahrain has been subject to recurring occasions for Shiite protest even before the Iranian Revolution, as well as to continuing Iranian-sponsored propaganda and subversion since the Revolution. A series of Bahraini Shiite demonstrations occurred in 1980. There were demonstrations over the American attempt to rescue the Iranian hostages; over the Iraqi execution of Muḥammad Bāqir al-Ṣadr; and during the celebration of the religious month of Muḥarram, during which local mullahs made antigovernment broadcasts. In December 1981 the regime uncovered a plot to overthrow the government involving a fairly large number of allegedly Shiite conspirators. Seventy-three persons, not all of whom were Bahrainis, were arrested, tried, and sentenced to prison terms. The conspiracy was linked to the Iranian-sponsored Islamic Front for the Liberation of Bahrain, led by an Iranian mullah, Hādī Mudarrisī. Mudarrisī's group had allegedly provided equipment and training and promised Iranian naval support.[22]

The regime's response to Shiite dissidence has been to increase its internal security measures and seek external assistance against subversion through the GCC. The regime has increased its surveillance of dissidents, arrested or rounded up potential dissident political leaders, and tightened its control of the press. Within the GCC Bahrain has expressed the need for a Gulf rapid deployment force to increase members' capabilities to respond to security threats.[23] On the other hand, as in Iraq, the Bahraini regime cannot afford to alienate its Shiites, the majority of its population. Thus, it has taken steps to respond to religious demands for greater enforcement of Islamic law by crackdowns on the sale of alcohol, on Western dress and "conspicuous consumption."[24] There are limitations, however, on the extent to which the Bahraini regime has been willing to go in compromising its pro-Western orientation. It has not totally banned the sale of alcohol, for example. Hence, it continues to remain vulnerable to fundamentalist religious protest and Shiite unrest.

Iran

While Iran has religious minorities, they are distributed among Iran's various ethnic groups, and their threat to the central regime is treated below in the discussion of ethnic dissent. The Sunni of Iran constitute less than 10 percent of its population and are composed of Arabs, Kurds, Baluchis, and Turkomans. There appear to be no organized politically active religious interest groups of Sunnis, as there are such Shiite groups in Iraq. Nor, on the other hand, is there any clear evidence of religious persecution of the Sunnis by Iranian authorities as there is of persecution of the religious minority of Bahais.[25]

Saudi Arabia

The Shiites in Saudi Arabia constitute a religious minority of approximately 5 percent of the Saudi population. They are concentrated, however, in Saudi Arabia's oil rich Eastern Province, where they provide approximately 50 percent of the workers in the oil fields.[26] Saudi Shiites have been socially and economically disadvantaged, reaching only lower echelons in the civil and military bureaucracy and obtaining

relatively poor health care, educational, and other social services in
the villages and towns of the Eastern Province. It has been reported
that the Shiite towns in the Eastern Province such as Hufuf and Qatif
have remained neglected while larger cities such as Dammam and Jubayl prospered; but also that Sunnis and Shiites in the Eastern Province
have shared the same sense of discrimination in the reallocation of
revenues generated from its oil resources.[27]

Saudi Shiites have also suffered religious discrimination, since in
the eyes of the Saudi Wahhabi religious leaders the Shiites have been
practicing "misguided religious rites."[28] Shiite women have been prohibited from teaching (unlike Sunni women) and Shiite literature and
history have been prohibited in local schools. Furthermore Shiites have
been prohibited from celebration of their emotionally charged *Ashura*
ceremony during the religious month of Muharram. In the *Ashura* a
mourning procession is formed in honor of the Imam Husayn.[29]

This proscription had serious repercussions in Saudi Arabia after
the Iranian Revolution. After Khomeini's return to Iran in 1979, Shiite
mujtahids in Saudi Arabia defied the ban and led *Ashura* processions
in late November. These became political demonstrations to protest
against Shiite discrimination, and for more equitable distribution of
wealth as well as to show support for Iran's Islamic Revolution. The
demonstrations turned into riots in a number of Eastern Province towns,
including the larger ones of Sihat and Qatif (the largest Shiite town),
in which a number of people were killed and 600 or so arrested and
imprisoned.[30] Some damage was done to property, including an oil
pumping station near Ras Tanura. This heightened the concern of
Saudi authorities over the potential threat of Shiite sabotage within
the oil industry.[31] The authorities initiated discussions to address Shiite
economic demands but on February 1, 1980 on the anniversary of
Khomeini's return to Iran, Shiite demonstrations again broke out,
turning into riots in which property was damaged and a small number
of people died.[32]

The Saudi regime thereupon made a concerted effort to forestall
the recrudescence of *Ashura* rioting among Eastern Province Shiites
in 1980. The government publicized plans for economic improvement
projects for the Province; some jailed demonstrators were released;
and the king made a political visit to the area. The economic projects
included electrical generation, street asphalting, new schools and hospitals, swamp drainage, improvements to lighting and sewage, as well
as home loans, particularly in Qatif. Other projects were included in
the Saudi Five Year Plan.[33] The promises of economic improvements
appear to have quieted the Eastern Province Shiites. It remains an
open question, however, whether the slowdown in Saudi Arabia's gen-

eral economic development as a result of decreasing oil revenues will
have any deleterious impact on these programs in the Eastern Province, and with that a return of the Shiite sense of discrimination.

The Siege at Mecca. The possibility of religious dissension within Saudi
Arabia from another direction was demonstrated by the siege of the
Great Mosque at Mecca, which began on November 20, 1979. The
siege involved a group of fundamentalist Islamic religious rebels, an
unexpected event in the strictly observant Wahhabi society of Saudi
Arabia. Wahhabism is practiced by over 90 percent of Saudi society.
Although the practice varies somewhat within Saudi Arabia, these vari-
ations have not been viewed as destabilizing.[34]

The rebel group has been estimated as varying from 200 to 1,000
in size. There were 170 rebels captured in all. The rebel group appears
to have been composed mainly of Saudis with a number of adherents
from Egypt, Kuwait, Sudan, Iraq, and North and South Yemen. Of
the sixty-three rebels who were beheaded, twenty-two were foreign
nationals.[35] It is not clear to what fundamentalist sect the rebel group
adhered. Its leadership included a Riyadh preacher, Juhaymān ibn Sayf
al-'Utaybī, but proclaimed Juhaymān's brother-in-law, Muhammad ibn
'Abd Allāh al-Qaḥṭānī, as *mahdī* ('messiah'), a concept alien to Wahhabism. Juhaymān may have been influenced by some Islamic reform
groups in India, the Sudan and Kuwait.[36] He had been arrested in 1978
in Riyadh for publishing pamphlets denouncing modernized practices,
including additional roles for women and accusing the Saudi royal family of corruption, sexual improprieties, and use of alcoholism. Juhaymān was released after questioning by the *'ulamā'* in Riyadh and
adjudged no risk to society.[37]

The recapture of the Great Mosque took two weeks and involved
a major effort by the Saudi National Guard, army, local police, and
reportedly an elite French antiterrorist squad was called upon while
the United States provided advice to the Saudi military. Saudi religious
leadership was also involved and issued a *fatwa* (decree) proclaiming
the rebels seditious and permitting fighting in the Mosque.[38] It is difficult to draw conclusions as to Saudi military capabilities for combat-
ting internal subversion from the experience of the siege. The
battleground was the holiest of Islamic mosques and the regime was
interested in capturing as many rebels as possible for purposes of in-
terrogation. On the other hand the siege pointed up Saudi vulnerability
to organized religious dissension. Notwithstanding Saudi Arabia's ban
on assembly other than in mosques, the siege demonstrated the inability of the Saudi regime to control its borders to prevent the infiltration
of arms and subversion. Investigations after the siege showed that the

rebel group may have gotten its weaponry from members of the Saudi National Guard and that the group may have stored weapons caches in remote desert areas.[39]

The Saudi regime reacted by tightening up its internal security force and organizing an industrial sabotage force to counter terrorist attacks on oil installations. It also indicated its willingness to broaden political representation by establishing a committee to plan a Consultative Council and reorganize provincial administration.[40] There are, however, limitations within the Saudi monarchical system on the amount of power it is able or willing to share. The regime also depends on Saudi religious institutions for the source of its legitimacy. Large numbers of pilgrims visit the Moslem holy places in Mecca and Medina, and Saudi universities attract foreign theological students. The religious visitors include people from radical states, and therefore these religious centers are potentially vulnerable to subversion. Indeed it was reported that many of the rebels involved in the siege met at the Department of Theology at the Islamic University of Medina. Three-quarters of the student population of that university is composed of foreign nationals, some of whom were attracted by Saudi government aid to students of religion.[41]

Kuwait

Shiites in Kuwait compose approximately 20–25 percent of the population, but they are not necessarily a cohesive social group. Some prominent Kuwaiti families are Shiites who either immigrated to Kuwait long ago and became successful merchants or emigrated from Kuwait to Iran, adopted Shiism, then returned to Kuwait. A third group of Shiites are found among the large expatriate labor force within Kuwait, either as transients or as resident aliens subject to ejection.[42]

The Iranian Revolution did spark demonstrations in Kuwait in support of Khomeini involving Kuwaiti Shiites and other disaffected groups such as aliens. This led to the politicization of Shiite pulpits and some reported bombings. Following the onset of the Iraq–Iran war, refugees settling in Kuwait contributed to further social unrest.[43] The regime reacted to the first incidents by deporting a Shiite leader of Iranian origin, 'Abbās Mutṛī, who was a nephew of Ayatollah Khomeini, and by enforcing its laws curbing freedom of the press. Such laws, for example, permit the authorities to shut down papers criticizing the regime for three days to two weeks. The regime also enacted a stringent public assembly law. The law prohibited assembly of more than twenty people without a permit, with certain exceptions including services at mosques. It authorized police attendance of public meetings and the break-up of private parties. It forbade criticism of Kuwait, religion, the Arab Nation, or foreign states. It also banned nighttime processions and demonstrations as well as bearing of arms at a public meeting.[44]

The Kuwaiti regime counterbalanced its prohibitions by opening participation in government through reinstitution in February 1981 of the National Assembly that had been shut down after 1976. When the Assembly did reopen as scheduled, only four Shiites took seats, as compared to ten Shiites in the last Assembly, and no radical Arab nationalists were elected.

North Yemen

In North Yemen the Shiite–Sunni split takes the form of the Zaydite–Shafiite split. The Zaydites who practice a form of Shiism different from that in Iran have achieved political predominance in the north. The conservative northern tribes in the rural areas are predominantly Zaydite, and Zaydites are becoming socially and politically prominant in the urban areas. This predominance was reinforced before the Republican Revolution of 1962–1970 by the regime of the Zaydite Imamate who was de jure both the spiritual and temporal leader of the state. The Shafiites, who compose more than half the population of North Yemen, adhere to a Sunni sect that follows the school of Islamic law begun by Muhammad ibn Idris al-Shafii. Their religious differentiation from the Zaydites is, however, not very pronounced. There are slight differences in prayer and oral traditions and at times both groups have reportedly used the same mosques for worship.[45]

The Shafiites tend to populate the southern area of the state and under the Imamate were socially inferior to the Zaydites. The southern tribes in the rural areas only begrudgingly accepted the Imam and bowed to his military superiority in the collection of taxes. In the urban areas, Shafiites were the merchants and craftspeople and had little social mobility as the government maintained controls over trade.[46] Although the Imam permitted the Shafiites their own courts, discrimination against the Shafiites continued through the Imam's power to appoint and remove judges.[47]

The discrimination against Shafiites contributed to the cause of the unsuccessful coup attempt of 1948. The attempt was organized by Ahmad Muhammad Nu'mān, a Shafiite, who became president of the Free Yemeni party, and obtained financial support from Shafiite merchants in Aden who had lived in Hodeida in the north. Other supporters included rival Zaydite clans, students with foreign educations, and disaffected tribesmen.[48]

The 1962 coup, which was led by army officers and supported financially by Shafiite merchants, ultimately did succeed in overthrowing the Imamate. Although Zaydites tended to support the Imamate and Shafiites the Republicans, each side was so riddled with factions, there was no clear religious split. Local political control devolved upon village leaders and tribal sheikhs during much of the civil war. And schemes promoted during the civil war to separate Zaydite and Shafiite populations by creating two states north and south of the capital city of Sana came to naught.[49] After the civil war the Zaydites regained positions of power by controlling the larger tribal forces and the military, although the Shafiites did improve their access to high-level government positions.[50]

The Iranian Revolution appears to have had little effect on North Yemen's Shiite community. Zaydite Shiism is sufficiently different from Iranian Shiism that no major challenge has been mounted on religious principles against the Republican regime, as in other Gulf states. Indeed it is particularly difficult to determine in North Yemen to what extent it is the religious distinction between Zaydites and Shafiites that creates potential for subversion against the central Republican regime. Shafiites, particularly in some rural southern areas, have supported the subversive National Democratic Front (NDF) which has been able to establish community centers, schools, hospitals, and clinics in those areas.[51] On the other hand, Zaydite tribal federations in North Yemen have also resisted the central government.[52]

Ethnic Dissension

Within the Gulf states there are significant ethnic minorities, be they ethnic groups, tribal collectivities, or aliens (residents and workers), that present challenges to the central regimes. These challenges arise from the group's sense of discrimination in the regime's allocation of the resources of the state. They also arise from the group's resistance to the central regime's policies, which foster national identity and thus threaten the ethnic group's historical, cultural, linguistic, and sometimes religious identities. Moreover, the central regimes view ethnic autonomy as threatening to their centralized authority. They view their alien populations, be they long-term residents or short-term workers, as breeding grounds for subversion and potential economic and political protest. Ethnic group responses to the various central regime's programs in the Gulf range from organized military resistance to pas-

Iran: The Kurds

Iranian Kurds have been estimated to comprise approximately 3 million to 3.5 million persons, which numbers include Kurdish refugees from Iraq. They are concentrated mainly at the northwest border with Iraq north of Kermanshah and south of Tabriz, and centered around Mahabad. As in Iraq, the Iranian Kurds are dispersed among urban and rural areas, they retain varying degrees of tribal affiliation, and are mainly Sunni, although there are pockets of Shiite Kurds.[59] Unlike the Iraqi Kurds, however, their Iranian compatriots did not engage in protracted conflict with the central regime. For a brief period after World War II Iranian Kurds did enjoy limited autonomy when, with Soviet assistance, they formed the Kurdish Republic of Mahabad within the Soviet-sponsored Autonomous Republic of Azerbaijan. However, after withdrawal of Soviet forces in 1946 and the collapse of the Azerbaijani autonomy movement, Kurdish autonomy was also suppressed, and little resistance was subsequently offered to the shah's regime.[60]

The Iranian Revolution of 1978–79 revived the repressed Iranian Kurdish autonomy movement. The Kurdish armed resistance to the new Khomeini regime appeared as a coalition composed of Kurdish nationalists under Sheikh 'Izz al-Dīn Ḥusaynī, a Sunni religious leader, together with the leftist Iranian Kurdish Democratic Party (IKDP), the Maoist Komeleh party, and the Marxist Fedayeen-i-Khalq. There are also reports of joint action with the leftist Mujāhidīn-i-Khalq.[61] At time of writing, there are reportedly 15,000–20,000 Kurdish guerrillas operating mainly outside of urban areas opposed by some 60,000 regime forces (regular army, Revolutionary Guards, and militia), notwithstanding the larger war with Iraq.[62] While the Iraq–Iran war continues, the Iranian Kurds can expect to continue to receive Iraqi assistance.[63] The question remains open as to whether such assistance might terminate in the event of a settlement with Iran; or even without such termination whether the Kurdish resistance can succeed in the face of larger Iranian forces that would be released from the Iraqi front.

Iran: The Ethnic Perimeter

Following the Iranian perimeter clockwise north of the Kurdish areas are located a number of distinct ethnic groups, of varying population size, with varying degrees of tribal affiliation, and with differing penchants for local autonomy. (See map 1.) The major ones are the Azerbaijanis (sometimes referred to as "Azeris"), the Turkomans, Baluchis, Qashqais, Arabs, Bakhtiaris, and Lurs. Under the Pahlevi shahs, Reza

Shah and Muhammad Reza Shah, the central regime implemented programs to integrate and nationalize these ethnic groups, particularly by destruction of their tribal affiliations. Education was in Persian and of the Persian heritage; administrative offices were denied to local leaders; some local leaders were simply purged and others exiled; and oil revenues created dependencies on the largesse of the central regime.[64]

The Iranian Revolution provided renewed opportunities for these perimeter peoples to regain control over their ethnic heritage. The groups that are predominantly Sunni, namely, the Kurds, the Baluchis, and the Turkomans, as well as the Shiite Azerbaijanis, plus the Shiite Kurds, boycotted the referendum for adoption of the new Islamic Constitution in 1979. They objected to its lack of recognition of autonomy or "home rule."[65] A review of the various efforts by these perimeter ethnic groups to press the central regime for greater autonomy follows.

Azerbaijanis. Azeris comprise the largest of the ethnic groups, estimated at 13 million persons. They are integrated into the commercial life of the country and do not have strong tribal affiliations. Immediately after World War II, Soviet forces permitted the establishment of a separatist Autonomous Republic of Azerbaijan. The region was retaken by the central regime after Soviet troop withdrawals. The new Islamic Republic sent forces into the region in 1979 to quiet Azeri autonomy demands. These demands, however, have been for more moderate home rule rather than strict autonomy as voiced by other groups.[66]

Turkomans. Although this group comprises approximately 500,000 and has expressed a demand for autonomy, their one serious protest involving the need for central regime military action in 1979 was not so much for autonomy as for redistribution of agricultural land. There were nonetheless a few uprisings reported as instigated by the Fedayeen-i-Khalq in the Turkoman region, which were easily suppressed by the regime.[67]

Baluchis. The Baluchis, who are tribally organized, comprise an estimated 500,000 persons and, like the Kurds, have harbored desires for an autonomous entity with compatriots on other sides of their borders—in this instance, Pakistan and Afghanistan. The shah in 1973–1977 aided in the Pakistani repression of an insurgency movement of Pakistani Baluchis seeking greater autonomy.[68] In Iran the Baluchis have backed up their demands for regional autonomy with the formation of the Islamic Unity party in 1979 and have gained support from Baluchi organizations in foreign states. After a number of clashes with regime forces the Baluchis appear to have established a free zone within their region in which they have resisted governmental control.[69]

Qashqais. The Qashqais are estimated to comprise approximately 400,000 persons. They are Shiites, organized in tribes, but also settled in both urban and rural locations in the southwest quadrant of Iran, including parts of oil-producing Khuzestan. Qashqai leadership had been exiled under the shah for participation in the Mossadeq interregnum, and had developed connections with the leadership of the emerging Khomeini regime as a result. Upon their return from exile at the onset of the Iranian Revolution, the Qashqai leadership, primarily Naser and Khosrow Khan, did not assert strong demands for autonomy. Khosrow Khan participated in the Iranian *Majlis,* the parliament. Although Naser Khan did propose the formation of a Confederation of Southern Tribes and a Union of Iranian Tribes, he was unable to concert sufficient support for their organization. The Qashqai leadership efforts appeared to be devoted primarily to recovery of tribal lands and gaining support from rival Qashqais, including those who had joined antitribal leftist groups.

The regime's attempts to repress Kurdish demands for greater autonomy and reassertion of "Persian" nationalism, however, appears to have turned the Qashqai leadership against the regime and toward organized military resistance.[70] Clashes between Qashqai forces and Revolutionary Guards have subsequently been reported. Qashqai leaders have been arrested and reportedly executed. Rioting occurred after the sentencing of Khosrow Khan.[71] It is difficult, however, to assess the likelihood of continued armed resistance by the Qashqais, particularly in the face of additional military effort by the central regime, which is likely to follow the denouement of the war with Iraq.

Arabs. Estimates of the Arab population of Iran, which is concentrated in the Khuzestan province, vary from 500,000 to 2 million.[72] Approximately one-half are estimated to be Shiite; the other half, Sunni. It is this Arab population that contributes a substantial part of the labor force involved in Iranian oil production. The shahs were sensitive to that situation and resettled large numbers of Persians into that region.

The unrest among the Arabs that followed the Iranian Revolution focused mainly on economic grievances, and riots occurred over demands for increased pay and promotion. Arab leadership, however, did express demands for more autonomy and reallocation of economic development resources to benefit their region. Revolutionary Guards reportedly put down the protests and also removed an Arab Shiite leader, Ayatollah Muḥammad Khaqani, after sabotage of an oil pipeline in June 1979. The sabotage of oil facilities in 1979 has generally been attributed to Iraqi trained groups, however.[73]

While Iraq had promoted the efforts of the clandestine Al-Ahwaz Liberation Front in its increasing demands for Khuzestan secession prior to the Iraqi invasion, no ground swell of popular support for Iraqi "liberation" greeted the invading forces.[74] Tested under fire, the Iranian Arabs appear to have demonstrated their considerable integration into the larger society, and armed resistance to the central regime to support demands for autonomy is thus highly unlikely.

Bakhtiaris and Lurs. These are tribally organized Shiite populations concentrated in the Zagros mountains south of the Kurds and north of Khuzestan. The estimated populations of these ethnic groups are approximately 570,000 Bakhtiaris and 500,000 Lurs.[75] There is little report of demands by these ethnic groups for autonomy and no report of armed resistance to the regime in support of such demands.[76]

Others. Other ethnic groups within Iran include Shahsevan, Basseri, Afshars, and others, whose total populations are in excess of 520,000, and whose dissatisfaction with the Khomeini regime, if any, has not been reported.[77]

General Implications. The Khomeini regime, like that of its predecessors, has evidenced strong desires to repress ethnic autonomy movements within Iran. These relatively dispersed and disparate perimeter ethnic groups have not demonstrated any significant ability to organize collective opposition to the central regime. There are various reports of alignments with the more active ethnic groups of ideologically directed opposition groups such as the Mujāhidīn-i-Khalq and Komeleh which have clandestine centralized organizations. On the other hand, the leftist opposition groups do not easily overcome resistance by the generally conservative ethnic/tribal leadership to leftist alignments. The Kurds are a notable exception. Certain of the groups at the Iranian borders—the Azerbaijanis, the Kurds, and the Baluchis—have more opportunities for foreign alignments than the others. After the return of Iranian forces from combat with Iraq, there may be less chance for the survival of armed resistance to the central regime, and most likely a return to the Pahlevi policies of repression of autonomy movements.[78]

The Traditional States: Aliens

The large alien populations within each of the Traditional states, although Oman to a far lesser extent, present different kinds of problems to each of their host regimes. Aliens have immigrated, both legally and illegally, and have been imported into the Traditional states on a large scale to fill manpower needs in civilian development projects, including the oil industries, and for their armed forces. The extent of the dependency by each of the Traditional states on aliens for their workforce and military manpower will be discussed below on a country-by-country basis. It should be recognized, however, that statistical accuracy on this subject is difficult. Indeterminate proportions of aliens in the populations are illegal; moreover, a considerable number of the alien workers in each Gulf state are hired under contracts that require repatriation after specified periods of time. Furthermore, to a lesser extent small percentages of the longer standing residents are permitted to convert their alien status from time to time into citizenship.

Each of the Traditional states has expressed great concern over their large alien populations. The problems envisaged include labor strikes and unrest and in the military equivalent, mutiny and disruption. These states also fear that such alien populations could become "fifth columns" and receive assistance from neighboring Gulf states— a fear expressed particularly about Iranian residents and labor. Also feared is ideological infection and political disruption, expressed particularly by Kuwait concerning its Palestinian population.

The response by the Traditional states to these actual and potential problems has been to develop labor policy priorities that in the first instance encourage employment of their indigenous populations, then employment of nationals of other Gulf sheikhdoms, then other Arabs. These states also attempt to diversify the national origins of their alien workforce.

In addition the Traditional states have tightened internal security measures and immigration control, conducting searches from time to time against illegal immigration. They have sought to regulate private enterprises contracting for alien labor and impose responsibility for maintenance of order among the workers upon the companies that employ them and at times the foreign governments whose nationals are under contract. They have segregated contract workforces and other aliens from their own citizenry. And they have maintained tight control over granting privileges of citizenship in order to avoid more permanent political problems.

Nonetheless there are occasional reports of alien unrest. It is expected that the potential problems will continue so long as the pace of economic development projects in the Gulf states outstrips their ability to provide manpower for them from their indigenous workforce. Let us examine the scope of these potential problems for each of the Traditional states.

Saudi Arabia. The total alien population estimated ranges from 3 million to 4 million inclusive of family members of alien workers and persons who will be repatriated after their contracted labor period.[79] Of this total the range of persons accounted for within the alien workforce is from just over 1 million to 2.5 million.[80] Estimates concerning the nationality of both the general alien population, including workers and residents, and those of the workforce alone also vary, and obviously may change over time. The largest single national group may be Yemenis, whose general population number may be 1 million, over 600,000 of whom are within the workforce.[81] The total non-Arab group of Asians within the workforce (Pakistanis, who predominate; Indians; Koreans; Filipinos; Bangladeshis; Sri Lankans; and Thais) has been estimated in 1983 at 1,235,000. An earlier (1980) estimate of Arab workers put their number at 930,000.[82] The Palestinians, who have been politically active in other Gulf states, notably Kuwait, have been estimated as totaling 180,000 in Saudi Arabia. Some 80,000 of these Palestinians are in the workforce.[83]

No precise figures are given for the numbers of aliens who may be serving in the Saudi armed forces. One report states that many contract expatriates fill skilled and semiskilled positions in the military.[84] Strikes among alien workers have been reported but have been made the responsibility of the employer or national government involved.[85]

Kuwait. Approximately 800,000 persons, or 59 percent of the Kuwaiti population, are recorded or accounted for as alien, and of the Kuwaiti workforce, 70 percent are aliens.[86] Of the aliens one of the largest Arab groups is the Palestinians, estimated at approximately 350,000. Another large Arab group is the Egyptians, estimated at 200,000.[87] There are differing reports as to the ethnic composition within the Kuwaiti armed forces. Although the bulk of the fighting force in the army appears to be of Bedouin origin, there are also "non-Kuwaiti professionals" in assistance functions, composed of Palestinians, Egyptians, and Jordanians.[88]

Of the alien groups, the Palestinians have been the most active politically. In 1976 the regime dissolved the National Assembly in the face of mounting protests, particularly by Palestinians, against the regime's ambivalent foreign policy in the Lebanese civil war of 1975–76 and Egypt's disengagement agreement with Israel in September 1975. Palestinians also demonstrated against other Egyptian moves of rapprochement with Israel after the closing of the Assembly.[89]

Other unrest and labor strikes involving foreign workers have also occurred, and the regime remains vigilant against illegal immigration.[90] In addition, the permanent alien population in Kuwait has put considerable pressure on the regime to relax its highly restrictive naturalization laws. The regime acceded to some of this pressure in 1980 by permitting naturalization for Arabs with fifteen years residency and non-Arabs with twenty years continuous residency, and permitting the government to set annual quotas for naturalization of aliens with particular expertise. In 1983 the National Assembly proposed a special quota of 1,000 and proposed to naturalize a number of persons serving in the army, paramilitary and police.[91]

UAE. Estimates set the alien population in the UAE as approximately 800,000 of its population of 1 million persons. Aliens constitute approximately 90 percent of the UAE workforce.[92] It is not clear if any one nationality predominates.[93] The Union Defense Force, which developed from the Trucial Oman Scouts, appears to have retained a substantial number of aliens in its ranks as well as a predominant alien officer class made up of Britons, Pakistanis, and Jordanians.[94]

UAE labor policy has attempted to encourage nationals to take unskilled jobs and promotes the hiring of Arabs over nonnationals. UAE immigration policy has tightened up its border and visa controls and illegal immigration investigations but loosened naturalization for Gulf Arabs from Qatar, Oman, and Bahrain to three years of residency.[95]

Bahrain, Qatar, and Oman. Of the three remaining Gulf sheikhdoms, Qatar has the smallest population and the largest proportion of aliens, estimated from 40–80 percent. Oman has reportedly few aliens, but it does have the largest proportion within its armed forces, estimated at approximately 25 percent. Bahrain reportedly has a population composed 35 percent of aliens, although no aliens are reported in its diminutive armed forces.[96]

Ideological Contests

There coexist in the Gulf a number of political value systems with significant international impact. These ideologies range from right to left and can be categorized as follows: (1) *religious-conservative* ideologies of fundamentalist Islam, best represented by Khomeini's Shiism and Saudi Arabia's Wahhabism; (2) *Arab-nationalist* ideologies represented by Iraq's Ba'thism; and (3) *Marxist-Radical* ideologies of South Yemen and the rebel groups sponsored by it, the NDF in North Yemen, PFLO in Oman.[97]

Before identifying the individual ideologies within each category that contend for adherents within the Gulf, some observations are in order concerning their impact on international politics. Each of these ideologies has been exported by its national proponent and used overtly or subversively to create alignments within other Gulf states with pro- or antiregime groups. How effective such export has proved or may prove is one of the considerations in this chapter.

None of these ideological systems is static. Each is in the process of development, sometimes developing schisms and factions that blunt its effectiveness. Sometimes the ideologies adapt effectively to different national environments, thereby increasing its effectiveness, but in so doing their exportability is blunted. For example, the more "Persian" the Shiism of Khomeini, the less acceptable it may be to Arab Shiites across the Gulf.

These ideologies are political. They are put to political uses by particular decision makers and thus become vulnerable to the political fortunes and failures of their proponents. For example, Nasserism suffered sorely with Egypt's perceived defeat in the 1967 Six Day War and Sadat's defusing of Nasserism succeeded with Egypt's perceived victory in the 1973 Yom Kippur War (October War).

Finally, it can be observed that these are mainly ideologies of regimes in power. These regimes are what might be called "orthocratic" in their outlook toward potentially competing political value systems. Their legitimacy allows for only one "correct" ideology. Hence these regimes typically brook no challenge or dissent within their own states. Within such states this need for legitimacy leads, among other things, to the organization of strong internal security measures.[98] Alien ideologies imported from other states are viewed as conspiratorial and subversive propaganda. The groups that adopt and promote such ideologies for the most part are oppressed minorities, often compelled to operate clandestinely. Occasionally the fate of the group espousing the minority ideology is abandoned by its outside sponsor for strategic reasons such as the sponsor's need for alignment or settlement with the host state. It is difficult, therefore, to make a general assessment of the potential effectiveness of these minority ideologies. They may succeed or fail to gain adherents and power depending on both their internal domestic and external international political environments, both of which are susceptible to change. The contending ideologies will be identified on a state-by-state basis.

Iran

The Iranian Revolution of 1978–79 swept into power not only the Ayatollah Khomeini but also Shiite mullahs and other ayatollahs. Most

of the ayatollahs have been provided the forum for ideological articulation and political organization of the Shiite Revolution through the
ruling Islamic Republican Party (IRP). Some, like Ayatollah
Shariʻatmadarī did not wholly accept the dictates of the new regime.
In any event the Iranian clergy continue to play a significant political
role.

Under the shah, the financial independence of the Iranian clergy
and the oppositional stance of Shiite doctrine attracted broad popular
support, particularly among the urban and rural poor. This oppositional role of the clergy was to some extent forced on them by the
need for self-defense against the shah's concerted efforts to crush all
political opposition, including clerical opposition. Moreover, Iranian
Shiism possesses a peculiar suitability for such an oppositional role,
with its tenets that sanctify the mosque as a haven from persecution
and its sanctification of personal martyrdom. For all these reasons the
Iranian clergy adapted well to the political task of bringing down the
regime.[99]

After achieving power in Iran through the IRP the Iranian clergy
appear to have lost their oppositional consensus. Their political ideologies range from extremist to moderate. The IRP itself is composed
of a number of factions, which stretch across the political spectrum in
degrees of independence from Khomeini's political philosophy. Six such
factions have been identified. All are loosely integrated. They are the
Maktabī, who are most closely aligned with Khomeini; the *Hojjatiya,*
who are more conservative and anticommunist; the *Mujāhidīn-i-Islam,*
the "independents"; the "traditionalist" clergy, including senior ayatollahs who are independent from Khomeini; the military who have
been indoctrinated through political commissars; and the *Pasdaran,*
Revolutionary Guards who are pro-Khomeini and *Maktabī.*[100]

Even after achieving power, however, Khomeini's oppositional political philosophy has been able to maintain its revolutionary fervor.
Other "devils" have replaced the shah, for example the United States,
especially during the hostage crisis, and Ṣaddām Ḥusayn during the
Iraq–Iran war. It is this fervor that has led the Gulf states to fear for
the export of the Shiite republican revolution into their states through
not only Iranian propaganda but also Iranian organized subversion and
potentially, Iranian military adventures.[101]

It is not clear whether this same ideological fervor can survive
Khomeini's death or incapacity. As Iran's ruling group makes its own
compromises and political accommodations inherent in the formulation
and execution of central policies, the ideological underpinnings may
well loosen, particularly in the absence of the Revolution's charismatic
proponent, Ayatollah Khomeini. Furthermore, in Khomeini's absence,

factionalism within the IRP may dilute the force of revolutionary Shiism. Indeed the death of Khomeini may well lead to a struggle for succession within the IRP, and with other opposition groups that may perceive opportunities to bid for recognition and power.[102]

The other ideological opposition groups within Iran, other than ethnic opposition groups, have generally been suppressed after the IRP achieved power, as they had been under the shah. This opposition is mainly leftist and organized around three relatively small groups: the *Tudeh,* Communist party; the *Mujāhidīn-i-Khalq,* Islamic-Marxists or left-wing Moslems; and the radical Marxist *Fedayeen-i-Khalq,* a faction of which conducts urban guerrilla campaigns against the regime.[103] In spring 1983 the regime conducted a purge against the Tudeh, arresting a large number of its already small membership.[104] It is not clear how large or small the base of support is for the other leftist groups. Nor is it clear how much external assistance these groups may receive or the effectiveness of any of their internal alignments with other ethnic opposition groups.[105] While the Iranian regime has not been able to destroy them, neither have these opposition groups at this time created a major threat to destroy the regime.

Iraq

Since 1968 Iraq has been ruled by the Ba'th ('Resurrection') party. Ba'thism developed in Syria during World War II under the guidance of Michel 'Aflaq, who was Greek Orthodox, and Salāh al-Dīn al-Bitār, both of whom were middle class, Paris-educated, Syrian nationalists. The major tenets of Ba'thism are pan-Arab nationalism and socialism, tenets that have appealed mainly to the new Arab elites composed of the salaried middle classes, students, and army officers concerned with social change.[106] Ba'thism's ideological opponents within the Gulf are accordingly adherents of conservative religious ideologies of the right and Marxist ideologies on the left. Within the broader Arab nationalist and socialist movement Ba'thism's chief competitor has been Nasserism. Nasserism opposed the collectivist leadership approach of Ba'thism in favor of charismatic leadership—namely that of President Nasser of Egypt.

Ba'thism was introduced into Iraq in 1949 by Palestinian refugees and returning Iraqi students who had studied in Syria and Lebanon. Ba'thism did not, however, emerge into a significant political force in Iraq until the mid-1950s.[107] The Ba'thists came to power briefly in 1963 after participating in the overthrow of Qāsim, who had five years earlier participated in the overthrow of the monarchical regime. The

Ba'thists lost power however, in 1963 after the failure of their attempted coordination with Syrian Ba'thists and Nasser. The succeeding ruling coalition was dominated by a Nasserite military leader, 'Abd al-Sālam 'Ārif. In 1968 the Ba'thists again gained power in a coup led by General Aḥmad Ḥasan al-Bakr. The Ba'thists have since consolidated their hold on Iraq by permeating social organizations, establishing a ruthless internal security organization, and politicizing the armed forces with Ba'thist cadres and cells.[108] Ṣaddām Ḥusayn, supported by a close-knit group of army officers from the Takriti area of Iraq, edged al-Bakr out of the top posts in the regime in 1979.

Since the Ba'thist consolidation of power after the 1968 takeover, the ideological opposition to the regime has been purged and is no longer considered a major threat. The other Arab nationalist socialist parties, such as the Nasserites, were too fragmented by the early seventies to remain a threat and the Iraqi Communist party was purged in 1978–79.[109]

Ba'thism in power in Iraq has been tempered by the regime's need to avoid alienation of its Shiite majority. The otherwise secular aspects of its ideological underpinnings are deemphasized and Ḥusayn pointedly pays attention to Shiite concerns. While the radical republicanism of the ideology has been of concern to the conservative regimes in the Gulf, Ḥusayn has underplayed this ideological threat in his dealings with the Traditional states, particularly to maintain alignments and financial support during the Iraq–Iran war.

Saudi Arabia

Saudi Arabia's Wahhabism has in this century already passed through a number of the phases other ideological systems in the Gulf are just entering. Under Ibn Saud, Wahhabism provided the revolutionary fervor with which to inspire his *Ikhwān* military force for the conquest of the Arabian Peninsula. Wahhabism then provided the legitimizing principles for the consolidation of Ibn Saud's rule and the integration of the disparate tribal elements within the Peninsula into the newly created Kingdom. Thereafter King Saud and his successors found ways in which to temper Wahhabism to the task of ruling and to overcome the resistance of Saudi *'ulamā'* to the Kingdom's accommodations with modernization. For example the use of radio broadcasting was tolerated because it also provided a means of spreading religion; the education of women was tolerated so long as their strict segregation from men was maintained. Indeed modern technology has reportedly been used in an ingenious manner to enforce the religious ban on sexual integration. Riyadh University apparently uses closed-circuit television to maintain the separation of the sexes while educating women.[110]

As oil revenues increased, particularly in the seventies, the regime also dedicated large sums for the promotion of Islamic causes. Such promotion has furthered the export by Saudi Arabia of its conservative-religious ideology. Thus, foreign assistance was provided to Muslim governments and political parties, and international Muslim institutions were established. These include the Islamic Conference, which since 1969 has hosted summit meetings of heads of Muslim regimes, the Islamic Council of Europe, and the Islamic Institute of Defense Technology. The Islamic Conference has spawned a news agency, broadcasting organization, bank, "solidarity fund," and clearinghouse for cultural centers. It has also served as the forum from which Saudi Arabia announced the formation of the GCC in 1981.[111]

Nevertheless, Saudi Arabia's conservative religious ideological principles have not been without challenge both from the right and from the left. None of these challenges, however, have as yet served as major threats to the viability of the regime. The challenge from the right has been evidenced by the attack in 1979 on the Great Mosque. The challenge from the left arises from small and clandestine ideological opposition groups. Such clandestine groups that have achieved public notice, notwithstanding suppression by Saudi internal security measures, include principally the Nasserite Arabic Peninsula Peoples Union, which sponsored coup attempts in 1966 and 1977, the Popular Democratic Party, which was formed of a union of Nasserites and Ba'thists in 1970, and the Marxist National Liberation Front.[112]

North Yemen

The North Yemen civil war of 1962–1970 originated in a republican coup led by a Nasserite military commander, 'Abd Allāh al-Sallāl. Egypt immediately provided troops to aid the republican forces. After the Egyptians withdrew in 1967, Sallāl was deposed and Nasserism waned in North Yemen. Nasserism waned generally in the Mideast after Egypt's defeat in the 1967 war. After Nasser's death in 1970, his successor, Anwar Sadat, shifted away from Nasserism and the ideology lost its force.[113] The republican regime that came to power in North Yemen under Qadi 'Abd al-Rahmān al-Iryānī offset the Nasserite influence with Ba'thist ministers. Al-Iryānī generally underplayed the ideological underpinnings of the revolution in order to reach accommodations with Saudi Arabia and the Saudi backed ideologically conservative tribes of North Yemen.

The succeeding military regimes have not maintained any well-defined ideological identity. Ideological opposition to the North Yemeni regime arises not only from northern tribes but also from the National Democratic Front (NDF), a coalition of dissidents sponsored by South Yemen. The NDF leadership in 1978 consisted of a coalition of two Ba'thists and a Marxist ideologue from the Arab Nationalist Movement (ANM) a radical Arab nationalist socialist party originated by George Habash (and renamed the Popular Front for the Liberation of Palestine, PFLP). Moreover, another opposition coalition, called the Islamic Front, was reported in 1981 as composed of Saudi-supported northern Hashid tribes and the conservative Moslim Brotherhood.[114] North Yemen, as a result, holds onto its republicanism on the slenderest of ideological foundations while beset by a complex ideological contest among conservative factions, Arab nationalist socialist factions, and Marxist factions.

South Yemen

The avowedly Marxist-Leninist regime in South Yemen traces its origins to the Arab nationalist socialist ferment of the 1950s. At that time the ANM became influential in South Yemen, then the British controlled Aden Protectorate. The ANM in the late fifties formed the National Liberation Front (NLF), which emerged to combat the British regime in the Aden Protectorate in 1963–1967. The NLF at the same time overcame the competition from the Egyptian-supported Nasserite Front for the Liberation of South Yemen (FLOSY). Egypt was at that time providing assistance to the republican regime during the civil war in Northern Yemen. The Marxist wing of the NLF predominated and gained control of South Yemen in 1969. The People's Democratic Republic of Yemen (PDRY) was thereby created.[115]

After it consolidated its power, the ruling group divided into two main factions within the Marxist-Leninist organization. One faction represented a pragmatic approach to policy and was led by Sālim 'Alī Rabī. The other represented a doctrinaire approach and was led by 'Abd al-Fattāh Ismā'īl. 'Alī Rabī alienated the Soviets by opposing their development of a naval base at Aden, and alienated the doctrinaire group by advocating improvement of relations with Saudi Arabia.[116] In a 1978 coup Ismā'īl took power and formed the Yemen Socialist Party (YSP). Ismā'īl proceeded to draw South Yemen closer to the Soviet Union with a Twenty-year Treaty of Friendship and an influx of Soviet and Soviet bloc advisors. A similar treaty was signed with East Germany in 1979, and with Czechoslovakia in 1981.[117] In 1980

Ismā'īl himself was replaced, in an apparently bloodless coup by 'Alī Nasser Muḥammad. It was reported that Ismā'īl alienated Soviet support with his overly doctrinaire approach to South Yemen's domestic and foreign policy. He failed to follow the Soviet line as the Soviets turned to improving relations with the conservative Traditional states. His replacement, 'Alī Nasser is a pragmatist, but one not willing to confront the Soviet Union.[118]

It is not clear to what extent the Marxism-Leninism of the PDRY has accommodated to Islamic practice within Southern Yemen. There are conflicting reports as to the regime's attitude toward religion. The regime has been reported as downplaying its secularism and publicly acknowledging Islam as the state religion while officially opposing feudalism and tribalism. It has also been reported as engaging in religious repression.[119]

Furthermore the regime has espoused the Arab nationalist cause, an ideological posture that furthers its efforts to achieve unification with North Yemen. In addition, the regime has sought to export its Marxist-Leninist revolution through the support of liberationist causes on the Arabian Peninsula, particularly in its support for the Popular Front for the Liberation of Oman (PFLO). Even after the suppression of the PFLO within Oman, the South Yemen regime has not renounced its support of that cause, and some five hundred or so Omani rebels are still provided refuge in South Yemen.

There appears to be no organized ideological opposition to the regime operating from within South Yemen. The regime, with Soviet bloc assistance, has nevertheless established an internal security force that appears capable of suppressing such opposition. A small but ineffective expatriate opposition group has operated from Cairo since the early 1970s, and for a brief period was hosted in Baghdad. Iraq lent its support to the group during a period of breakdown of Iraqi relations with South Yemen, 1979–1981. The breakdown was apparently occasioned by the purge of the Iraqi Communist party, and general weaning away from Soviet influence. The Iraqi regime also pursued some Communists who fled to South Yemen and assassinated one. Diplomatic relations between the countries were then ruptured. After 'Alī Nasser gained power, however, he sought to repair the relationship with Iraq.[120] Iraqi support for the South Yemeni opposition group, accordingly, diminished.

Oman: The Dhofar Rebellion

The rebellion in Oman's westernmost and relatively isolated Dhofar province originated in tribal discontent against the prior Sultan, Sa'īd ibn Taymūr.[121] In 1965 the ANM became involved and transformed the rebellion into an Arab nationalist movement in opposition to the sultanate itself, similar to the Arab nationalist contests in North and South Yemen. The rebels then obtained external support from Egypt, Iraq, and Palestinian groups. By 1968 and after the advent to power of the NLF in South Yemen, the Dhofar rebellion became more radicalized. With NLF support the rebellion extended its ideological objectives as suggested in its new name, the Popular Front for the Liberation of the Occupied Arabian Gulf (PFLOAG). It also lost its Nasserite support with Egypt's general withdrawal from the Peninsula after the 1967 defeat by Israel, but gained assistance from the Soviet Union and People's Republic of China. The radicalization of PFLOAG into a Marxist-Leninist rebel force probably lost some tribal support due to the anti-Islamic bent of the new ideology, but it also widened the attraction to the rebel cause of other dissident groups in northern Oman. By 1970 these dissident groups had formed a coalition named the National Democratic Front for the Liberation of Oman and the Arabian Gulf (NDFLOAG), but posed no significant military threat to the regime.[122]

The regime itself underwent a change in orientation as Sultan Sa'īd ibn Taymūr was deposed in 1970 by his son, Qābūs. The new sultan gradually inaugurated economic development programs for the Dhofar, offered amnesty to defecting rebels, and augmented the Omani Armed Forces with foreign military assistance. By mid-1972 PFLOAG forces had extended their control in the border region and attempted in vain to push eastward by attacks on the coastal villages of Taqah and Mirbat east of Salalah, the capital city of Dhofar. These assaults were repelled and thereafter the sultan's forces maintained successive lines of defense, gradually pushing the rebels back to the border. In this the Omanis were assisted by an Iranian contingent as well as by British advisors. By mid-1974 the PFLOAG had renounced its larger goals as evidenced by the retraction of its name to the Popular Front for the Liberation of Oman (PFLO). By the end of 1975, the sultan proclaimed the rebellion officially over. During this same period of retreat, various sources of PFLO support dropped away: the Chinese in 1973, the Iraqis in 1975—both as a consequence of their reconciliation with the Iranian regime, and even the South Yemen regime moderated its support in 1975–76.[123]

The PFLO has not, however, been totally eliminated. There are various reports of small enclaves of PFLO combatants within Dhofar and a number still across the border in South Yemen.[124] A recrudescence of PFLO activity accompanied the regime of the Marxist hardliner, Ismā'īl, in South Yemen in 1979–80. There were also reports of stepped up propaganda and subversion from across the South Yemen border after the withdrawal of the remainder of the Iranian contingent following Khomeini's accession to power.[125] Since Ismā'īl was deposed and succeeded by the more pragmatic regime of 'Alī Nasser in South Yemen, PFLO activity has reportedly decreased and South Yemen has taken steps to normalize relations with Oman. South Yemen is, however, reportedly still seeking expatriate Omani student support for its cause and engaging in propaganda. And the PFLO has continued to seek financial and other support from a range of Arab countries. In so doing, however, it has become victim to the rivalries between its putative benefactors. Support for the PFLO cause, accordingly, has suffered from contests between Iraq and Libya prior to the Iraq–Iran war, and contests between Syria and Iraq since that war.[126]

Other Lesser Actors

Generally, the other lesser actors in the Gulf, all of which are sheikhdoms—Bahrain, Kuwait, Qatar, and the UAE—depend upon legitimating principles that uphold the personalized dynastic rights of their sheikhs. They have accommodated themselves, however, to the ideological cross-currents within the Gulf by espousing Arab national causes, particularly those of the Palestinians. They have also accommodated their regimes in varying degree to the religious pressures of the "Islamic revival."[127] Because of their large expatriate populations and the risks of various ideological "infections", each of these states has increased its internal security apparatus, censorship of its press, and control over public expression of criticism of their respective regimes. The Gulf sheikhdoms have also looked to coordinate their internal security measures and countersubversion controls through the GCC. Notwithstanding their efforts, these states have not remained impermeable to ideologically animated opposition groups. These groups operate clandestinely but occasionally emerge into public notice with reports of bombings, strikes, protests, and propaganda. The more significant ideological challenges to these regimes are briefly listed below:

Bahrain. The leftist groups are most notably the National Front for the Liberation of Bahrain and the Popular Front for the Liberation of Bahrain, both of which had links with the PFLO and have recently espoused a common platform. The ANM, renamed the PFLP, has also reportedly been active in Bahrain.[128]

Kuwait. The PFLP has also been active in Kuwait as have various other Palestinian political groups. Although political parties have been banned, some members of the National Assembly are reportedly linked to Arab nationalist groups and others to conservative-religious ideological groups such as the Moslem Brotherhood.[129]

Qatar. There does not appear to be any active political opposition, although the regime has tightened its internal security since 1979 as have other Gulf states.[130]

UAE. There are scant reports of political opposition groups within the UAE, although the Moslem Brotherhood may have a following and Ba'thism appears to have attracted some of the younger intelligentsia.[131]

International Implications

How do religious cleavages, ethnic dissension, and ideological contests within the Gulf impact upon the international behavior of the Gulf states? We need to consider two broad international implications. The first relates to the potential for these divisions in the political communities of the Gulf states to incapacitate a state. The Gulf state that is susceptible to disintegration in its political community will not be capable of engaging in international behavior. Its military capabilities will be diverted to the reintegration of the state and it may present opportunities for intervention by other states. The second relates to the potential of ideological contests to cause a radical change of regime. The Gulf state that succumbs to such a regime change may in turn radically shift its alignments and foreign policy orientations. That shift may promote foreign adventures and prevent diplomatic interchanges.

Having identified the significant religious cleavages, ethnic dissension, and ideological contests in the Gulf, we can now explore their implications for the current international politics of the Gulf—its dynamic balance of power system. How unstable are current international politics of the Gulf as a result of these divisions, and what potential do they have for destabilizing the system in the future?

Implications for the Current International System

One conclusion that is possible from examination of disintegrative effects of the cleavages in the political communities of the Gulf states and the potential of Gulf ideological contests for radical regime changes is that all of the major actors and most but not all of the lesser actors are currently fairly well integrated and resistant to radical change of regime. Each of the major actors—Iran, Iraq, and Saudi Arabia— currently has an orthocratic regime organized by a single-party system, as in Iran (the Islamic Republican Party) and Iraq (Ba'thists), and/or by fundamentalist religious legitimacy as in Saudi Arabia (Wahhabism) and Iran (Khomeini's Shiism). Each of these regimes has extensive internal security systems for the purpose, among others, of suppressing dissent and enforcing ideological conformity. Moreover, both Iran and Iraq have highly politicized their respective armies with ideological indoctrination and political commissars. The effects are integrative in the sense that they counteract the centrifugal societal forces within their respective states from religious dissension and from ethnic cleavage.

Moreover, such internal security systems have so far proved sufficiently effective to have divested opposition groups of broad-based popular support. This has indeed forced dissenting groups underground and encouraged subversive activity. On the other hand, it has also restrained the scope of minority opposition activity—even in the case of assassinations of high-ranking regime officials, as for example in Iran, and somewhat larger lethal protests such as the siege of the Great Mosque in Saudi Arabia. While such subversive activities have caused and may cause temporary interference with governmental operations they have not proved sufficient to bring down regimes or incapacitate the states.

Our current view of the relatively integrative effects of ideological orthodoxy and internal security systems in the major Gulf actors should not, however, obscure from a historical perspective some inherent disintegrative effects. Orthocracy breeds factionalism. Factionalism, typically expressed as contests between hard-liners and moderates within these regimes, in turn creates the opportunities for power struggles. Power struggles invite coups and broader based bids to overthrow the regime.

From a historical perspective it can be recognized that each of the major actors has succumbed to regime overturns within the past twenty-five years that have radically reoriented its foreign policies. Iran's most radical regime change occurred in 1978–79 with the Iranian Revolution, which brought the Ayatollah Khomeini to power. Iran, however, had also suffered major reorienting overturns in 1951–53 when the "nationalists" came to power under Mossadeq and thereafter in 1953 when Mossadeq was ousted in a coup. In 1963 radical regime change was threatened when major disturbances attended the implementation of the Pahlevi regime's land reform program, the so-called White Revolution. This program sought to institute land distribution, nationalization of forests, privatization of state factories, profit-sharing for workers, female suffrage and rural literacy. Indeed, the Ayatollah Khomeini first drew national attention in Iran by his outspoken opposition to the shah's programs during the Muḥarram upheavals of 1963.[132]

Iraq's major regime change occurred in 1958 with the overthrow of the monarchy. Other regime reorienting coups followed in 1963 and 1968 bringing the Baʻthists to power, and to a lesser extent in 1979 when Ṣaddām Ḥusayn edged al-Bakr out of power. To a lesser degree and without a revolution a confrontation occurred with major modernization demands in Saudi Arabia during the reign of King Saud (son of Ibn Saud) whose resistance to them led to his ouster in 1964 in favor of his brother, Faisal.[133]

One result of the perceived potential for internal overturns of these regimes is the degree of their attention to the development of the loyalty of their armed forces. Such loyalty is secured by indoctrination and political supervision through cadres and commissars and by periodic purges as in Islamic Republican Iran and Baʻthist Iraq, or by maintaining counterforces, such as the National Guard in Saudi Arabia and the Revolutionary Guards in Iran.

Similar regime overturns have occurred among the minor actors. In North Yemen the major regime overturn occurred in the 1962 republican coup and protracted civil war that ensued into 1970. North Yemen has since suffered coups in 1974, 1977, and 1978. South Yemen went through its major reorientation upon the withdrawal of the British in 1967 and consolidation of power by the NLF in 1969. South Yemen has since suffered coups in 1978 and 1980. Oman's major regime orientation occurred in 1970 with the deposition of Sultan Saʻīd ibn Taymūr. The sultan, like King Saud in Saudi Arabia, unsuccessfully resisted nationalist demands for modernization.

The Gulf sheikhdoms—Bahrain, Kuwait, Qatar, and constituents of the UAE—on the other hand, appear to have accommodated themselves to various modernizing demands. Their regime changes have occurred so far more by way of intradynastic overturns. Indeed, among the constituents of the UAE five of the seven ruling sheikhs in 1977 had gained power through dynastic coups or assassinations.[134]

Given the incidence of major overturns of Gulf regimes within the past twenty-five years, an interesting question is why there has not been a more radical change in the international politics of the Gulf as a result of the ideological reorientations of such regime changes? The essential answer is that the regime overturns have not fundamentally altered the structure of the dynamic balance of power system in the Gulf. The regime changes have not eliminated any major actors or generated new ones. They have not produced a radical alteration of the relative distribution of capabilities among the Gulf actors.

Two further general conclusions are possible. The first is that the divisons within the political communities of the Gulf states have been functional for the maintenance of the dynamic balance of power system of international politics of the Gulf. The second is that the potential regime changes, particularly from ideological contests have not been dysfunctional for those international politics and may also have reinforced its dynamic balance of power structure.

How have divisions within the political communities reinforced the dynamic balance of power structure of Gulf international politics? In the first place there are significant ethnic and religious cleavages within the two major actors with relatively superior military capabilities, Iran and Iraq. These cleavages are insufficient, as we have observed, to incapacitate these states over the long run. But they are sufficiently pronounced to create additional potential allies to external actors. The Iraqis and Iranians, for example, have each supported Kurdish opposition to the other's regime. The possibility of the diversion of armed forces for internal threats from ethnic and religious unrest, to some extent has impeded the full use of their relatively superior military capabilities by the major actors, Iraq and Iran.

In addition to a considerable extent the religious and ethnic cleavages within the Gulf are cross-cutting. The disintegrative effects of any one cleavage may be constrained by a counteractive cleavage. So for example, the Kurds on both sides of the Iraq–Iran border have been rent by ideological factionalism, even to the point of combat. The result is to undermine the Kurd's centrifugal demands for increasing autonomy and lessen their effectiveness against the forces and resources of the central regimes in each of the states. There are cross-cutting effects of religious affiliation also. The Azerbaijanis, for example, although the largest of the Iranian ethnic groups, are predominantly Shiite. They have not as significantly challenged the Islamic Republican regime as have the Kurds.

How have regime overturns through ideological contests proven functional for or reinforced the dynamic balance of power structure of Gulf international politics? In the first place, it is noteworthy that no one ideological force has been dominant in the Gulf. As a result no major actor shares the same ideological penchant as any other. Each are actual or potential ideological contestants of the other. There are obvious ideological polarities among Iranian Shiism, Iraqi Ba'thism, and Saudi Wahhabism. There are also ideological polarities between North Yemen's ideologically weak republicanism and South Yemen's Marxist-Leninism as well as polarities among these republican regimes and the Gulf sheikhdoms.

Indeed, the only natural ideological alignments within the Gulf appear presently among the constituents of the GCC. On closer examination, even among the GCC there exist ideological divergencies. There are ideological strains, for example, between Oman, which is the least Arab nationalist and the most pro-West, and Kuwait, which has diplomatic connections with the Soviet Union. Yet, these ideological differences in the Gulf generally have not prohibited diplomatic intercourse, or even alignments between the major actors or with lesser actors.

There are, however, two notable exceptions to this generalization in the current context of Gulf international politics. One is the extremism of Khomeini's Shiite revolution and the other is the Marxist-Leninism of South Yemen. The fervor of both of their revolutions has inhibited alignments. To some extent, the fervor of South Yemen's revolution, which transpired in 1969, has subsided. It remains to be seen whether the Iranian Revolution will follow the same course. Alliances with Iraq, for example, were inhibited during the period of ideological fervor following the Ba'thist coup of 1968. Thereafter the fervor subsided and by 1975 Iraq was pursuing alignments with the Traditional states.

Generally, however, ideological contests in the Gulf have not prevented diplomatic intercourse. There have been diplomatic dealings between ideological enemies and this dynamic balance of power flexibility has also enabled states to shift support from ideological friends to obtain settlements. Such settlements included the North Yemen civil war in 1970; settlement of the Iraq–Iran boundary struggles in 1975; and resolution of the Dhofar rebellion in 1976. These settlements have been obtained consistent with switches in alignment in the dynamic balance of power at the expense or sacrifice of the lesser ideological ally. Thus for example in the aforementioned settlements there were switches from alignments with the conservative tribes in North Yemen, the Iraqi Kurds, and the PFLO, respectively.

Implications for the Future

The potential divisions within the political communities of the Gulf states and the potential radical regime changes currently reinforce the dynamic balance of power structure of the Gulf or at least do not undermine it. On the other hand (as shown in chapter 2) the international system of the Gulf has undergone radical changes of structure within the twentieth century. And the major actors have succumbed to radical regime changes with consequent reorientations of their foreign policies within the last twenty-five years. Without the gift of prophesy we cannot therefore conclude either that the current structure of the international system of the Gulf will continue or that it will remain a dynamic balance of power. Let us consider instead what possibilities exist that changes to the structure of the international system can result from cleavages within the political communities of the Gulf states and radical changes in their regimes.

Six radical changes within the Gulf states appear to have the potential for restructuring the current dynamic balance of power system. They affect each of six Gulf states: Iran, Iraq, Saudi Arabia, Kuwait, Bahrain, and North Yemen. Before exploring these possibilities two caveats are in order. First, these are only possibilities. Without clairvoyance, there is no reliable way to assign probabilities to their occurrence. They are indeed the stuff that scenarios are made of. Second, for convenience these changes will be explored on a state-by-state basis. Were any of them to occur, however, it is likely that such changes would not occur in a vacuum, and that changes in one state would not be insulated from changes in others. Indeed, far more complicated scenarios could be developed from the possibility of simultaneous or sequential occurrence of changes identified below.

Iran. The regime and political community changes in Iran with significant international political consequences are usually viewed as resulting from a succession crisis after Khomeini. Without Khomeini the ruling IRP may not maintain cohesion or control over the country. Factionalism within the IRP and fragmentation of central authority in Iran would encourage the larger autonomy-seeking ethnic groups within the state to reassert their demands for autonomy. This same breakdown in the ability of the central regime to maintain its authority at the Iranian perimeter could invite Soviet intrusion directly or indirectly into Azerbaijan and similar Iraqi intrusion into Khuzestan. The Soviet Union could support an autonomous Azerbaijan with military assistance, including by means of the deployment of Soviet forces. Similar pressure could be asserted by Iraq, which would have less fear of repeating its 1980 miscalculation of central regime breakdown, were the Soviets to divert Iranian attention to Azerbaijan. An Iraqi invasion into Khuzestan under such circumstances would have greater chance of success without the need to guard Iraq's relatively exposed approach to Baghdad. Depending on Soviet motives and opportunities, it is not clear that the USSR would welcome an Iraqi intervention, or vice versa, the Iraqis a Soviet intervention.

Centrifugal and also countervailing pressure could be expected in such circumstances by the ethnic perimeter groups between Azerbaijan and Khuzestan. Soviet and Iraqi encouragement of Iranian Kurdish dissension and resistance to the central regime could be expected. The Soviet Union, assuming its continuing entrenchment in Afghanistan, could also directly or indirectly encourage Baluchi autonomy at the southeast perimeter in order to increase the dispersion of whatever central regime military forces may exist.

Ethnic groups to the south of the Kurds may, however, see their own autonomy just as threatened by the Iraqis and Soviets as by the central regime. They could offer resistance to Soviet military advances to the south from Azerbaijan and Iraqi military advances to the north from Khuzestan. Such groups as the Bakhtiaris, Lurs, and Qashqais would be advantaged by operating on their familiar terrain of the Zagros Mountains. They could serve as potential allies to western forces willing to support their autonomy and resist the dismemberment of Iran by the Soviet Union or Iraq.

This latter part of the scenario is not as farfetched as it may sound. A similar situation occurred in mid-1946 as the central Iranian regime under the mercurial Premier Qasavam accepted communist Tudeh party participation in the government. Qasavam's tilt to the left also undermined Iranian resistance to the Autonomous Republic of Azerbaijan that had been established with Soviet assistance and was being maintained with the support of Soviet troops. The Qashqais coalesced with the Bakhtiaris, some Kurdish tribes, Khuzestan Arabs, and other southern tribes, and obtained British support for their demands for similar recognition of their ethnic autonomy and the removal of Tudeh influence.[135]

Iraq. Changes within the central regime with international implications probably involve an unseating of the Ba'thist control over the state. Coups by disaffected military officers may initiate such a process. Opportunities could arise for example in the event of serious Shiite dissension that the central regime could not dampen. Disintegration of central authority in Iraq also presents opportunities for the Soviet Union as well as Iran. The Soviets gain by assisting whatever faction seems most likely to reinvite Soviet influence within the regime. Any hostile anti-Soviet faction that gains power has to reckon with the Soviet capability of assisting Kurdish autonomy, particularly the left-wing Iraqi Kurdish factions. Playing a Kurdish card, however, is risky for the Soviets because recrudescence of active Kurdish resistance would divert Iraqi military efforts and advantage the Iranians.

Iran, at least in its present Shiite revolutionary phase, would welcome any faction contending for power in Iraq that supported Iraqi Shiite causes. Iranian fomentation of Iraqi Shiite dissent could further debilitate the central regime and create opportunities for direct or indirect Iranian intervention into Iraqi affairs to "protect" Shiite coreligionists. Such intervention would also seek to encourage Kurdish autonomy to divert Iraqi military efforts. The Iranians would benefit from joint and effective Kurdish resistance to the Ba'thist central regime. Yet they would be harmed by continuation of such resistance to an Iranian-supported Iraqi Shiite regime or, worse, joint resistance with Iranian Kurds to the Iranian regime.

Saudi Arabia. Scenarios for regime changes within Saudi Arabia with international implications tend to focus on ideological groups. The most likely candidates are those Arab nationalist and possibly leftist ideologies that may have penetrated the Saudi military, or conceivably members of the extensive royal family. Conditions of social and political disintegration that may precede such a successful "free officers" type coup or succession struggle with radical princes would have to be imagined. Lessening Western dependency on Gulf and, particularly, Saudi oil would diminish oil revenues, deflate development projects, and could contribute to social unrest as social benefits of the Saudi welfare state are denied. Massive social unrest might also result from Saudi involvement in a Gulf military action in which Saudi oil production was damaged, its foreign reserves reduced, its alien workforce frightened off, and its economy shattered as a result.

The groups most likely to be first affected by Saudi economic disaster and, therefore, most likely to pressure the military and internal security resources of the state would be the economically disadvantaged Shiites in the Eastern Province and noncontract alien workers. If social protest reached the level of the technological and professional classes of the alien workforce, the Saudi economy could be seriously affected. Under such circumstances the divergence between the affluence and advantages of the royal family and the rest of the population could become politically intolerable. A military officers group with Arab nationalist and leftist leanings seeking to restore the economy, put down protest, and make the monarchy its scapegoat for social ills could move against the central regime. Similarly, a military or National Guard force imbued with Islamic fundamentalism could assert contending cures for such social ills. The fundamentalist group might seek the establishment of an Islamic republic, albeit of a Wahhabi and not a Shiite nature.

In each instance, the left-wing or the right-wing takeover in Saudi Arabia, would be imagined as reorienting its foreign relations away from Western alignments. What regional support such a new regime may obtain for its new orientations may depend on its ideological leanings. An Arab nationalist and left-wing regime would look to Iraq and probably the Soviet Union. An Islamic fundamentalist regime could look to Iran and possibly Pakistan.

A resurgent and republican Saudi Arabia, whatever its ideological bent, would pose an immediate threat to the Gulf sheikhdoms. Unless contention for power within a republican Saudi Arabia paralyzed its military forces, republican ideological fervor emanating from Riyadh would have little difficulty penetrating the surrounding sheikhdoms. Each of Saudi Arabia's neighbors would in such circumstances desperately seek regional and superpower allies. The GCC would have little capability of sustaining itself without Saudi Arabia. Protection of the territorial integrity and security of the central regimes of the lesser actors in the Gulf would become a serious problem.

Kuwait. Kuwait has no significant religious or ethnic group with a geographical base capable of breaking away from the central regime. The critical threats to the regime therefore result from the possibility of left-wing or right-wing ideologically inspired coups. It is conceivable that left-wing or right-wing ideologies have penetrated the ruling family or the military or security forces and could surface in a succession crisis. There could also be struggles for power initiated during a succession crisis or internal security crisis by a left-wing Arab nationalist group or a right-wing Islamic fundamentalist group.

A power struggle within the regime or between the regime and other contending ideological groups would attract the interest of Kuwait's northern and southern neighbors, Iraq and Saudi Arabia. A struggle involving the Shiite minority in Kuwait could also attract the interest of Iran. An embattled central regime that has already established diplomatic relations with Moscow might also seek direct assistance from the Soviet Union. Accordingly, a regime-threatening crisis in Kuwait may be viewed as inviting potentially multilateral international intervention.

The implications for the international politics of the Gulf result from the effects of such international intervention. The one neighboring state most likely to intervene militarily in a Kuwait crisis is Iraq. During such a crisis the Iraqis could be expected to grab Bubiyan and Warbah, as well as some Kuwaiti coastline on the pretext of protecting the Iraqi port of Umm Qasr. The ability of Iraq to hold onto any captured Kuwaiti territory in the face of international pressure from the Gulf states and the superpowers would serve as a bellweather to Iraqi predominance in the Gulf. Thus the most significant implication for Iraqi intervention into Kuwait is its potential for additional Iraqi military moves in the Gulf, and possibly appeals by Kuwait for Soviet assistance that would involve the Soviet Union more directly in the Gulf.

Bahrain. Bahrain is a similar bellweather state for indications of potential Iranian hegemony in the Gulf. Of all the Gulf sheikhdoms, Bahrain presents the greatest opportunity for Iranian intervention in the event of a regime threatening crisis. Indeed, Iran under the Khomeini regime is viewed as likely to create such opportunity by stirring up Shiite dissension. The international contest that would be generated by factions seeking external assistance would most likely involve Saudi Arabia, and possibly Iraq in the event of an Arab nationalist faction. An embattled central regime might also seek U.S. assistance, because a radical changeover would jeopardize the maintenance of American naval facilities at Bahrain. As in Iraq, the significant international implications of such a Bahraini crisis would be the ability of Iran to maintain its intervention in the face of potential international resistance. If that were to occur, such intervention by Bahrain could serve as a prelude for other Iranian military moves in the Gulf.

The Unification of North and South Yemen. The disintegration of the central regime in North Yemen has international political implications because it would invite multiple international interventions. South Yemen and Saudi Arabia would both have a stake in the outcome of any regime threatening crisis. An embattled North Yemeni regime might seek assistance from either or both of the United States and Soviet Union. In such a crisis the South Yemenis would seek to support either the already active National Democratic Front or any other prounification regime that it could install. The Saudis, on the other hand, would actively promote secession of the areas under control of the northern tribal confederations or installation of a more conservative, pro-Saudi regime.

If the outcome of such a North Yemeni crisis was the establishment of a radical left-wing and pro–South Yemen regime, a unification with South Yemen might ultimately result. Such a united Yemen might well result in a Soviet-supported regime and would constitute a threat to Saudi Arabia. The threat would be evident in a comparison of the potential manpower resources for the military forces of both states. (See appendix B for a hypothetical combination of the military capabilities of the united Yemens.) There would be an additional threat to Saudi Arabia from the development of a potential fifth column or sabotage and subversion among the substantial numbers of Yemeni workers in Saudi Arabia. Even if military manpower resources were commensurate or even if sophisticated weaponry enhanced those of Saudi Arabia, there would remain the problem for Saudi Arabia of dividing its security forces to counter threats on both coasts. Any military engagement by the Saudis in a crisis on the east coast would leave their west coast vulnerable to military intrusions by a unified hostile Yemen. In the face of military contests on both coasts the Saudis would probably need to concentrate on guarding their oil-rich Eastern Province. Yet sacrificing the Islamic holy places such as Mecca and Medina on the west coast would have a telling effect on the ability of the current regime to maintain itself in power.

Other Scenarios. The six scenarios just outlined are by no means the only situations that may affect the current dynamic balance of power in the Gulf. They are viewed, however, as the ones with the most likely immediate effects. Other scenarios involving disintegration or radical regime changes in the other Gulf states are conceivable, but their impact on the international politics of the Gulf would appear less immediate or not as destabilizing for the current dynamic balance of power. For example, a radicalization of Oman would have to presuppose a withdrawal of U.S. CENTCOM forces and facilities from this pivotal Gulf state. A disintegration of the UAE would have to presuppose the same outcome as in the Bahrain situation for a demonstration of Iranian hegemony in the Gulf, but there is less opportunity for direct Iranian intervention as in Bahrain. A radical regime change in South Yemen that retracts the Marxist-Leninist orientation of the regime would reduce the potential of the regime for destabilizing the international politics of the southwest Arabian Peninsula. There would be a great likelihood of Saudi resistance to any radical regime change in the Wahhabi sheikhdom of Qatar. Even so, there are always possibilities of requests for superpower assistance by any embattled Gulf regime. Let us therefore consider the interests of superpowers in the Gulf in order to weigh the likelihood of any superpower response and the potential changes in the international politics of the Gulf that may ensue.

5 Superpower Competition in the Gulf

We have already examined the international political environment of the Gulf, its potential for instability, the implications of the rifts within its political communities, and the risks of radicalization of its regimes. This is the same environment in which the superpowers, the United States and the Soviet Union, pursue their respective and competing interests.

The Soviet Union in the Gulf

In the absence of any clear picture as to the motives of Soviet foreign policy, Soviet interests are conventionally depicted as pursuing three objectives in the Gulf. These three Soviet interests are control over the Gulf, by direct invasion; influence over the Gulf, by indirect intervention; and interference with the transmission of Gulf oil supplies to the West. None of these Soviet interests necessarily forecloses any of the others, all of these interests are viewed as threatening to vital U.S. interests in the Gulf. None of these interests is entirely free from debate as to its likelihood of achievement or credibility as a threat to the interests of the United States in the Gulf. Most of the debate focuses on the first interest: Soviet potential for control over the Gulf by direct invasion.

U.S. assessments of Soviet motivations and capabilities vis-à-vis the Gulf divide most noticeably over the issue of the interest of the Soviets in controlling the Gulf. The extreme positions of the debate may be portrayed as follows. One view sees the Soviet Union as motivated programmatically; as possibly ideologically but at least geopolitically committed over the long run to extending its control over Southwest Asia by fulfilling a manifest destiny to extending its territorial reach to the Indian Ocean and warm water ports. A modification of this programmatic position sees Soviet commitments if not to direct control at least to extending its influence over the entire Southwest Asian region. In this region the Gulf states become stakes in this "Great Game."[1]

The extreme position of the opposite view sees the Soviet Union concerned pragmatically only about maintaining its Southwest Asian security perimeter, particularly against potential Western security threats in the so-called Northern Tier of Turkey, Iran, and Pakistan. A modification of this pragmatic position sees the Soviet Union prepared to extend its influence into the Gulf but only opportunistically whenever the occasions arise to exploit U.S. weaknesses in the region.[2]

Proponents of both the programmatic and pragmatic viewpoints argue cogently but are limited by the outward signs of Soviet behavior and Soviet capabilities as guides to possible future behavior. The current behavior of the Soviet Union, its invasion of Afghanistan, installation of advisors in South Yemen, military arms supplies to South and North Yemen, Treaties of Friendship with Iraq and South Yemen, and diplomatic entree to Kuwait, are all subject to different interpretation. They provide no conclusive way to assess future behavior.

Similarly divergent views are expressed when assessing Soviet capabilities for future moves. Proponents of the programmatic viewpoint tend to see current Soviet capabilities as expandable over the long term. Such capabilities are therefore viewed as creating a major conventional as well as nuclear threat to future projections of U.S. power into the region because of the relative Soviet advantage of proximity to Southwest Asia. The pragmatists tend to view current Soviet capabilities as inadequate for a major military move toward the Gulf. They see projections of Soviet power limited by potential resistance by Gulf states either to direct invasion or to Soviet alliance. (The Soviet military capabilities subject to these assessments are described in appendix C.)

In one respect there is a commonality of the two viewpoints. Neither accord to the Soviets any interest in controlling the Gulf or extending influence into it in order to secure oil supplies for the Soviet Union. To what extent and by what date the Soviet Union, which currently exports oil, will become a net importer, are questions that have engendered their own minidebates. One U.S. view has been expressed by the Central Intelligence Agency, which had in 1977 predicted a conversion by the Soviet bloc into net importers by 1985. After this prediction was discredited it was revised in 1981 to forecast such conversion by 1990. There are probably sufficient unknowns in the assumptions for such predictions to maintain the debate without coming to any conclusions.[3]

Soviet Invasion of the Gulf

The most divergence between the programmatic and pragmatic views of Soviet intentions occurs on the question of the likelihood of a direct invasion by the Soviet Union of the Gulf in order to achieve control. Such an invasion is usually viewed as originating across the Iranian border and proceeding in one or two steps through Azerbaijan across the Zagros Mountains into Khuzestan, and from there conceivably across the Gulf. Believers in programmatic Soviet motives see the capabilities of the USSR as providing an overwhelming force advantage to support such an invasion. They can cite, moreover, a certain amount of precedent for these Soviet moves. As noted in chapter 2, parts of Azerbaijan were occupied by Bolshevik troops in 1920 and all of Azerbaijan was occupied by Soviet troops from 1941 to 1946. From this viewpoint the United States would be deterred from countering these moves because of the Soviet advantages of proximity.[4]

The advocates of the viewpoint that Soviet intentions are pragmatic look at the same Soviet capabilities and see the ability of the United States to deter any direct or preemptive Soviet invasion of Khuzestan. Such Soviet moves would be set back either by Soviet force limitations in the dropping of airborne troops and the landing of naval infantry or by geographical limitations of fighting through three hundred or more chokepoints in the Zagros mountain chain, which shields Khuzestan from invasion from the north and east.[5]

The problem with the debate on this issue of the likelihood of a direct Soviet invasion of the Gulf is that each side focuses on different Soviet battles in such an invasion. One is an engagement in northern Iran, primarily over Azerbaijan, which the programmatic viewpoint sees most likely as a Soviet victory. The other engagement is in the south, over Khuzestan, which the pragmatic viewpoint sees most likely as a Soviet defeat. Moreover, each of these paper battles attempts to anticipate a strategic calculus more favorable to their point of view. It is unlikely, however, that the values of the variables in any Soviet strategic calculus would be known until an actual attack. These variables include the following:

1. Soviet military objectives—Azerbaijan, Khuzestan, the Strait of Hormuz, or even the Gulf states.
2. Soviet departure points. A number of Soviet air bases are available across the Transcaucasus, Afghanistan, and locally in South Yemen; a number of naval bases are available around the Bab al-Mandab; and troops are maintained nearby in the Soviet Union and Afghanistan.
3. Timing considerations involved with a preemptive fait accompli; a protracted struggle; logistical support and communications.
4. The size and quality of opposition forces—regional states, Western powers, the United States.

5. The possibility of diversion of Soviet and/or American attention and capabilities outside of the Gulf theater.
6. The availability of credible nuclear deterrents by both the superpowers.

Another problem with the debate is that it relies to some extent on an assessment of Soviet capabilities. However, weapons technologies and capability enhancements keep changing to overcome tactical and strategic problems. There is a problem in trying to assess future military possibilities using present assessments of weapons capabilities. Moreover, as learned from the American experience in assessing Japanese capabilities on the eve of Pearl Harbor, there is a natural inclination to underestimate the opponent's technological expertise.[6] It should be assumed that both superpowers are attempting to narrow the gaps presently perceived in their respective long-distance and rapid deployment forces that are projectable into the Gulf theater.

In the absence of any firm basis for assessing the likelihood of a direct Soviet invasion of the Gulf, any conclusions on this question should remain tentative. If anything, a direct Soviet invasion of Iran would require such a major military commitment by the Soviet Union that it would be risked only for significant stakes. If such a move were a prelude to strangulation of the West, it is unlikely to expect American reactions to cleave to conventional warfare in a theater in which the Soviet Union has substantial military advantages. Under such circumstances a direct Soviet invasion of the Gulf could be expected to invoke general and global contingency planning by the West for similar major Soviet military moves. The threat of such a direct invasion, therefore, although credible, should be assigned the same order of probability as have threats of other projections of Soviet power into Western Europe or Japan.

If on the other hand Soviet strategists see an opportunity to "readjust" Soviet borders by "liberating" Azerbaijan without any major military commitment to control all of Iran, that is the harder case. What remains unknown in this scenario is the degree of resistance to Soviet conquest which Iranian forces could offer and the willingness of the central regime to invite Western assistance. The problem for Western decision makers in this scenario is that the Soviet grab of Azerbaijan, without more, poses no immediate threat of Soviet seizure of Western oil sources in the Gulf, but it vastly increases the risk of such seizure. It is quite likely that there would be Iranian resistance to the Soviet invasion and that the Iranian regime would seek U.S. assistance. It would be expected that the United States would respond to this request and deploy forces to deter any further Soviet moves into Iran.

Soviet Influence in the Gulf

The ability of the Soviet Union to extend its influence into the Gulf by means of indirect intervention is constrained by the current dynamic balance of power environment of the Gulf. Such extension of influence requires firm alignments, strengthened by ideological ties in order for the Soviet Union to develop proxy states. It also requires domestic political environments hospitable to the fostering of Marxist-Leninist parties that would be capable of taking power in a regime crisis. Neither of those situations obtains in the current Gulf. The only state with which the Soviets have ideological ties is South Yemen.

In the absence of an environment hospitable for the development of proxy states and Marxist-Leninist parties, the Soviet Union is compelled to play dynamic balance of power politics in establishing its influence within the Gulf. Soviet strategies in the Gulf can be described generally as bargaining for alignments with the major actors, Iraq and Iran, even to the point of sacrificing the Communist parties in both states and even to the point of dishonoring the Soviet Treaty of Friendship with Iraq in not supplying weaponry at the outset of the Iraq–Iran war. The Soviet refusal to supply weapons for Iraq not only provided Moscow with the opportunity to bid for closer relations with Iran, it also prevented the possible elimination of Iran as a major actor by an Iraqi victory in the 1980 war.

With respect to the other Gulf states the Soviets have attempted to maintain their availability for alignment as a counter to local threats. The problem for the Soviet Union in extending its influence through dynamic balance of power strategies is that such influence is of relatively short duration. Except for South Yemen, which has ideological ties to the Soviet Union, each of the Gulf states that has relationships with the USSR seeks to preserve its own dynamic balance of power flexibility in those relationships.

The limitations on the extensions of Soviet influence in the Gulf can be illustrated by a brief review of the Soviet Union's relationships with the Gulf states. In the first instance there is little relationship with Saudi Arabia, and no formal diplomatic relations between Riyadh and Moscow have been established. Moreover Saudi Arabia, which is ideologically opposed to atheistic communism, has banned all Marxist-Leninist parties. Hence the Soviets have few overt means of extending influence over Saudi Arabia.

The most influence the Soviets have achieved over a major Gulf state has been in Iraq. Soviet entree to Iraq by the provision of extensive military assistance to Iraq was formalized through the 1972 Treaty of Friendship and Cooperation. Alignment with the Soviet Union was sought in earnest by Iraq to support Iraq's oil nationalization program, to counter the shah of Iran's massive arms program, to obtain weaponry after the Arab–Israeli War of 1973, and to put down the renewed revolt of the Iraqi Kurds in 1974.[7]

After the Algiers settlement with the shah and termination of Iranian assistance to the Kurds, as well as the growth of oil revenues enabling Iraq to obtain European, particularly French weaponry, Iraqi dependence on Soviet arms support diminished. Iraqi flexibility in its alignment with the Soviet Union was then demonstrated by its purge of the Iraqi Communist party and criticism of the Soviet invasion of Afghanistan.[8] Indeed the Iraqi estrangement from the Soviet Union by the time of the Iraqi attack on Iran in September 1980 enabled the Soviets to adopt a neutral role in the conflict, supported by a virtual embargo of Soviet military supplies to its erstwhile ally. It was reported that the Soviet Union did permit the resupply of some minor pieces of military equipment and did assist with the repair of a Russian-built electrical plant, but generally maintained its posture of neutrality. After the war turned and Iran began to press Iraq in the summer of 1982, the Soviets recommenced the supply of weaponry.[9] France nonetheless appears to have remained a key supplier of weaponry to Iraq.

The Soviet Union used this dynamic balance of power flexibility in its relations with Iraq as a means of rapprochement with Iran. Without demonstrating direct support for Iraq's enemy, the Soviets did advantage that enemy in a number of ways. One of these was to conclude a Treaty of Friendship with Syria in October 1980 and to assist with Syrian armament. Syria was aligned with Iran. It is not clear that any Soviet arms for Syria were transferred to Iran. There are reports that a number of Soviet bloc or arms clients have supplied Iran with arms.[10] Nevertheless, Soviet approaches to Iran have not blossomed into alignment. Moreover, Iran under Khomeini has also demonstrated its interest in flexibility with any relationship with the Soviet Union by purging the Iranian Communist party.

Similar dynamic balance of power limitations on the extension of Soviet influence into the Gulf are evident in the Soviet relationship with South and North Yemen. The Soviet Union increased its influence in South Yemen after a purge of its radical Marxist National Liberation Front regime in 1978. The new ruling group strengthened its ties to the Soviet Union by increasing arms purchase and military advisors from the Soviet bloc, including East Germans and Cubans, and signing a Treaty of Friendship and Cooperation in 1979.

This gave South Yemen further opportunity to promote border clashes with North Yemen in 1979 as well as to aid the National Democratic Front guerrillas operating within North Yemen. It also created an opportunity for increased Soviet assistance to North Yemen, which had taken a more pronounced Western turn in its officially nonaligned foreign relations since 1976.[11] At the outset of the 1979 border war with South Yemen, North Yemen turned to the Saudis and the United States for increased military assistance. The Carter administration responded with an almost $400 million arms package to be paid for by the Saudis. The Soviet Union, however, offered a $700 million arms package on easy credit terms. The Saudis perceived that the North Yemen regime was then capable of a large-scale rearmament with both arms packages and slowed deliveries of U.S. arms to North Yemen.[12] This increased North Yemen's reliance on the Soviet connection. Such reliance may also have been induced by the North Yemeni's belief that the Soviets would be able to keep a rein on South Yemen, while giving North Yemen a counterweight to Saudi influence. Thus, it would appear that the Soviets chose a dynamic balance of power strategy of fostering an alignment with North Yemen rather than encouraging a South Yemeni conquest. The South Yemenis in turn have attempted to preserve some flexibility in their relations with the Soviet Union by entertaining the possibility of financial assistance from Saudi Arabia.[13]

With respect to other Gulf states the Soviet Union is an available source of military assistance and serves as a counterweight to pressures by pro-West states. This appears to be the situation with Kuwait in that Soviet arms sales offer a counterweight to military adventure by Iraq and probably pressure by Saudi Arabia. From the Kuwaiti viewpoint, a strong Iraq increases the risks of an Iraqi takeover of Kuwaiti territory, as did occur in March 1973. Thus, as the Soviets increased their arms supplies to Iraq in 1973–74, Kuwait also sought military assistance from the Soviet Union and concluded an arms supply agreement with Moscow in April 1974. After the Algiers Agreement of 1975 and the lessening of Iraqi dependency on Soviet military assistance, the Soviet Union pursued its opportunities to maintain good relations with Kuwait. A further major Soviet arms assistance deal was concluded with Kuwait in 1976. Given Kuwait's relatively large Palestinian population, the relations with Moscow relieved some pressure on the regime created by its American connections. Soviet arms assistance to Kuwait, accordingly, evidences the interests of both sides in maintaining a flexible dynamic balance of power alignment without major commitments that would alienate similar relations with other Gulf states. Similarly in the territorial dispute of 1977 between Oman and Ras al-Khaymah, in which the UAE was not sympathetic to the plight of its constituent, the Soviet Union became available to support Ras al-Khaymah's cause.

In sum, the Soviet Union is able to maintain its position in the superpower competition in the Gulf, not so much by seeking to extend its influence ideologically but more by playing the dynamic balance of power role of keeping its military assistance available to all Gulf states.

Possible Soviet Interference with the
Transmission of Gulf Oil

The transmission of oil supplies from the Gulf as well as other commerce with the Gulf ordinarily passes through two strategically located and relatively narrow waterways. The Strait of Hormuz commands entry into the Gulf itself and the Bab al-Mandab commands entry into the Red Sea and ultimately the Suez Canal. Normal traffic through the Strait involves approximately 70–80 ships daily and over half the oil involved in international trade. Although, the Iraq–Iran war has been estimated as cutting down this traffic to 50–60 ships daily, carrying approximately 20 percent of the West's oil supplies. The Bab has been estimated as handling approximately 50 ships daily and approximately 10 percent of Western Europe's oil supplies.[14]

How susceptible to blockage are the Strait and the Bab? The Strait is approximately 100 nautical miles long and 21 nautical miles wide at its narrowest point, and has a depth in its shallower shipping channel of about 67 meters and about 88 meters in the deeper channel. At its narrowest point, and for some 15 nautical miles, the Strait is within the territorial waters of both Iran and Oman. The current shipping lanes are within Oman's territorial waters and are about 1 mile wide with a safety zone of approximately 1 mile between them. If need be, the shipping lanes could be relocated within Iran's territorial waters. Indeed, west of the Strait the shipping lanes currently pass to the north and south of the Tunbs Islands, which are controlled by Iran.[15]

The Bab is a little over 14 miles wide at its narrowest point and supports two shipping lanes in a channel 9 miles wide and over 180 meters deep. These lanes are to the west of Perim Island, which is in the possession of South Yemen. The shipping lanes are also within the territorial waters of three other states: North Yemen, Djibouti, and Ethiopia, each of which also lays claim to Perim Island.[16]

These waterways are, accordingly, narrow enough to constitute chokepoints susceptible to blockage by a concerted naval effort. Such a naval effort would need to be able to defend itself from attack and among other things prevent any minesweeping or salvage operations from clearing any blockage. The most likely candidates for such sustained naval operations are the superpowers.

Soviet control over these two chokepoints could inflict serious economic loss on Gulf commerce as well as delays in Western military deployments. Bypassing the Strait by the transshipment of oil and gas through pipelines as well as transshipment of other civilian supplies by overland desert routes would probably be costly. There has reportedly been discussions within the GCC of the construction of another pipeline from Kuwait to Oman, thereby bypassing the Strait. Saudi Arabia already has a pipeline crossing the Arabian Peninsula from the east coast to the west coast port of Yanbu. But its capacity of 1.8 million barrels per day is less than one-quarter of the estimated 8 mbd passing through the Strait.

Moreover, the petroleum shipped from Yanbu must exit the Red Sea either through the Suez Canal or the Bab. Limitations currently exist with either of those choices. The Suez Canal, also a potential chokepoint, needs to be widened to accommodate supertankers. It presently accommodates tankers of 140,000 tons fully laden. Plans to widen the Canal by 1985 to accommodate tankers of 260,000 tons fully laden have been adversely affected by the global slump in supertanker usage. The supertanker slump has been linked to the global oil glut.[17] There is, in addition the Suez to Mediterranean pipeline (Sumed) with a normal capacity of 1.6 mbd (2.35 mbd at full design capacity) that bypasses the Canal and could otherwise augment oil transshipment through the Canal.[18] Any blockage of the Suez Canal or of the Bab that forces shipping to bypass the Bab adds another approximately 6,000 miles to the transshipment of goods around the Cape of Good Hope.

The capability of the Soviet Union to interfere with shipping through the Strait and the Bab is a function of the naval and air bases to which it has access within the Gulf and at its perimeter across the Soviet and Afghanistan borders. Within the Gulf Iraq has afforded the Soviet navy access to the Iraqi ports of Umm Qasr and Basra. Such access depends in turn on the state of the relations between the Soviet Union and Iraq. When Iraqi relations with the Soviet Union are estranged it is unlikely that the Soviet navy would be made welcome at Iraqi ports. Moreover, such access can be jeopardized by the breakdown of relations between Iraq and Iran. During the current Iraq–Iran war Soviet naval access has been blocked by vessels that have been sunk in the Shatt al-Arab and the Iranian naval blockade of Umm Qasr.

With respect to Soviet access to the Bab, the Soviet Union has obtained better air and naval facilities in South Yemen as a result of its stronger relations with South Yemen, given their ideological nexus. The Soviet Union has access to the South Yemen port of Aden as well as to Socotra Island off the South Yemen coast. It is also reported that the Soviet Union is constructing a new naval base at the Bay of Turbah, near Perim Island.[19] In addition, the Soviet navy has facilities across the Red Sea at the port of Aseb on the Ethiopian coast and the Dahlak Islands off that coast. South Yemeni air bases are some 500 to 1,000 nautical miles from the Strait.

For longer range interdiction strategies the Soviet Union has its own air bases across its borders, and across the Afghanistan border, which is 350 nautical miles from the Strait. It also has naval facilities in the Indian Ocean and at the Chagos Archipelago north of the U.S. base at Diego Garcia.[20]

What inferences one draws from this assessment of the Soviet Union's capabilities to interdict the transmission of commerce, particularly oil, through the Gulf chokepoints are subject to the same debate over the likelihood of direct or indirect ground force invasion into the Gulf. It is difficult to imagine an isolated Soviet move to block oil transshipments without greater political objectives. The international repercussions of any such action would be enormous. In addition to the Western needs for Gulf oil, a large number of states depend on access to these chokepoints for their normal commerce. In addition to the seven Gulf states whose maritime commerce requires access to the Strait (all states of the area but North and South Yemen and Oman), seven other countries also depend on access to the Bab to varying degrees for their maritime commerce: North Yemen, Sudan, Ethiopia (a Soviet ally), Saudi Arabia, Egypt, Israel, and Jordan.

More significantly, any Soviet strategy for any such isolated interdiction moves would need to take into account the substantial capabilities of the United States, and to a lesser extent its allies, in countering such moves. The United States has clearly committed itself to maintenance of maritime passage through the Strait in the face of Soviet threats of interdiction, although primary responsibility for normal maritime passage is retained by Oman.[21] CENTCOM navy and air facilities within the Gulf and at its perimeter support the U.S. commitment as well as the implicit capability of maintaining passage through the Bab al-Mandab. We will take a closer look at CENTCOM's ability to deter Soviet interference with Gulf commerce below.

In addition to CENTCOM forces the French maintain facilities at Djibouti, close to the Bab, reportedly with a force of 11 naval vessels, facilities for aircraft and a 5,000-man contingent of the Foreign Legion.[22] Such facilities are not trouble-free, however, since the former French colony is subject to potential conflict between its two major ethnic groups, the Afars and Issas.

The United States in the Gulf

American interests in the Gulf have been articulated in the Carter Doctrine of 1980 and President Reagan's 1981 corollary to the doctrine. Those interests can be expressed as a containment of Soviet expansion in the Gulf and the protection of Gulf oil supplies, from threats from within the Gulf, particularly the threat of regime change in Saudi Arabia. From a broad historical perspective the Carter Doctrine was a radical departure from prior post–World War II American policy in the Persian Gulf area. For the first time a U.S. administration promised unilateral military action in the region. The United States had run out of major allies in the Gulf who could ostensibly be relied upon to join in collective action. Gone was the original Baghdad Pact, which became the Central Treaty Organization; gone was CENTO's successor, the shah of Iran, whom the United States promoted as the Gulf policeman after the British withdrawal; gone were the twin pillars of collective security buttressed by American military assistance, Iran and Saudi Arabia. The Carter Doctrine recognized the reality of the Gulf international political environment in which the United States would have to operate: the Gulf offered no powerful allies, only potentially powerful enemies.

President Reagan's corollary to the Carter Doctrine which stated a U.S. commitment to the defense of the Saudi regime, recognized the insufficiency of protecting the Gulf only from the threat of Soviet invasion. The Reagan corollary recognized the possibility of threats from within, and the need for U.S. forces to be prepared to intervene in any regime threatening crisis in Saudi Arabia.

The chosen instrument for pursuing these American interests in the Gulf is the rapid deployment force (RDF) now known as CENTCOM. The current Gulf policy of the United States can be described as that of developing CENTCOM's dual mission to provide military containment to the "external" threats of Soviet expansion and to provide military assistance to counter the "internal" threats that affect Gulf oil supplies, particularly in the event of a Saudi Arabian regime change. Such military assistance takes two forms. One is the conventional supply of weaponry, training, and to some extent coordination and military advice, to Saudi Arabian and other Gulf sheikhdom forces. The other is the preparation for deployment of CENTCOM forces into the Gulf in the event of crises. Let us examine how well CENTCOM may perform such a dual mission.

Containment of the Soviet Union

How well can CENTCOM defend the Gulf against a direct Soviet invasion? Appendix D provides data on CENTCOM's present and projected capabilities over the next five years as contemplated by the Reagan administration. There is probably a rough equivalence of CENTCOM capabilities to current Soviet capabilities for Gulf action

as described in appendix C. The comparison, however, would be mis-
leading if it leads to the conclusion that the United States has the
capability to deter all Soviet threats or to defend against a major commitment of Soviet forces to the invasion of the Gulf. For major Soviet
moves the Soviets have the advantage of proximity and with it greater
rate of resupply and reinforcement. CENTCOM forces are disadvantaged by the distances involved for resupply and reinforcement from
the United States as well as from Soviet interdiction threats at many
points on the long sea and air logistical support lines.

To overcome such disadvantages of distance CENTCOM has attempted to obtain operational facilities both at the perimeter of and
within the Gulf. The CENTCOM facilities at the Gulf perimeter, while
substantial, are not altogether trouble free, however. Closest to the
Bab al-Mandab are facilities at the former Soviet naval base at Berbera,
in Somalia, as well as at Mogadishu in the same country, to which the
United States has access. Similar access rights have been accorded the
United States by Kenya to airfields at Nairobi and Nanyuki and the
port of Mombasa. Somalia and Kenya, however, are rivals. Moreover,
the access rights are in contingency agreements, with usage of the
facilities to some extent controlled by the host country.[23] The United
States has also obtained similar access rights to Egyptian airfields,
although at time of writing it is unclear what rights, if any, have been
granted the United States for the use of Egypt's military base at Ras
Banas on the Red Sea.[24]

The least politically trouble-free perimeter facilities for
CENTCOM are at Diego Garcia. Diego Garcia, however, is more than
2,000 nautical miles from the Strait of Hormuz. The air and naval base
there has a runway long enough for B-52 bombers and a sheltered
harbor that can accommodate an aircraft carrier and support ships.[25]
The United States also has access to NATO air bases in Turkey. It has
been reported that such bases at Konya, Van, Kars, Erzerum, Mus,
and Batman are being upgraded for CENTCOM use. Although not
wholly free from debate as to their effectiveness or from political complications, the Turkish bases are well situated to counter some hostile
military moves from bases within the Soviet Union.[26]

There are in addition key CENTCOM facilities for countering Soviet invasionary forces within the Gulf. These facilities pose certain
political problems for CENTCOM that will be discussed in more detail
below. Suffice it here to take note of the extent of CENTCOM's reach
within the Gulf. Facilities to which the United States has access within
the Gulf are in Oman. The facility closest to the Strait of Hormuz is
an air base at Khasab on the Musandam Peninsula that is expected to

have a 4,500-foot airstrip and facilities for prepositioning of supplies in 1984. The major air base to which the United States has access is at Thumarit, close to the South Yemen border. It is reportedly "hardened" and has the advantage of being out of the path of the monsoons that affect other air facilities at Masirah Island as well as naval and air facilities at Muscat. There are in addition air base facilities at Salalah and naval and air facilities at Seeb.[27]

Soviet strategists would also have to take into account the small U.S. flotilla that patrols within the Gulf, which has regular access to the naval base at Jufayr on Bahrain.[28]

At these facilities on the perimeter and within the Gulf the United States has apparently only access rights. The facilities remain under the control of the host country. Moreover, the United States has not been accorded similar access rights to military facilities in the one key Gulf state CENTCOM is charged with defending: Saudi Arabia. Instead CENTCOM has sought indirect ways of obtaining access to Gulf states. Foremost of these is the pre-positioning of materiel and maintenance services for future use. For example, plans have been reported to supply Saudi Arabia with more spare parts and maintenance sets for F-15's and to supply 1.5 times the number of upgraded tanks as Saudi Arabia could use for its own military forces, as well as for Saudi Arabi to maintain extra fuel stocks.[29] Furthermore, the United States has supplied Saudi Arabia, Oman, and the Gulf sheikhdoms with sophisticated air defense systems, including F-5 and F-15 fighters and Hawk missile batteries. These systems currently depend on CENTCOM-maintained AWACS surveillance as well as training and technical advisors.[30] After Saudi Arabia takes control of the five AWACS it has purchased from the United States, scheduled for delivery in 1985 it is unclear, however, how much involvement CENTCOM will continue to have in the air defense coordination of the Traditional states. The United States has reportedly obtained Saudi Arabia's agreement to continue to supply the United States with early warning information after delivery of the Saudi AWACS.[31]

Compared to the extent of U.S. troop deployments and base facilities in Europe and the coordinated allied military efforts of NATO, the U.S. presence in the Gulf through CENTCOM is a far more tentative deterrent force. Moreover, compared to clear American commitments to the defense of Western Europe, the United States has pointedly not committed itself to maintenance of the territorial integrity or regime of the one Gulf state most subject to the direct Soviet threat of invasion: Iran. Iran is one state in which the United States has, since the deposing of the shah, no access rights to facilities, no pre-positioned materiel, and no military assistance program. It is by no means clear that CENTCOM's forces could deter a Soviet direct invasion of Iran, at least across the border into Azerbaijan and possibly to Teheran. Nor is it clear that CENTCOM's forces could defend Khuzestan from the next phase of such invasion, at least unilaterally.

This uncertainty as to CENTCOM's capability to defend the Gulf against a direct Soviet invasion may be reflected in the divergence of views within the RDF, CENTCOM's predecessor, over Gulf strategy. This divergence may be due to the same philosophical dispute as exists over Soviet intentions and capabilities in the Gulf area. It may also be occasioned by the kind of interservice rivalry one would expect from a joint command. Nonetheless, it is reported that the U.S. army views the RDF as primarily a defense force deployable against Soviet ground forces in the Zagros Mountains barriers, assuming sufficient early warning of Soviet mobilization of division strengths across the Transcaucasus and Caucasus. The navy and marines, on the other hand view the RDF as geared for rapid, and possibly preemptive, local deployment of marines on beachheads and oil fields, with the slower army forces to follow.[32]

At the policy planning level, a number of rationalizations are available for handling these strategic debates. One of these is to ascribe "flexibility" to CENTCOM, particularly because the nature of its proposed engagement cannot clearly be foreseen. Another would be to upgrade CENTCOM's deterrent capability against Soviet intervention primarily by viewing American troop landings as laying a tripwire for additional force escalation outside of the Gulf. The third reaction might be to expect rapid local cooperation when the chips are down, particularly when confronted by the more credible threat of Soviet invasion of other Gulf states.

None of these rationalizations, however, can escape the immediate political problem for any defense against a Soviet invasion of the Gulf through Iran, the need to obtain Iranian cooperation for CENTCOM's mission. The army's view of that mission certainly requires some Iranian invitation and local assistance if it intends to take advantage of Zagros terrain. This invitation is hardly forthcoming under the present circumstances of the Khomeini regime. Even assuming that Iranians will have sufficient fears of a Soviet occupation or invasion as to issue such an invitation no matter what the present antipathy to the United States, there is a second problem. The USSR has a general advantage of proximity, hence a capability of massive reinforcement at a faster rate than that of the United States. Therefore, U.S. combat aircraft would be needed to interdict and harass Soviet logistical lines. Even assuming local Gulf state assistance in providing air base facilities it is not clear that CENTCOM has sufficient numbers of such aircraft to offset Soviet advantages of relative rates of reinforcement. Nor indeed is there any assurance that the Soviet air forces would not attempt a preemptive first strike to destroy local basing facilities so as to constrain effective deployment of CENTCOM's non-carrier-based aircraft.

There is in addition a third problem with the army's scenario of a Soviet invasion. It is not at all clear that Soviet strategists would concede the defensive advantage of the Zagros Mountains in planning an Iranian invasion. They might just as likely plan a massive parachute force assault over those mountains to secure Soviet reinforcement routes and generally effect a fait accompli.[33] To counter such a preemptive first strike, the United States would need a far more credible deterrent capability than presently provided by CENTCOM. Furthermore, underlying that credible deterrent would need to be clear public statements of commitment to defend Iran. Those are not provided in the Carter Doctrine or the Reagan corollary. Nor do these commitments appear to be politically feasible in the face of the current anti-U.S. posture of the Khomeini regime.

Moreover, the naval and marine view of CENTCOM's mission appears to concede Iran, or at least the bulk of it that lies outside of the range of U.S. warships and beyond coastal areas that could be secured by marine landings. Even then it would be unrealistic to expect uncontested naval activity and marine landings in Iran. The same Soviet constraints against the deployment of CENTCOM's army contingent apply to the deployment of marines and naval forces. Soviet air forces are equally capable of preemptively or otherwise striking at local basing facilities critical for the sustenance of marine landings.

The conclusion to the foregoing analysis is that it is difficult to conceive of CENTCOM as an effective deterrent to a concerted Soviet invasion of present-day Iran. There may yet be some grounds to viewing CENTCOM as more effective in deterring a direct Soviet invasion of Saudi Arabia, Oman, and the Gulf sheikhdoms. There are much firmer grounds, however, to viewing CENTCOM forces as a deterrent to Soviet attempts to interfere with the transmission of Gulf oil and commerce, under the present circumstances. Isolated interdiction moves by the Soviet Union, without any grander strategy such as larger scale military invasion, would be checked by available U.S. and allied countermoves. Since it is unlikely that such isolated interdiction moves would occur, it is generally unclear how effective a deterrent force CENTCOM can be against a direct Soviet invasion. Let us turn, therefore, to consider the potential effectiveness of CENTCOM in performing the other part of its dual mission.

Protection of the Gulf from Internal Threats

The naval and marine view of CENTCOM's mission obviously emphasizes its task of protecting Saudi Arabia and Oman in particular, and the Gulf sheikhdoms generally, from internal threats. In the absence of a concerted Soviet military threat, U.S. naval and marine forces are capable of relatively rapid deployment of smaller forces to secure beachheads, port facilities, and coastal oil facilities in confrontations with potentially hostile Gulf state forces or revolutionary forces. A critical element, however, to this effective deployment of CENTCOM forces is local Gulf state cooperation. If the military contest warranting such deployment is to secure oil facilities and the transmission of oil supplies, invitation by the central regime of some threatened state or some faction with ostensible authority in the event of civil strife would be substantial assistance in countering contested marine landings or sabotage against the oil facility targets. Such invitation would counter the fear that oil facilities were merely being seized by CENTCOM forces for the United States' own uses. Moreover, local cooperation would be needed during such contests for logistical and intelligence support for CENTCOM. Even in anticipation of such deployment CENTCOM's effectiveness relies heavily on available local military cooperation and assistance in the following ways.

1. Pre-positioning of supplies, fuel, water, spare parts and armed vehicles, as well as U.S. technicians for the maintenance of pre-positioned weaponry and early warning systems are required. Not all of these items require storage, although one could assume for security purposes a U.S. preference for such storage rather than distribution among Gulf state forces.
2. Facilities for resupply, refueling, and maintenance of military equipment of all kinds, including tanks and other armed vehicles, aircraft, and warships are required. Not all of these facilities need be within the Gulf region or close to expected theaters of combat. Some facilities can be on the perimeter of the Gulf.
3. Early warning detection of potential combat needs to be maintained. The AWACS being operated from Saudi Arabia, for example, are suited for this purpose. There are also probably early warning systems on NATO bases in Turkey.
4. Base facilities for tactical aircraft in addition to those based on aircraft carriers are needed. It has been reported that the exclusive use of eight or nine Gulf air bases are required for five of the wings of such CENTCOM aircraft. Additional facilities will be

needed for the additional five wings to be assigned to CENTCOM as well as for helicopters.[34]

5. Security for base facilities, both ground security from sabotage as well as from attack by irregular or regular forces and from air attack, must be maintained.

6. Military exercises must be permitted. Some extraregional exercises such as in Egypt, also have provided analogous climate and terrain simulation conditions. There have also been a number of small-scale exercises by the RDF involving Oman, such as Operation Bright Star involving the landing of 1,000 marines, coordinated with Egyptian, Somalia, and Sudanese assistance.[35]

The central problem, therefore, for the effective deployment of CENTCOM forces in the Gulf, particularly for the protection of oil supplies from internal threats but also for containing Soviet expansion in the Gulf, becomes one of maintaining the cooperation of Saudi Arabia, Oman, and the Gulf sheikhdoms for such deployment. Therein lies the central dilemma of U.S. Gulf policy, since the very states it seeks to protect are reluctant to maintain the type of firm alignment with the United States that would assure that cooperation. Why the Traditional states reject such firm alignments can be explained best in terms of the international politics of the Gulf.

U.S. Gulf Policy and the Dynamic Balance of Power

U.S. policy planning toward the Gulf needs to operate in the same dynamic balance of power environment as does policy planning for the Soviet Union and the Gulf states themselves. This environment, whose hallmark is the distrust of both one's allies and one's enemies leads to considerable frustration. The U.S. policy style has little patience for such dynamic balance of power games. Friends should be friends; enemies, enemies. If a friend needs assistance, you provide it if you can. If the assistance needs to be provided in advance of any conflict in order to deter such conflict and if the most efficient form of such assistance is to deploy forces in bases on the threatened territory, then a friend should welcome such bases. This expectation does not work in the Gulf.

The dilemma of seeking to assist Gulf states that reject U.S. bases there is reflected in the incredulity that U.S. policy planners manifest at the unwillingness of Gulf states to allow U.S. control over local base facilities, at the same time as such states, particularly Saudi Arabia, express concern about the credibility of the U.S. commitment to their defense.

The rejection of firm alignments with the United States is often credited to an ideological incompatibility between U.S. interests and Arab ideological positions, sometimes expressed in the form of latent anti-Americanism in Arab populations. The most voiced example of ideological incompatability is the conflict between U.S. support of Israel and Arab hostility toward Israel over Palestinian and Arab security issues. Such incompatability exists, but so do other ideological incompatabilities within the region, as described in chapter 4. Such incompatabilities have not prohibited security arrangements between a radical Iraq and a conservative Saudi Arabia or Saudi overtures to a Marxist-Leninist South Yemen. Moreover, in a dynamic balance of power even ideological compatability does not create firm alignments. A good example of this is Syria and Iraq, which share a common Ba'th ideology. Even within the GCC, where there are commonly shared principles of monarchism, strains exist between Oman and Kuwait, Kuwait and Saudi Arabia, Saudi Arabia and Oman. It is a reasonable guess that in such a dynamic balance of power even total U.S. support for Palestinian causes would not create invitations for U.S. controlled bases within the Gulf.

Rejection of firm alignment with the United States is also often credited to suspicions that U.S. based forces would pose a threat to the security of the oil fields they were designed to protect. The suspicion is that such forces would seize Gulf oil fields in the event of an OPEC price squeeze or an Arab oil embargo. This fear, however, needs to be reconciled with the threats voiced by local states to sabotage oil facilities and fields against any such seizure. It may be that either the seizure or the sabotage, or both, would work, but the consequences would be dire, both for the flow of oil and for the maintenance of any alignment. On the other hand it may be that neither threat, of seizure or of sabotage, would be credible and each side would seek to preserve the alignment rather than risk the loss of the oil supplies the alignment sought to protect.

There may also be local suspicion that U.S. bases would permit greater U.S. interference into local affairs, as was suspected of the Soviet Union in Egypt. Furthermore there might be concern that once such bases were established, the U.S. force would be harder to eject, as Cuba discovered with respect to Guantánamo. Nevertheless, these concerns need to be reconciled with the fact that large numbers of U.S. advisors are needed to train and supply local security forces and possibly maintain sophisticated air defense systems. These advisors are housed, if not based, in the Gulf states. Furthermore, the need for large-scale naval deterrent forces patroling the Gulf region has not yet been rejected by Gulf states even though such naval forces may carry the specter of gunboat diplomacy.

These U.S. policy frustrations cannot simply be credited to ideological incompatibility or local fears and suspicions. They are created by the reality of current Gulf international politics. The dynamic balance of power induces the need for flexibility in one's alignments and relationships with one's allies. U.S. controlled bases would restrict or prevent such flexibility.

The one Gulf state closest to the United States in shared security interests is Oman. Yet Oman has drawn closest as a counterweight to Saudi Arabian local predominance. Oman needs a U.S. parachute if local security efforts bilaterally with the Saudis, or collectively with the GCC, tailspin. Were Oman to face again a recrudescence of the PFLO activity against its regime, in the absence of any other major actor Oman would be compelled without U.S. assistance to strike a bargain for Saudi or GCC aid. The U.S. connection permits Oman some leeway to avoid a bargain with too high a price or to avoid defeat if local assistance efforts fail. On the other hand, even Oman keeps U.S. basing facilities under its own control as a lever against U.S. pressure that may be incompatible with Oman's local alignments.

Kuwait is the example of ultimate balance of power flexibility. Like Oman, Kuwait is concerned about Saudi predominance, but it is just as concerned about Iraqi pressure. As a counterweight to Iraq and Saudi Arabia, Kuwait has sought Soviet assistance. Kuwait also benefits from U.S. assistance to the GCC as a counterweight against the Soviet Union. Kuwait also exemplifies the influence of domestic considerations upon the choice of which superpower to seek as a counterweight in the Gulf. It would appear that Kuwait's choice is greatly influenced by its large Palestinian population, which has occasionally pressured the regime on foreign policy issues.

Although Saudi Arabia for ideological reasons eschews diplomatic relations with the USSR, it does not need a Soviet counterweight to Iran or Iraq because it has a willing source of military assistance in the United States. On the other hand, Saudi Arabia wants the flexibility of playing dynamic balance of power politics in the Gulf without undue U.S. pressure. Too close a connection would provide the United States with the leverage that would come with threats to withdraw its security support.

Nor are there any incentives currently in the international politics of the Gulf for the Traditional states to seek a firmer alignment with the United States. As we have observed, much of the dynamic of the current Gulf balance of power is provided by the relative superiority of military capabilities of Iran and Iraq over that of the other Gulf states. Furthermore Iran and Iraq have ample ways to exercise that superiority, whether by assertion of territorial claims, or internal intervention for ethnic, religious, or politically ideological reasons, to the detriment of the lesser states. The rivalry of Iraq and Iran, currently exacerbated by an ideological struggle, inhibits any condominium over the Gulf by both of these powers. While that rivalry continues and until there is a radical change in the structure of the dynamic balance of power system in the Gulf, Saudi Arabia and the other GCC members can be expected to seek alignments with one or the other of Iraq or Iran as a counterweight to the predominance of either of them. Saudi Arabia and the other GCC members can also be expected to switch out of such alignments as their perceptions of predominance change.

Furthermore, there are a number of other alliance partners available to the GCC states from outside of the Gulf system. While the superpower competition in the current context of Gulf international politics continues the GCC states can obtain alignments with the United States or the Soviet Union. And these Gulf states also have available as potential alliance partners other major actors in contiguous international systems such as Egypt or Syria in the larger Middle East or Pakistan in Southwest Asia.

For all these reasons, therefore, under the current conditions of the dynamic balance of power in the Gulf, the essential dilemma of pursuing U.S. interests in the Gulf without any firm alignments with Gulf states can be expected to continue. It is precisely because CENTCOM relies for its effectiveness on the maintenance of cooperation of those Gulf states in the face of that dilemma that we need to consider the formulation of a new U.S. strategy in the Gulf.

6 A New United States Gulf Strategy

The current U.S. Gulf policy as represented by the Carter Doctrine and the Reagan corollary depends on the development and deployment of CENTCOM as the principal strategy for safeguarding Gulf oil supplies and commerce. The principal shortcoming of this strategy is that it undertakes to counter too broad a range of threats to U.S. interests and it risks being ineffective in the international political environment of the Gulf. CENTCOM is simply not capable of countering all the threats to the security of Gulf oil supplies and commerce that the current policy seeks to protect. These threats range on three levels from superpower competition from the Soviet Union on one level; threats from the advancement of territorial claims in the international politics within the Gulf region on another level; and threats from radical regime changes and divisions within the political communities within the Gulf states on yet a third level.

The international political environment in which U.S. Gulf policy must presently operate is the dynamic balance of power. In this environment alignments are fragile and diplomatic relations flexible. The U.S. CENTCOM strategy will founder if it is based upon the expectation of firm alignments for the assurance of continuing local cooperation for CENTCOM effectiveness.

The prescription offered here is to narrow the range of threats to which CENTCOM should respond, and to broaden the means by which the United States should be prepared to counter the other threats to Gulf security. These means include dependency on the U.S. global deterrence forces, and not primarily CENTCOM, for countering Soviet invasionary threats; and dependency on local GCC forces, not primarily on CENTCOM, for countering some internal regime threats. That leaves CENTCOM's primary role as countering threats from within the Gulf arising from territorial objectives pursued by the major actors as well as those regime threats that the GCC could not handle, such as a radical takeover in Saudi Arabia. This new CENTCOM strategy also requires two other strategies for an effective U.S. Gulf policy. One is a reliable energy policy that will reduce long-term dependency on Gulf oil supplies and will increase the capability of the United States to deal with short-term supply disruptions. The other is a diplomatic strategy of pursuing as firm alignments as possible with the Traditional states and flexible relations with the other Gulf actors, including Iraq and Iran.

In proposing a new U.S. Gulf strategy we should be careful to distinguish between the prescription that is offered for the current dynamic balance of power and the possibilities that such environment could radically change. In a different type of international system alternative strategies may be required. The potential changes to the international politics of the Gulf that can be derived from discussions of Gulf instability in earlier chapters will be considered in this one. To the extent that some of these changes are deterimental to U.S. interests in the Gulf, the new U.S. Gulf strategy should be effective to resist these changes; to the extent that some of these changes may be beneficial to U.S. interests in the Gulf, the new strategy should be flexible enough to accommodate to such changes.

**Countering the Range of Threats to U.S.
Interests in the Gulf**

The three levels of threats to security of Gulf oil and commerce escalate from three international political arenas: the global arena, wherein threats emanate from the Soviet Union; the regional arena, wherein threats emanate from the competition among the major actors and lesser actors for increasing capabilities; and the arena within Gulf states, wherein contestants over the nature of the regime and the political community may invite international assistance or otherwise create preconditions for international intervention.

CENTCOM's present mission appears to be that of countering all levels of threats, although more focus is usually given to the first and last, namely, Soviet threats and securing oil facilities against threats from internal regime changes. That mission appears to be framed too broadly. As we observed in the discussion of Soviet threats, CENTCOM's rapidity of deployment is seriously disadvantaged in countering a major Soviet invasion of Iran by Soviet advantages of proximity. Proximity gives the Soviets advantages of surprise and of resupply and reinforcement. While the probability of such invasion may not be high except in support of a grander Soviet strategy against the West, countering the threats of such invasion would take more than CENTCOM's present force projection.

Deterrence of a direct Soviet invasion of Iran requires a clearer commitment of Western retaliation than provided in the Carter Doctrine. Any Soviet attempt to cut off Gulf oil supplies by invasion should be treated as the same *casus belli* as any Soviet invasion of Western

Europe or Japan. Deterrence of a Soviet invasion of the Gulf should therefore become an integral part of Western deterrence strategies generally. Although CENTCOM may be an adjunct for such strategies, it is unrealistic to expect CENTCOM forces to bear the brunt of the deterrent role.

CENTCOM forces can play a much clearer role in deterring Soviet attempts to interfere with the transshipment of oil and commerce through the Gulf chokepoints. Soviet strategies for such interference may, however, be somewhat improbable in isolation from grander Soviet designs. Even so, CENTCOM forces do need to offer a credible deterrent to any Soviet strategies that might blockade the Gulf and Arabian Peninsula. This CENTCOM capability will support the credibility of U.S. assistance generally to Saudi Arabia, Oman, and the Gulf sheikhdoms.

Countering the third level of threats from within the Gulf caused by radical regime changes and divisions within political communities is equally problematic for CENTCOM in the current dynamic balance of power environment of the Gulf. As we have observed CENTCOM faces a major dilemma in operating in this Gulf environment. To operate effectively CENTCOM needs to obtain local cooperation. Yet local Gulf states refuse to enable CENTCOM to station forces in their states to give them maximum protection, and CENTCOM may be denied local cooperation for even minimum operations within the Gulf.

Closer examination should therefore be made of the ability of the Gulf states themselves to counter threats to their own security. In particular Saudi Arabia and the GCC profess to be able to maintain their own collective security. At this third level, threats to the maintenance of regimes and the integrity of political communities, GCC capabilities to counter such threats may well be sufficient, with the exception of internal threats to Saudi Arabia. American military assistance through CENTCOM should be used to enhance GCC capabilities. Furthermore, it would be anticipated that CENTCOM deployment would be readily available in the event of any internal threat to the Omani regime, notwithstanding any GCC involvement. Oman is a critical element of CENTCOM's own Gulf capabilities.

Against second level threats emanating from the major actors in the Gulf, Iran or Iraq (or even Saudi Arabia were a radical regime to take power), it is unlikely that GCC forces would be able to offer much resistance. Therein lies a clearer role for the CENTCOM mission—to maintain U.S. availability to assist a Gulf coalition seeking to counter a bid for predominance by a major actor. Such a role need not contemplate CENTCOM as a first resort or call for the most rapid deployment by CENTCOM. There may be other available coalition partners such as Egypt and Pakistan. No doubt CENTCOM could assist in the transport of such external forces to the area of combat in the Gulf. It is this role that more clearly fits both CENTCOM's capabilities and the dynamic balance of power of the Gulf.

The Necessity for an Energy Policy

To be effective the new U.S. Gulf strategy needs an energy policy to enable this country to handle Gulf oil supply disruptions that CENTCOM cannot prevent. An effective energy policy will encourage the reduction of U.S. and Western dependency on Gulf oil imports and encourage the development of efficient mechanisms for coping with Gulf oil supply disruptions.

The concern over oil supply disruptions is generated by the common observation that the facilities and installations involved in the oil extraction, production, and transmission process are peculiarly vulnerable to sabotage and destruction from military action. These oil facilities include tanker terminals, loading platforms, pumping stations, gas and oil separation plants, refineries, and others. It is also noted that the major Gulf actors, Iran, Iraq and Saudi Arabia, possess a concentration of such key oil facilities.

The Vulnerability of Gulf Oil Facilities

The concentration of such facilities at tanker terminals, at ports and at offshore loading platforms, it is true, creates attractive military targets, but probably only for large-scale military attacks. Even then, such facilities may be heavily defended and can resist destruction for a long time, as the Iraqis discovered in their focused bombardment of the Iranian terminal port at Kharg Island during the first three years of the Iraq–Iran war.

What and where are these oil facilities? Saudi Arabia has two major terminal ports on the east coast, Ras Tanura and Juaymah, and has constructed a third east coast terminal port at Jubayl, as well as a fourth major terminal at Yanbu on the west coast. A 1980 report lists three other major Saudi terminals for loading oil, together with seven major offshore loading platforms; Iran has four major terminals and two loading platforms. Five other Gulf states have among them fifteen terminals and nineteen offshore loading platforms.[1] Destruction of the loading terminals and platforms of a lesser Gulf sheikhdom may not necessarily block its oil exports.

Somewhat less concentrated but also significant facilities that offer attractive targets for major military action are pumping stations, gas and oil separation plants, and refineries. It has been reported that eight critical pumping stations service two-thirds of the Gulf oil that was shipped through two Saudi east coast ports and the Iranian port at Kharg Island; and that twenty-two refineries service the three major actors plus Kuwait, the UAE, and Qatar.[2] In the event of refinery destruction, crude oil could be shipped to refineries outside of the Gulf. It is not clear how quickly damage to pumping stations or separation plants can be made or what alternatives may exist in the event they may be destroyed.

In addition there are a series of installations that are critical for the oil extraction and transmission processes but are far more numerous or dispersed. These include stabilizer plants, gas and water injection plants, tank farms, pipelines, power plants, and port facilities. These installations represent less efficient targets for major military attacks but would be attractive to minor military action.

Finally, the most numerous and dispersed targets for military attack are the oil wells themselves and their interconnecting pipes. In 1980 it was reported that the six Gulf oil producers other than Saudi Arabia possessed among them eleven major onshore oil fields, thirty-one major offshore fields, and 2,035 active wells. Saudi Arabian oil fields cover 70,000 square miles. Seven major Saudi onshore fields are found within 10,000 square miles, and five of these contain 800 wells and 3,000 miles of pipe.[3]

The dispersal of such extraction facilities, while vulnerable to minor military action and even sabotage, makes it difficult to succeed at causing significant economic damage without a major and comprehensive effort that would probably be better spent attacking key terminal facilities.

There appears to be scant public information, for obvious security reasons, on the nature and efficiency of defense systems, public or private, for oil facilities. GCC members are aware of the vulnerability problem. At their organizational meetings the GCC discussed plans for defensive measures for oil facilities, including stockpiling of oil and equipment, utilization of underground facilities, and construction of a pipeline bypassing the Strait of Hormuz.[4]

It is difficult to assess the vulnerability of oil facilities to sabotage. There have been scattered reports of isolated incidents of sabotage.

For example, such incidents were reported in Dubai in 1981 and 1982 and it has been reported that Iraqi Kurds attempted to cut the Iraqi pipeline into Turkey.[5] A far greater problem, it has been suggested, may exist in the event of civil strife and the likelihood of foreign technical personnel leaving the oil facilities in the event of danger.[6]

The answer to the problem of oil supply disruptions caused by internal regime takeovers or civil strife, or for that matter GCC attempts to restore order or the old regime, is not found in gauging the degree of vulnerability of Gulf oil facilities, or the degree of additional protection to be afforded by CENTCOM intervention. There are just too many unknown elements in such calculations. Hence the need arises for sound energy policies of the United States and the West generally for coping with such disruptions. The ability to cope is a function of the willingness of Western governments to implement policies to decrease such dependency and control the effects of disruptions.

The Dependency of the West on Gulf Oil

It is difficult to assess the current degree of dependency by the West on Gulf oil. Like a moving target, the assessment shifts according to the different statistical bases used. See Appendix E for the 1982 statistics showing relative percentages of oil as a primary energy source and Gulf oil as a percentage of oil consumed.[7]

What is the likely future dependency? Debate occurs among energy experts on the future supply and demand by the noncommunist world, concerning oil generally, as it does over the specific question of future supply and demand by the West concerning Gulf oil. Much of the debate has been occasioned by the oil glut of 1982–83, which led OPEC in March 1983 to reduce its marker price for crude oil from the high of $34 per barrel to $29 per barrel, and to impose a production limit of 17.5 million barrels per day. One side of the debate predicts increasing demands for oil and higher prices; the other side decreasing demand and stable or lower prices.

The problem is one of prophesying unknowns, and each side of the debate is quick to remind the other of prior false prophesies.[8] Two of the unknowns in the debate should be highlighted here because of their international political implications. First, it is not known what effect the termination of the Iraq–Iran war will have on the need for both sides to restore their economies, as well as their arsenals, by radically increasing oil production for export. Increased production would pressure OPEC and oil prices generally. Saudi Arabia's oil minister, Sheikh Yamani, for example, anticipated that the Iraq–Iran war would end in 1982 and that together both States would produce another 6–7 mbd.[9] Part of the unknown is the extent to which the oil production facilities of both sides will have suffered destruction by the time of such termination. Second, it is not known to what extent the Soviet Union may become a net importer of oil in the future, and in particular of Gulf oil. The Soviet Union has been reported as increasing its oil exports in 1983 from 1.5 million barrels per day to almost 2 mbd. Yet it has been estimated that the Soviet Union would stop exporting and start importing by 1990.[10]

There are a host of other unknowns concerning the viability of OPEC itself as a cartel and its ability to coordinate pricing and production with non-OPEC oil producers such as Britain and Norway in the North Sea, Mexico, and the Soviet Union. Furthermore, there are other unknowns involved in calculating the long-term effects of the oil glut on exporter relations with the international oil companies. Saudi Arabia, for example, has used Aramco for approximately 80 percent of its oil sales, and for the balance it has used its own Petromin company. It has been reported that Saudi Arabia has organized another company, Norbec, Ltd., to compete with Aramco by sales of Saudi oil to the spot oil market. This spot market has increased its volume with the oil glut and general avoidance by the major oil companies of long-term supply contracts.[11] Norbec and similar distribution companies, which form part of so-called downstream operations (a reference to all processing and sale of crude oil petroleum products) also put pressure on OPEC and oil prices. In addition, Kuwait has acquired West European distribution channels. The more the major oil producers, such as Saudi Arabia and Kuwait, control downstream operations, the greater their leverage over the supply of oil. Generally speaking, the greater the concentration of downstream operations in the hands of the Gulf exporters, the more Western dependency increases.

Reduction of Dependency over the Long-Term

Given all of the unknowns in the prediction of future dependency by the United States and the West generally on Gulf oil imports, it will be assumed for purposes of this analysis that some measure of dependency will continue in the future. For policymakers this is a more prudent assumption than the opposite assumption of a vanishing dependency. The Reagan administration has announced that it has abandoned the U.S. policy goal of energy independence and expects the United States to remain dependent on oil imports for another twenty years.[12] As suggested, a new Gulf strategy would reverse that decision and seek to implement a number of long-term policy measures that can reduce dependency on Gulf oil imports by the United States and the West. Using a simple matrix these measures can be categorized according to their operation domestically or internationally and according to their intended effects of increasing the supply of oil from sources outside of the Gulf, and OPEC, or decreasing the demand for oil.

Domestic Increase of Supply. Domestic increases to the supply of oil occur primarily through private and governmental stockpiling. Private stocks include crude oil at refineries, terminals, and in pipelines, as well as refined oil held for resale by wholesalers and retailers and also by consumers. These private stocks, however, are subject to economic costs of storage and commercial strategies. Commercial strategies seek to increase stocks in anticipation of higher demand and potential emergencies, such as during the Iraq–Iran war, and sell them at higher profits as supplies become scarcer. In times of excess supply stocks are reduced, as has occurred in the recent oil glut. Another strategy of the major oil companies during the current oil glut is to avoid long-term contracts and shift the cost of inventorying, hence stockpiling, to the oil producers. Given these fluctuations, it is not clear what the ultimate capacity of private stockpiling may be. Nor is it clear what the efficacy may be of imposing government regulations to increase the incentives for private stockpiling as a long-term dependency-reducing measure.[13]

A more viable energy policy measure would be to increase the capacity and rate of fill of the governmentally controlled Strategic Petroleum Reserve. The SPR was established in 1975 in response to the embargo of 1973–74. Its current objective is to accumulate 750 million barrels of oil. At the end of September 1983 the SPR was estimated as holding approximately 350 million barrels of oil in salt dome storage, enough to replace imported oil for approximately ten weeks. It has been estimated that salt dome storage capacity is only 398 million barrels, and thereafter more expensive storage methods such as steel tanks will be needed. There have been disagreements between the Reagan administration and Congress over fill rates and budgeting for additional storage capacity. At the administration's preferred fill rate of 145,000 barrels per day (bd), it will take some eight years or so to achieve the 750 million barrel goal. Congress originally mandated a 220,000 bd fill rate. However, a Congressional Conference Committee has been reported as compromising at a 186,000 bd rate and eliminating funding for additional storage capacity.[14] This current policy toward SPR stockpiling is too shortsighted. Both capacity and fill rates should be increased because the SPR represents one of the few clearly beneficial and uncontroversial means of overcoming oil supply emergencies.

There are in addition a number of other domestic supply increasing measures that a sound energy policy could encourage. These include maintaining incentives for switching from oil to alternative fuels and increasing domestic supply of oil through Alaska and other continental oil exploration. The most politically difficult incentives to maintain during an oil glut are those that encourage alternative energy sources, such as synthetic fuels, shale oil and tar sands oil extraction, and natural gas transmission from Alaska. Many such projects undertaken by private oil companies have been abandoned during the recent oil glut. They, together with other energy research and development projects such as nuclear fusion, should be encouraged as an integral part of a long-range strategy to reduce dependency on oil imports.[15]

Decreasing Domestic Demand. Domestic decreases in demand can be encouraged by continuation of conservation and energy efficiency measures, although these are vulnerable to swings in the national economy. Such measures have had a cumulative effect on the reduction of Gulf oil imports to the United States from the reported peak of 8.8 mbd in 1977 to a low of 2.8 mbd during February and March of 1983. The latter represented approximately 2.3 percent of American oil consumption. In addition, energy efficiency (measured as the amount of energy needed to produce $1 of GNP) reportedly dropped by 25 percent in the decade from 1973 to 1983.[16]

International Increase of Supply. The United States does participate in international efforts to increase the supply of oil by stockpiling, primarily through membership in the International Energy Agency (IEA). The IEA was established in November 1974 by sixteen nations of the Organisation for Economic Cooperation and Development (OECD) in response to the Arab oil embargo of 1973–74. The IEA requires its members to maintain stockpiles equal to at least 90 days of their oil imports.[17] The IEA reported that in the summer of 1983 its members had a 5.3 billion barrel oil stockpile, equivalent to approximately 95 days of oil imports. The same considerations that lead to the need to increase the United States' SPR, would encourage a policy of increasing IEA member stockpiles, more so since many IEA members import far more Gulf oil than does the United States. Since the duration of any oil supply disruption would be unknown, there is no reason to be satisfied with current levels of stockpiling.

There are other means of increasing the supply of oil from outside of the Gulf that are not as susceptible to governmental policies. These are more a function of the economic incentives for oil exploration and the potential for an increase in the capacity of non-Gulf/non-OPEC producers. However, none of these free market efforts are free from potential OPEC or Gulf state interference or cooptation. For example, exploration for oil in the continental shelf of the South China Seas was recently permitted by the People's Republic of China. Kuwait Petroleum Corporation, it was reported, has acquired a partnership interest in a U.S. venture drilling in that new region.[18]

North Sea production by Great Britain and Norway has reportedly increased from 1982 levels of approximately 2 mbd to a peak of 3 mbd in 1983. Not all of this is for export, however, and production is expected to decline within two years, with proved reserves exhausted by the end of the decade. Mexico, however, has proved reserves of some 57 billion barrels and produced approximately 3 mbd in 1982. These non-OPEC producers have little incentive to undercut OPEC pricing and increase demands on their reserve capacity.[19] Moreover, OPEC is aware of the problem of price and production competition from outside of the cartel and has attempted to discuss an informal agreement with these producers as well as the Soviet Union on ways to avoid a price war.[20]

Suggestions are sometimes voiced for the West (OECD at least, through the IEA) to engage in collective bargaining with OPEC to contract for assured supplies of OPEC oil at reasonably rising prices. It is unlikely that the political obstacles to such negotiations will be overcome and even more unlikely that such negotiations would reduce Western dependency on Gulf oil in any event. Moreover, OPEC has sufficient problems in enforcing its own agreements with its producer members without expecting it to be able to enforce with such members more comprehensive international agreements with consumer nations as well.[21]

Decreasing International Demand. Decreasing the demand for Gulf (or OPEC) oil by international agreements confronts the same problems of lack of economic incentives at the national level. Most of the international measures that have been taken up by OECD have addressed emergency situations. Some long-range oil reducing steps have been taken, however. At the Venice Summit of 1980, the participating countries set goals of doubling coal use and reducing oil from 53 to 40 percent of energy use by 1990; and at the Tokyo Summit of 1981 a collective import ceiling of 24.6 mbd by 1985 was agreed upon (with the United States agreeing to a ceiling of 8.5 mbd).[22] It has been reported that demand for oil has been dropping among the six Western nations that account for 60 percent of global oil consumption. A drop of 3.8 percent was reported for the first half of 1983 as compared with the same period in 1982. It was also reported that the 24 OECD nations attained an average decline of 2.5 percent of demand for oil in the third quarter of 1983 as compared to the same period in 1982 (although U.S. demand increased by 1 percent during that period).[23] This drop in demand is probably attributable to the sluggish world economy (as compared to the relatively improved U.S. economy during the same period). As the world economy improves, the greater will become the need for the international conservation measures.

Coping with Short-Term Oil Supply Disruptions

The same matrix used above to consider long-term measures to reduce dependency on Gulf oil can be applied to the formulation of measures to be taken in coping with short-term or emergency disruptions to Gulf oil supplies.

Domestic Measures to Increase Supply. The size of the SPR during the time of any emergency will control the degree to which it can deter consumer panic, private hoarding, and consequent price increases. Government regulations are needed, however, to control the withdrawal rates and institute pricing mechanisms for oil withdrawn from the SPR in emergencies. Too rapid a depletion will undermine the antipanic strategy whereas pricing too low will encourage private stockpiling and risk higher prices for such stocks later.

Some governmentally regulated measures are already in place. Under the Energy Policy and Conservation Act of 1975 (EPCA) the president has authority to require refiners and importers to hold 3 percent of their product in storage during an emergency.[24] In addition, the Department of Energy (DoE) has developed emergency plans for increasing supply through production increases from the Naval Petroleum Reserve, increased Alaskan pipeline capacity, electricity transfers and natural gas substitutions. Conceivably other emergency measures permitting increased coal usage or high-sulfur oil consumption could also be instituted at the time of an emergency.

Domestic Measures to Decrease Demand. A number of emergency conservation measures have already been adopted in the EPCA and 1979

Emergency Energy Conservation Act. These affect the use of fuel in commercial buildings and automobiles in conjunction with state conservation contingency plans. There are also federal standby regulations for the allocation of crude oil to refineries, control over refined product mix (such as for heating oils, aviation fuels, gasoline), allocation of products to end users and control over prices. In addition, the Standby Petroleum Allocation Act of 1982 continued the presidential authority to adopt price controls in an emergency after the expiration of such provisions in the EPCA.[25]

Other less popular but stronger allocation measures would probably also be proposed during an emergency. Those most likely to be hotly debated are rationing and domestic "disruption" tariffs. A tariff or charge on oil imports would radically reduce demand by increasing the cost of imported oil. The objective of such a disruption tariff is to deprive the oil exporter of the benefit of the transfer of wealth occasioned by high prices. The government that collects the tax or tariff is then free to rebate it directly or indirectly to the oil consumers.

International Measures to Increase Supply. The IEA has instituted a highly complex emergency allocation system that is triggered when oil interruption exceeds 7 percent of supply. The formula has not yet been tested in a real crisis and has attracted considerable criticism. Part of the problem is attributed to the absence of France from the IEA, although France does participate in a similar European Community sharing system with overlapping members. The United States is also accused of a lack of apparent commitment to the IEA system by its lack of leadership in energy policy matters and the possibility that the complex voting procedures in the IEA can be used by the United States to avoid commitments to collective action.[26] The greater the U.S. investment in its own energy policies, therefore, the more credible the U.S. commitment to the IEA will appear.

International Measures to Reduce Demand. The measure most recommended is coordinated disruption tariffs among the OECD. These measures, however, would be the most difficult to institute. They would incur the most resistance at the domestic level, hence be even less politically attractive internationally.[27]

This energy policy is intertwined with the new U.S. Gulf strategy because it provides the assurance that the United States can cope with oil supply disruptions resulting from Gulf crises. This is significant not only for the United States but also for the Gulf states. For the United States it relieves the pressure to deploy CENTCOM for every Gulf crisis that threatens an oil supply disruption and supports a CENTCOM strategy that does not require deployment to Gulf troublespots first or fastest. For the GCC states a U.S. energy policy provides assurance that the United States has nonmilitary alternatives to sustain it through Gulf oil disruptions to counter their fear that a desperate America will deploy its Gulf forces to seize oil supplies whether invited or not.

U.S. Diplomacy in the Gulf

There should be three major objectives for American diplomacy in the Gulf in support of the new Gulf strategy. The first concerns U.S. relations with the GCC states; the second concerns U.S. relations with Iran and Iraq; the third, U.S. relations with the Yemens. The first goal is to achieve as firm alignments with the GCC states as is possible in the dynamic balance of power environment of the Gulf. Such firm alignments are prerequisites for maximizing the degree of local cooperation CENTCOM depends upon for its effectiveness.

Nevertheless, there are serious limitations on achieving firm alignments with the GCC states. As we have already observed the dynamic balance of power itself encourages the need by these states to retain flexibility in their diplomatic relations. Such flexibility is preserved with each other and the United States notwithstanding the collective security arrangement of the GCC and the major arms purchases and military assistance programs from the United States. There is an additional limitation that U.S. diplomacy should also recognize from its experience in attempting to establish a firm alignment with the shah of Iran. Firm alignments are not bought with offers of sophisticated weaponry. Nor does the provision of sophisticated weaponry and military assistance by the United States enhance the capabilities of the GCC states to resist internal regime changes. Indeed, radical regime overturns in the Traditional states would risk the loss of sophisticated defense weaponry to a hostile regime that could turn them over to the Soviet Union or against the United States or its Gulf allies.

With respect to U.S. diplomatic relations with Iraq or Iran the options are more complex. During the first three years of the Iraq–Iran war, the United States has been pursuing a policy of strict neutrality. The advantages from the U.S. point of view are clear so long as neither side in the conflict threatens to extend it to the Traditional states or to block the Strait of Hormuz. The United States announced its intention to intervene to safeguard the transmission of commerce through the Strait in the face of Iranian threats to close it in retaliation for possible Iraqi use of French Etandard bombers and Exocet missiles acquired to destroy Iranian Gulf oil facilities. Generally, however, escalation of the Iraq–Iran conflict to the larger Gulf did not occur in the war through 1983 and the American willingness to protect Gulf oil facilities in the GCC states from either combatant remained untested.

In the event, however, that one side were to achieve a clear-cut victory in the Iraq–Iran conflict that retarded the recovery of capabilities of the other side, the victor would threaten to become predominant in the Gulf. The territorial claims of the victor could be pursued with more impunity against the Traditional states in the absence of a countervailing force from the loser. A new CENTCOM strategy would be better off attempting to forestall the potential predominance of a victor in the current or any future Iraq–Iran conflict by making military assistance available to the loser, than by addressing the consequences of such victory by deployment of CENTCOM forces in the Gulf.

A diplomatic policy, therefore, of redressing the potentially risky situation that may result from the current or any future Iraq–Iran struggle leads to the need to flexibly assist the potential loser in such a struggle. The assistance should be by making military assistance available, not by deployment of CENTCOM forces. If such CENTCOM deployment is needed, it should be to contain the next move by any potentially predominant victor at the borders of the GCC states.

Similarly, the United States should remain open to the possibility of Iran's seeking U.S. assistance in order to resist potential Soviet pressure in the future. The United States should in such a situation signal its availability to supply military or economic assistance, as part of its general policy of seeking to contain Soviet expansion of influence in the Gulf.

The third objective of the U.S. diplomatic policy in the Gulf is to remain flexibly available to provide military and economic assistance to North and possibly South Yemen. The same dynamic balance of power policy has been pursued by Saudi Arabia. The objectives are to compete with the Soviet Union for influence in these two states. South Yemen is the harder case and least likely to evidence any interest in U.S. assistance. North Yemen has already evidenced its interest during the 1979 crisis with South Yemen, but the United States conceded the influence to be attained from military assistance to Saudi Arabia.

In sum, a new U.S. Gulf strategy will redirect CENTCOM's efforts to countering threat levels within its capabilities and to operating more effectively within the current dynamic balance of power environment of the Gulf. This strategy will not mean any slackening of the proposed development of CENTCOM's contingents and capabilities. It requires all presently available facilities within or at the perimeter of the Gulf to which CENTCOM has access.

The new Gulf strategy, however, does not rely on CENTCOM

alone for its effectiveness. There needs to be a clear restatement of U.S. commitments to retaliation against a Soviet invasion of the Gulf by U.S. global deterrent forces. There needs to be a far greater effort in the United States and the West to develop an effective energy policy that will decrease dependency over the long run on Gulf oil supplies and increase our ability to cope with short-term disruptions. And there needs to be a diplomatic strategy that will seek as firm alignments as possible with the Traditional states, while remaining open to flexible alignments with other Gulf states. In aid of this there should also be a continuation of U.S. military assistance programs to other potential alliance partners to the GCC states, such as Egypt and Pakistan.

The strands of this new U.S. Gulf strategy are intertwined. The GCC states that seek to implement their own collective rapid deployment force to respond to members' regime-threatening crises need the assurance that CENTCOM will not intervene for fear of oil supply disruption. The GCC states that may need CENTCOM in crises that they cannot handle also need the assurance that CENTCOM will not refuse to withdraw after its intervention for fear of oil supply disruption. The U.S. energy policy and U.S. dynamic balance of power diplomatic strategy will provide these assurances and in turn assist in the maintenance of the local cooperation CENTCOM will need in order to be effective.

Possible Objections to the New U.S. Gulf Strategy

The new U.S. Gulf strategy will be open to a number of objections. (1) If countering most internal regime threats is left to the GCC, will not the new policy risk oil supply cutoffs that possibly could have been avoided if CENTCOM had been involved? (2) How will the West be protected against Gulf oil producers who purposely cut off oil supplies, for example by another embargo, thereby wielding the so-called oil weapon? (3) What assurance is there, particularly in the dynamic balance of power, that the GCC will remain on the scene to perform such threat-countering functions?

Risk of Gulf Oil Supply Cutoffs
from Internal Regime Takeovers

The first objection to the new strategy presupposes that CENTCOM would be more capable of preventing or prevailing over oil supply cutoffs during coups and their aftermath or during civil strife than would the GCC. This is an untested proposition. Generally, GCC forces would be expected to have more rapid deployment into Gulf trouble-spots than would CENTCOM. GCC forces are already based in the Gulf. Delivery from Diego Garcia of CENTCOM's first-strike force of an amphibious battalion of 1,800 or so marines is anticipated to take 48 hours after notice. (See appendix D for further information.) Moreover, internal regime takeovers do not necessarily involve oil supply cutoffs. Factions or parties contending for power within a regime would be unlikely to wish to destroy the oil resource facilities upon which they would depend to support and/or rebuild their state after gaining power.

The Likelihood of Another Gulf Oil Embargo

The question of likelihood is posed in the context of using CENTCOM to secure Gulf oil supplies by military means in the face of a concerted effort by Gulf states, and other Arab oil producers, to cutoff such oil supplies, as occurred during the 1973–74 embargo, or to engage in a serious price squeeze, as occurred in the rapid price escalation of 1979. The context requires some clarification. The scenario presupposes that the leadership of the action is the current Saudi regime and that the motives associated with this oil weapon are to induce Israeli concessions on withdrawal from post-1967 territorial gains or on Palestinian or other Arab ideological issues. Without Saudi leadership or major participation it is doubtful that any production cutoff could succeed.

The context of the question also depends to some extent on the degree of implementation of effective energy policies by the United States and the West generally for reducing dependency on Gulf oil and for coping with supply disruptions. Obviously, the less the West depends on Gulf oil and the more efficacious the measures to cope with emergency disruptions, the less effective an oil embargo or price squeeze might be. Indeed, a truly effective energy policy would be measured by its very ability to deter such supply-disrupting moves.

Before considering the issues involved in answering the question, it would be worthwhile recalling the origins and effects of the 1973–74 embargo and the 1979 price escalation.[28] The 1973–74 embargo was not the first. There had been a one-month embargo by Saudi Arabia alone against oil shipments to the United States, the United Kingdom, and the Federal Republic of Germany at the time of the June 1967 war against Israel. This earlier embargo did not succeed because Saudi

Arabia could not sustain the financial losses the embargo was causing, and other countries such as Iran and Venezuala increased their oil production.

The 1973–74 embargo was directed against the United States, The Netherlands, South Africa, Portugal, and South Yemen.[29] It was lifted against the United States in March 1974, but not against other countries until May 1974. The embargo was imposed by the Arab members of OPEC. Their ostensible political objectives were to induce Israeli withdrawal from occupied territories and to punish U.S. financial support for Israeli military purchases. These political objectives were not attained, except insofar as the embargo may have widened the split between Europe/Japan and the United States over aid to Israel. The embargo did succeed in cutting oil production by 25 percent by most of the Arab members of OPEC. Iraq unsuccessfully advocated expropriation of U.S. oil interests and withdrawal of Arab investments in the United States and refused to cut its production.[30] Libya cut its production only 5 percent. The effect on the United States was to create a shortage of only 5 percent of its oil needs, less than that of the earlier 1967 embargo by Saudi Arabia alone. The real achievement of the embargo was an increase in prices to 400 percent over preembargo levels.

The embargo also succeeded in provoking a hostile U.S. reaction. The statement by the United States in November 1973 that it would consider countermeasures if the embargo were continued indefinitely or unreasonably was taken by Saudi Arabia as a threat of military retaliation. So were Kissinger's remarks in December 1973 that force could not be ruled out "where there is some actual strangulation of the industrialized world."[31]

The OPEC price squeeze of 1979 took advantage of the panic over potential oil shortages following strikes by Iranian oil workers in October 1978 and the elimination of Iranian oil exports during the Iranian Revolution in January and February 1979. Saudi Arabia increased the concern over potential shortages by its announcement in April 1979 of an 8.5 million barrels per day production ceiling as a reaction to the March 1979 Egyptian–Israeli peace agreement. There was very little cut in oil production, however. OPEC escalated prices from $12.70 per barrel for Arabian light crude oil in September 1978 to $26 per barrel by the end of 1979, albeit with some variation among OPEC members.

Could such an embargo or price squeeze be concerted again by Gulf producers? The matter is still the subject of some debate.[32] On one side is the observation that Arab oil producers, particularly Saudi Arabia, are engaged in executing ambitious industrialization and modernization plans. This side maintains that even if these plans were cut back, these regimes cannot afford the error of the Pahlevi regime in Iran in dinting the revolution of rising expectations without creating massive social unrest and threats to overthrow the regimes. On the other side is the observation that the Gulf oil producers have vast foreign investments and deposits. Saudi Arabia's foreign investments, for example, have been estimated in excess of $200 billion, earning income possibly of $20 billion per annum.[33] This side maintains that such investment incomes are sufficient to sustain the Gulf oil producers' economies on a subsistence scale in the absence of oil revenues. This latter view is then countered by the observation that such foreign investments would become the targets of moves by the West to freeze Gulf producers' assets in retaliation. Other retaliatory economic countermeasures would also be available such as denial of technology transfers and embargo of Western goods and services. The response is that even if retaliatory countermeasures could work, they would be too late. The real effects of an oil-supply cutoff are to create panic within and among Western consuming nations. Arab states would be able to threaten to or create a dangerous split in the Western alliance. Under such circumstances the West would be willing to negotiate political concessions.

These responses then lead to the final exchange of views, with one side alleging that if panic did indeed takeover, the West would be likely to use force to seize the oil fields and restore production. This too is countered by the other side's view that oil fields and installations would be debilitated or sabotaged before sufficient Western military forces could seize them or Soviet bloc forces would be invited to defend them.

It is unnecessary to pursue the debate any further, except to observe that it leads to a consideration that is too easily overlooked in contemplating Gulf actions, the international political context. From the perspective of Gulf international politics a producers' embargo or price squeeze is unlikely to occur when the Traditional states need Western alignments, particularly with the United States. When such alignments are rejected, as for example during the 1973 Arab war against Israel or following the Camp David peace accords in 1979, production-cutting threats by Gulf producers are easier to make. When the Traditional states, however, have serious concerns as to their own security, as for example during the Iraq–Iran war, avenues for Western alignments need to remain open. Oil embargo or price squeeze moves would be unlikely. Given the uncertainties, therefore, of the outcomes of debates and of the international situation, there is additional reason to promote an effective U.S. energy policy.

*Will the GCC Remain Available
to Counter Internal Threats?*

Whether the GCC will remain available to counter internal threats is a good question since alliances tend to be short-lived in a dynamic balance of power. The GCC appears therefore to be an anomaly since it professes to be a more permanent collective security arrangement. It has developed the hallmarks of a collective security organization such as NATO, including coordinated planning and joint military exercises.[34] Like NATO, its members share a common political orientation, which in the case of the GCC is "monarchism," and a common interest in preserving their regimes from proponents of a hostile republican ideology who encourage the overthrow of their regimes by subversion as well as by external attack. Moreover, leadership for the GCC is provided by Saudi Arabia, which has the financial wherewithal to support the organization and has the largest contingent of military forces to contribute to it.

Yet the GCC also has its membership strains. Kuwait, which has diplomatic relations with the Soviet Union, is quite leery of Oman's close connections with the United States. Kuwait, like other members, mistrusts Oman's acceptance of the Camp David accords and eagerness to restore Egypt to the Arab community. Moreover the GCC developed because of an anomaly in the dynamic balance of power system created by Khomeini's ideological threat to the region. The Iraq–Iran war does not follow the expected pattern of relatively short-lived dynamic balance of power engagements. It has become protracted. Iran has rejected a number of opportunities to settle the war after it repelled the Iraqi invasion. Iran for ideological reasons has proclaimed war objectives, including the end to the regime of Ṣaddām Ḥusayn, which inhibit settlement with Iraq.

Accordingly, one answer to the question of the longevity of the GCC is that it will endure so long as there is concern by its members over the ideological threat of Iran and relative superiority of Iranian forces over Iraq's. Were Iran to be defeated or stalemated, and the ideological fervor to subside, it is not clear that the GCC would survive. GCC members may then see as much strategic advantage in retaining their pre-1981 flexibility without the collective security arrangement. In such event there is a possibility that the GCC might disband as a security organization. It may still continue to function as a common market without dismantling its economic cooperation arrangements.

This question concerning the continuation of the GCC leads to the consideration more generally of the possible changes to the international system of the Gulf and the potential challenges they would raise for the new U.S. Gulf strategy.

The Long-Term Challenges to U.S. Gulf Strategy

Earlier chapters identified the current dynamic balance of power system in the Gulf as an unstable one. In particular the Iranian Revolution introduced an element of ideological competition into the international politics of the Gulf that has given rise to the protracted Iraq–Iran war and the creation of the GCC as a collective security pact. Both of these activities are unexpected in a normal or "stable" dynamic balance of power. In addition a number of territorial disputes between Gulf states have been identified as well as cleavages within the political communities of Gulf states and potentially radical regime changes that have destabilizing implications for the current system.

While these additional destabilizing elements are possible, we have no way of knowing the extent to which their eventuation is probable. It is just as possible that the current dynamic balance of power system will restabilize. The Iranian Revolution's fervor may subside; the Iraq–Iran war may be settled; relationships between the Gulf states may resume their pre-1978 patterns. On the other hand, it is also possible that the current dynamic balance of power system will be transformed. Let us consider the sources for such transformation.

A transformation of the Gulf international system would occur in the event of radical changes to its structure, which is composed of a number of major actors and a distribution of their capabilities. These changes would be systemic in the sense that a radical change in one element, such as a radical redistribution of capabilities, would also incur a radical change in the other element, the number of major actors. So, for example, the most likely transformations from a dynamic balance of power would be to an imperial system, in which a single major actor possessed predominant capabilities, or to a bipolar system, in which two major actors possessed superior capabilities. What are the sources for such transformations?

Transformations may result from the interactions of the actors within the system, indicated in earlier chapters, for example in the pursuit of territorial claims. They may also result from interactions with actors from outside of the system, for example a Soviet invasion of the Gulf. It is also possible for transformations to result from radical changes to the capabilities of the Gulf actors. One serious possibility that should be mentioned is the development or introduction of nuclear weaponry into the Gulf.

The Gulf state most likely to "go nuclear" first is Iraq. Iraq's nuclear development program at Osiraq was somewhat retarded by the Israeli bombing strikes in 1981. Notwithstanding substantial damage to the actual reactor at Osiraq, Iraq's nuclear weapons development program itself was not put out of commission.[35] No other Gulf state appears to have obtained the same opportunity or stage of development for nuclear weapons development as has Iraq. It is not clear to what extent Iran can catch up to Iraq in nuclear weapons development. The nuclear reactor supplied to Iran by the United States was reportedly safeguarded from diversion for weapons development. Reportedly, no other Gulf state has any nuclear facility.

On the other hand, other Middle East states, Egypt, Pakistan, Libya, and Syria have actual or potential nuclear weapons programs.[36] Gulf states, particularly Saudi Arabia, could look to such nuclear states as Pakistan or the superpowers, or even Egypt in the future, for nuclear protection against a successful Iraqi nuclear weapons program or for the provision of nuclear weapons. The Iraqi program still faces Israeli threats of preemptive strikes such as that against Osiraq. It appears unlikely for ideological reasons, however, that any Gulf state could negotiate with Israel for such nuclear assistance.

Notwithstanding the multiplicity of sources for transformations of the current dynamic balance of power in the Gulf, there are a limited number of likely effects of such transformations. They create different challenges, however, for protecting U.S. interests in the Gulf. The two major types of transformations of the international politics of the Gulf are more likely an eventual hegemony by one or other of the major actors that achieves predominance, or a bipolarization of the system. Each transformation entails different risks for U.S. policy in the Gulf. Both types of transformation entail risks of Soviet intervention into the Gulf in different forms.

Of all these transformations, the least risky for U.S. policy is a bipolarization in which the United States directly participates. Examples would include a concerted effort by GCC states with CENTCOM and other military assistance to oppose the predominance of one of the two major actors. Were Iran to defeat Iraq and threaten intervention in Bahrain, the GCC states would look to the United States to help deter Iran. Similarly, were Iraq to defeat Iran and threaten to takeover Kuwait, the United States and others would become the source for deterrence. Thus, the deterrence of potential hegemony would create the need for bipolarization of the system.

The form of Soviet intervention into such bipolarization may vary according to the source of the potential predominance. The threat of Iranian hegemony by defeat of Iraq can be countered by Soviet pressure on behalf of Iraq. The Soviets could, for example, move troops across its border into Iran, or airlift Soviet forces into Iraq. The risk for U.S. Gulf policy is that Soviet military moves against Iran may not be limited to protection of Iraq. They may just as easily be dedicated to the promotion of an Iraqi defeat of Iran, and hence hegemony by Iraq. The Soviet Union has a similar opportunity for intervention were the threats reversed and Iraq the potential hegemonist. In the face of Iranian defeat, the Soviets can as easily intervene into Iran to partition it as they could put pressure on Iraq to prevent such defeat.

In any of these forms of Soviet intervention bipolarization may also result. The emerging bipolarization of the Gulf system, however, would assume more of the superpower rivalry with Soviet leadership of one bloc and U.S. leadership of the other. Again, while risky for U.S. Gulf policy, all of these forms of bipolarization invite U.S. involvement and opportunities to safeguard Gulf oil supplies directly.

There are other forms of bipolarization, however, which may exclude U.S. involvement or impede the ability of the United States to safeguard Gulf oil supplies. Such bipolarization would eventuate from a radical anti-American regime in Saudi Arabia. Such a regime may look to either of the other major Gulf actors for security or to the Soviet Union directly. U.S. protection might be sought by other Gulf sheikhdoms, but so might Soviet protection. Were a radical Saudi regime to seek an alignment with Iraq, the independence of Kuwait would be jeopardized. Were a radical Saudi regime to seek an alignment with Iran, the independence of Bahrain, Qatar, and the UAE may also be jeopardized. In each of these instances the major Gulf actor, be it Iraq or Iran, may seek to form a bloc to oppose the radical Saudi regime and its major actor ally. Were none of the jeopardized states to seek U.S. protection, the ability of the United States to safeguard Gulf oil supplies would clearly be threatened.

Why should the United States and its allies nonetheless automatically fear for the cutoff of Gulf oil supplies in any of these bipolarizing situations? Why would not even a radical Saudi regime, just like a radical Iraq or a radical Iran, need to continue to sell oil to the West? In the first place, it is not clear what the implications may be for Western oil supplies if the Soviet Union were directly involved in protecting the security of any of the major Gulf states in these bipolarizing situations. There is no necessary implication that such Soviet involvement would betoken Soviet control over oil supplies to the West. A bipolarization that ranged a radical Saudi Arabia and Iraq against a Soviet assisted Iran, for example, might increase the need of Iraq and Saudi Arabia for Western oil sales to generate defense revenues. On the other hand, a Soviet supported radical regime in Saudi Arabia which also protects Kuwait or the UAE against either or both of Iraq and Iran increases the risk of Soviet manipulation of Western oil supplies.

Is the same range of risks to Western oil supplies present in bipolarizations of the Gulf without Soviet involvement? Why would not a radical Saudi Arabia, whether or not aligned with Iraq or Iran, seek to sell oil to the West to generate government revenues, particularly defense revenues, no matter how anti-West its ideology? The answers, like the question, are speculative. There are risks, however, that a radical regime may for ideological reasons be capable of subsisting on lesser governmental revenues and hence a decreased production and export of oil, than the current regime. This probably would not obtain in most situations, since it would be expected that such regime's defense expenditures would be high, particularly where the regime felt threatened by other major Gulf powers or their superpower allies. There are also risks that a radical Saudi regime would engage in subversion of or intervention into neighboring Gulf sheikhdoms. Were such efforts successful an ideologically anti-Western group of Gulf states may exercise considerable control over Gulf oil supplies. Again, making the unlikely assumption of no increased need for governmental and defense revenues by such a group, there would be additional risks of manipulation of oil prices and production within or outside of OPEC. There would also be additional risks of invitation of Soviet protection against Western military intervention.

The New U.S. Gulf Strategy over the Long Term

The risks to U.S. interests in transformations from the current dynamic balance of power system demonstrate the need to focus CENTCOM on meeting the level of threats beyond the capabilities of the GCC states. CENTCOM's ability to assist the GCC states in the opposition to the predominance of either major Gulf state, Iran or Iraq, can forestall the transformation of the international system of the Gulf into an imperial system under Iranian or Iraqi hegemony, as the case may be. CENTCOM's ability to assist the Saudi regime in opposing a radical takeover can forestall the transformation of the Gulf into a bipolar system that might jeopardize the security of the Gulf sheikhdoms. Where the Soviet Union may become involved in such potential transformations, by alliance with a potentially predominant major actor or radical Saudi forces, deployment of CENTCOM will be critical.

On the other hand, were none of the possible transformations to occur, and instead the current dynamic balance of power system to restabilize, it is possible that the GCC might disband. In the absence of the GCC there is no reason to assume that CENTCOM would be called upon to play its role in countering regime-threatening crises to the Gulf sheikhdoms that require external assistance. Such assistance can be sought bilaterally from Saudi Arabia or possibly as in the Dhofar rebellion from a number of external actors. Only if that assistance were insufficient would the threatened regime or its allies be likely to resort to CENTCOM. The availability of CENTCOM in such situations would be equivalent to its availability in the event that GCC forces were unable to overcome a similar crisis. The new U.S. Gulf strategy should, therefore, have no trouble adapting to a dynamic balance of power Gulf system without a GCC.

7 Conclusions

How Unstable Is the Gulf?

Critics of the current U.S. policy in the Gulf, as enunciated in the Carter Doctrine and the Reagan corollary, have focused on the instability or stability of domestic and international politics in the Gulf to support their positions. The extreme positions of the critics view the Gulf as either too unstable to permit an effective deployment of CENTCOM, the chosen instrument of U.S. Gulf policy, or sufficiently stable to dispense with the need for deployment of CENTCOM. The dilemma of U.S. Gulf policy as mirrored in these criticisms is that CENTCOM does need some measure of stability in the U.S. relationship with the Gulf regimes in order to obtain local cooperation upon which CENTCOM depends for effective deployment.

How accurate are these perceptions concerning instability and stability in the Gulf? And, even assuming instability, how dangerous is such Gulf instability for the achievement of U.S. policy goals in the Gulf?

International politics of the region at the present time have been viewed in this book as a dynamic balance of power system. Much of the dynamic is occasioned by the actions and interactions of the two actors with superior military capabilities to the others, Iran and Iraq. Iran, however, has introduced its revolutionary ideology into its conduct of international politics, thereby inhibiting alignments and threatening to pursue a rivalry with Iraq until Iranian predominance is achieved. The third major actor, but with relatively inferior capabilities, Saudi Arabia, has reacted to this dangerous rivalry by forming a collective security organization of the Traditional states, the GCC. Our first general conclusion is that the current dynamic balance of power international system has become unstable. Moreover, this international political instability within the Gulf raises the possibility that the dynamic balance of power structure of the Gulf system may change.

What are the likely sources of change within the Gulf international system? What are their likely effects? Two significant sources for changes within the Gulf were reviewed: territorial disputes and changes to political communities and regimes from religious cleavages, ethnic dissension, and ideological contests. Their destabilizing character was measured in terms of their likely effects on the international politics of the Gulf. Four territorial disputes of current regimes were identified as possibly destabilizing. These were the Iraq–Iran territorial disputes; the Iraqi claims over Kuwaiti territory; Iranian claims over Bahrain; and South Yemen's unification with the North under a Marxist regime. Furthermore, were a radical regime to take over Saudi Arabia in the future, other destabilizing territorial claims would most likely be generated.

These territorial disputes were identified as destabilizing because of their potentially radical effects on the international politics of the Gulf. Were either Iraq or Iran to prove victorious in their territorial struggles, the victor would constitute a threat to the other Gulf states. Iraqi predominance would encourage its advancement of claims against Kuwait; Iranian predominance would encourage its intervention into Bahrain. Were South Yemen able to unite with the North under a Marxist regime, the Soviet Union's toehold on the Arabian Peninsula would be expanded and Saudi Arabia and Oman threatened. The potential for subversion would increase as would the territorial threat to Saudi Arabia's Red Sea coast and Oman's Arabian Sea coast. Were a radical regime to take over Saudi Arabia, the Gulf sheikhdoms at the Saudi perimeter would be threatened.

Six particular instances of cleavages within political communities and radical changes of the regimes of the Gulf were identified as possibly destabilizing for the international politics of the region. These were ethnic disintegration in Iran; religious cleavage in Iraq; radicalization within Saudi Arabia; radicalization of Kuwait; religious cleavage in Bahrain; and disintegration in North Yemen. Ethnic disintegration in Iran would permit Iraqi predominance within the Gulf; religious cleavage in Iraq would permit Iranian predominance. Iranian disintegration would also encourage Soviet intervention. Radicalization of Saudi Arabia could encourage intervention by ideological allies—from Iraq (or the Soviet Union) on the left, and/or Iran, possibly, on the religious right. If successful, such radicalization could bipolarize the Gulf by international alignments on ideological principles. Radicalization of Kuwait would encourage Iraqi intervention; religious revolution in Bahrain, would encourage Iranian intervention. Disintegration in North Yemen would encourage South Yemeni intervention seeking unification with the North under a Marxist regime.

How Dangerous Is Gulf Instability for U.S. Policy?

The consideration of the effects of instability within the Gulf is speculative. There are no clear signs that any of the foregoing possibilities will eventuate. Iraq and Iran may exhaust each other in their current conflict with neither proving predominant. The ethnic populations in Iran may remain loyal to the central regime as may the religious populations in Iraq. The invasion of Khuzestan by Iraq in 1980 did not dislodge the loyalty of the Arab population of Iran; and the prospect of invasion of Iraq by Iran in 1983 has not appeared to dislodge the loyalty of Iraq's Shiite populations. Furthermore, Iraq may choose to repress its claims to Kuwait to maintain alignments with the GCC states. Iran may choose to repress its claim to Bahrain to undermine the GCC opposition to Iran and alignment with Iraq. The internal security apparatuses within the Gulf states may well continue to prevent internal dissension from threatening to overthrow their regimes. In other words, the dynamic balance of power system could be maintained without increasing any of the risks to the supply of Gulf oil that U.S. policy is dedicated to securing.

There are, moreover, elements of instability within the Gulf that are countervailing to each other and contribute to the maintenance of this dynamic balance of power. The potential for ethnic disintegration in Iran as well as for religious cleavage and ethnic (Kurdish) dissension in Iraq, to some extent impedes the full use of their military capabilities. Ethnic and religious dissension in particular deprives each of their central regimes of the full use of their armed forces for external adventure or defense or the full use of their populations as reserves for those forces. Ethnic and religious dissension provides the regime's enemies with internal alignments that can assist in subverting the regimes and diverting their military efforts. Ethnic dissension and religious cleavages in North Yemen also provide potential resistance to any forcible annexation by the South or unification under Marxist principles.

The current international system in the Gulf may be unstable, but it presents no clear dangers for the achievement of U.S. policy goals. The problem, however, arises out of its very instability. There is no assurance that a dynamic balance of power will continue. The system could be transformed for many reasons, including the effects of destabilization by the threats from within that we have just described, as well as by nuclearization and greater Soviet intervention or invasion.

Some of these possible transformations are less risky for U.S. interests in the Gulf than are others. The less risky ones include bipolarizations in which the United States is involved, for example in the protection of GCC states from the predominance of either Iran or Iraq, or from the Soviet Union. The riskiest transformations include systems in which any of those powers achieve predominance or bipolarization in which the United States is not involved, for example after a radicalization of Saudi Arabia.

A New U.S. Gulf Strategy

The different threats to Gulf oil and commerce that U.S. Gulf policy
seeks to safeguard have been identified in this book. Threats emanate
from the Soviet Union outside of the Gulf; from within the Gulf threats
emanate from territorial takeovers and radical changes to Gulf regimes
or political communities. In countering the Soviet Union, U.S. Gulf
strategy cannot depend on CENTCOM alone to deter the threat of
direct Soviet intervention. To implement such deterrence will require
a clear commitment by the West to emply its global deterrent forces.

In countering the threats of regime overthrows and territorial takeovers, the lesser Gulf sheikhdoms can be expected to utilize the GCC
for their collective security. Within the current, dynamic balance of
power system, even the Iraqi threats to Kuwait and the Iranian threats
to Bahrain, so long as neither presages a bid for hegemony in the Gulf,
may be countered by the GCC with the availability of other Middle
East or Southwest Asian actors such as Egypt and Pakistan. For these
threats CENTCOM can play a supporting role by providing the GCC
states with military assistance and the possibility of direct deployment
of CENTCOM forces in conjunction with those of the GCC if their
efforts are inadequate.

Where CENTCOM's role in protecting Gulf oil supplies becomes
critical and the need for commitments clearest is in countering destabilizing events that could transform the current dynamic balance of
power. These events include all crises that the GCC cannot handle,
including bids by radical groups to take over the Saudi regime and bids
by Iraq or Iran to dominate the Gulf. All of these situations carry the
risks of bipolarization or hegemony in which the United States may be
excluded or impeded in trying to safeguard Gulf oil supplies.

For a U.S. Gulf policy to be truly effective it needs to pursue three
strategies. One of these is the CENTCOM strategy outlined. The other
two involve energy policy and diplomacy. The United States and the
West need an energy policy dedicated to reducing long-term dependency
on Gulf oil and to coping with emergency supply cutoffs. There can be
no assurance that a military strategy alone can prevent oil supply disruptions for the United States. Moreover, a military strategy without
an energy policy will be no assurance for the Gulf states that the United
States is willing to avoid the dilemma of distrust arising from the possibility that it could deploy its Gulf forces to seize oil facilities, whether
invited or not. The United States also needs to pursue a diplomatic
strategy that seeks to maintain the cooperation of the Traditional states

necessary for CENTCOM's deployment through as firm alignments as are possible and to pursue flexible alignments with the other Gulf states.

Together these three strategies—for CENTCOM, energy policy, and dynamic balance of power diplomacy—would constitute a new U.S. strategy for achieving the policy goals of the United States in the Gulf. The strategy seeks to maintain these goals in the current international political environment of the Gulf and to counter transformations of the unstable dynamic balance of power system that could result from threats from within.

Appendix A
Proved Oil Reserves of the Gulf States, January 1, 1982

Gulf State	Billion Barrels	Percentage of Proved Reserves		
		Of the Gulf	Of OPEC	Of the World
Saudi Arabia	167.9	45	38	25
Kuwait	67.7			
Abu Dhabi	30.6			
Subtotal of Traditional states	266.2	72	61	40
Iran	57.0			
Iraq	29.7			
Subtotal of major Gulf producers	352	95	80	52
OPEC	439			65
World	670.7			

Sources: BP Statistical Review of World Energy 1982, British Petroleum Company, 1983, p. 2; "How Much Oil and Gas," Exxon Background Series, Exxon Corporation, New York, May 1982, pp. 11–12.

Appendix B
The Military Capabilities
of the Gulf States[1]

States:	Iran	Iraq
Population:	41.5 million	14.3 million
GNP (1981)[2]:		$31.83 billion
GDP (1981)[3]:	$121.7 billion	
Oil exports (1983)[4]:	±2.4 mbd	.65–.8 mbd
Defense expenditure (1982–3)[5]:	$6.9–$13.3 billion	$7.72 billion
Foreign aid (1983)[6]:		$13 billion
Army:	150,000	475,000
Navy:	20,000	4,250
Air Force:	35,000	38,000
Total regular armed forces[7]:	205,000	517,250
Reserves:	550,000[8]	75,000
Militia[9]:	2.5 million	450,000
Combat vehicles[10]:	1,720	5,760
Combat vehicles on order[11]:	150	440
Combat ships[12]:	27	40
Combat ships on order:		10
Combat aircraft[13]:	70–75	330
Combat aircraft on order[14]:	100+	197
Air defense[15]:	Hawk and Improved Hawk; SA-7 SAMs	Various SA-2 to SA-7's; French SAMs

States:	Saudi Arabia	Kuwait	UAE
Population[16]:	8–12 million	1.45 million	1.13 million
GNP (1981)[17]:			$32.6 billion
GDP (1981–82)[18]:	$152.2 billion	$20.22 billion	
Oil exports (1983)[19]:	5 mbd	.863 mbd	1.1 mbd
Defense expenditure (1981–1984)[20]:	$22 billion	$20.2 billion	$2.9 billion
Army:	35,000	10,000	46,000
Navy:	2,500	500	1,500
Air Force:	14,000	1,900	1,500
Total regular armed forces:	51,500	12,400	49,000
Reserves[21]:	35,000		
Militia[22]:	8,500	18,000	
Combat vehicles:	1,820	724	604
Combat vehicles on order[23]:	240	344	38
Combat ships[24]:	17	15	15
Combat ships on order:	8	8	5
Combat aircraft:	170	49	43
Combat aircraft on order:	26	12	36
Air defense[25]:	Improved Hawk; Shahine	SA-7; Improved Hawk	
Air defense on order[26]:	Shahine	Shahine	Improved Hawk

States:	Oman	Bahrain	Qatar
Population:	970,000	400,000	260,000
GDP (1981)[27]:	$6.2 billion	$4.5 billion	$6.8 billion
Oil Production (1982)[28]:	.335 mbd		.340 mbd
Defense expenditure (1983):	$1.77 billion	$.253 billion	$.166 billion
Army:	19,550	2,300	5,000
Navy:	2,000	300	700
Air Force:	2,000	100	300
Total regular armed forces:	23,550	2,700	6,000
Reserves[29]:	3,500		
Militia[30]:		180	
Combat vehicles:	54	146	225
Combat vehicles on order:	15		8
Combat ships:	7	2	46
Combat ships on order:	5	2	1
Combat aircraft[31]:	37		11
Combat aircraft on order:		16	14
Air defense:	British SAMs	Various SAMs	Various SAMs

States:	North Yemen	South Yemen
Population:	7.2 million	2 million
GDP (1981):	$2.8 billion	$1.1 billion
Foreign aid[32]:	USSR/Saudi Arabia	USSR
Defense expenditure (1982):	$.527 billion	$.159 billion
Army:	20,000	22,000
Navy:	550	1,000
Air Force:	1,000	2,500
Total regular armed forces:	21,550	25,500
Militia[33]:	25,000	30,000
Combat vehicles:	1,293	770
Combat ships:	13	21
Combat ships on order:	2	
Combat aircraft:	75	113
Combat aircraft in storage:	17	Some
Air defense:	SA-2s; SA-7s	SA-2s; SA-7s
Air defense on order:	Improved Hawk	

Two Hypothetical Combinations of Gulf States:
The GCC and a Unified Yemen

Combination	GCC	Unified Yemen
Population[34]:	12.21–16.21 million	9.2 million
GDP[35]:	$189.4 billion	$3.9 billion
Defense expenditure[36]:	$47.3 billion	$.69 billion
Army:	117,850	42,000
Navy:	7,500	1,550
Air Force:	19,530	3,500
Total regular armed forces[37]:	145,150	47,050
Reserves/militia:	65,000	55,000
Combat vehicles:	3,573	2,063
Combat ships:	97	34
Combat aircraft:	341	188

Appendix C: Soviet Gulf Capabilities

The Soviet Union maintains the following forces in Southwest Asia, which, it is assumed, are capable of being deployed into the Gulf region.[1]

Armed Forces. A total of 28 Soviet army divisions, representing approximately 267,000 troops at full strength, are maintained in the three military districts of the Caucasus, Transcaucasus, and Turkestan. It is reported that, with the exception of the one airborne division of 7,000, these forces are at category 3 of combat readiness or at less than approximately 50 percent strength. A complement of 2 artillery units in this Southern Theater has an unspecified number of men. Two marine (naval infantry) regiments, with approximately 2,100 troops, serve with the Pacific Fleet. In addition the Soviets are reportedly deploying approximately 110,000–120,000 troops in Afghanistan, of whom possibly 12,000–15,000 are in combat (with reported losses of approximately 1,000 per year).[2] Elsewhere in the Gulf, the Soviets have 2,000 troops in Iraq; 1,500 in South Yemen; and 500 in North Yemen.

Combat Vehicles. The numbers of tanks, armored personnel carriers and similar armored fighting vehicles accompany the Soviet Southern Theater forces is difficult to assess. Among the 28 divisions there is 1 tank division, which apparently has fewer than the 335 tanks found in European divisions. There are also motorized infantry divisions, which apparently have fewer than the 266 tanks each found in European divisions.[3] There is 1 airborne division, which may also have combat vehicles, as will the Afghan forces.

Combat Ships. The Soviet Union's Indian Ocean fleet is a detachment of its Pacific Fleet and consists of 2–3 submarines, 8 combat ships, and 14 support ships.

Combat Aircraft. These are also difficult to assess. Probably some unspecified number of long and medium range bombers may be available for the Gulf as well as tactical aircraft, possibly 450–600.[4]

Appendix D: CENTCOM Capabilities

CENTCOM's military capabilities designated for deployment in the Gulf, the Middle East, and Southwest Asia, are as follows.[1]

Armed Forces. CENTCOM's most rapidly deployable Gulf force is the Marine Amphibious Brigade of 12,000 men stationed at Diego Garcia and supplied by 13 pre-positioned supply ships. There is in addition a Marine Amphibious Force composed of 1.33 marine divisions, 1 marine air wing, plus support personnel. (A marine air wing usually consists of 180–200 aircraft and 12,000–15,000 persons.) The balance of the second marine division, plus one other marine air wing are also scheduled for assignment to CENTCOM. Accordingly there may ultimately be a complement of possibly 120,000 to 140,000 marines.

The army has 1 parachute division of 17,000 troops, 1 helicopter assault division of 18,000 troops, 1 helicopter brigade of 2,500 troops, and 1 mechanized infantry division of less than its full strength of 19,000 troops, plus rangers and special forces. There are 2 other army divisions to be assigned to CENTCOM (with an unspecified number of troops, possibly 37,000). The total complement of army personnel is currently 130,000.

Naval and air force complements of CENTCOM are 42,000 and 30,000 personnel, respectively. Total armed forces in CENTCOM fully mobilized at present amount to 292,000 persons and are expected to be increased by additional assignments to almost 460,000.

Combat Vehicles. There are fewer than 1,000 combat vehicles with the Army Mechanized Division and Marine Amphibious Brigade. There will be an unspecified increase with the assignment of additional army and marine divisions.

Combat Ships. CENTCOM has been assigned 3 aircraft carrier battle groups composed of some 18 surface combat ships plus the Middle East Force (Persian Gulf) of 1 command ship and 2 destroyers. The normal Indian Ocean Detachment from the Seventh (Western Pacific) Fleet is 1 carrier battle group with 6 surface combat ships. There are also 17 pre-positioned supply ships assigned to CENTCOM.

Combat Aircraft. These include 28 B-52H long-range bombers and 210–285 aircraft onboard the carriers. These forces also possibly include 5 antisubmarine air squadrons and a number of adjunct services such as an AWAC wing, reconnaissance, and refueling. There are currently 7 tactical fighter wings and 4 tactical fighter groups assigned to CENTCOM with a total of 10 wings altogether as its complement. Accordingly there are possibly 520 aircraft plus another 220 to come, apart from the additional marine air wings. The total complement of combat aircraft could therefore reach approximately 1,000.

Additional projected airlift capabilities by 1987 include: 279 C-141 Starlifters with in-flight refueling from a fleet of KC-10 tankers (ultimate complement of 60); 50 C-5B Galaxies by 1988; 8 SL-7 fast deployment ships (with conversion to roll-on/roll-off capabilities by 1985).

How Rapidly Deployable Is CENTCOM?

This question cannot be answered with specificity because to some extent it depends on some imponderables that remain incalculable until the time of deployment. These include destinations, departure points, availability of base facilities in the Gulf, availability of local logistical support (particularly fuel and water), degree to which landing or destination areas are contested, degree to which sea and air lines of logistical and communcations support are contested, and availability of European, North African, and Middle Eastern refueling and transit points. Current estimations appear to be as follows:

One amphibious battalion of 1,800 marines (possibly from an aircraft carrier) can be landed within 48 hours after notice. The balance of the Diego Garcia Marine Amphibious Brigade (the air group and service support group) would be delivered within 7 days;

One brigade of 3,000 army paratroopers can be delivered, not necessarily all by parachute drop, within 4 days. Two more brigades, completing the division of 17,000 troops, can be delivered within 5 days.

Within 2 weeks, assuming the most favorable conditions, approximately 45,600 combat forces will have been delivered. The balance of the fighting force, the army's mechanized division of an additional 19,000 troops with tanks and artillery, can be delivered within 35 days.[2]

Appendix E
Western Dependency
on Gulf Oil, 1982

	Gulf Oil Imports (million metric tons)	*Net Oil Imports (million metric tons)*	*Gulf Oil as a Percentage*		
			Of Net Oil Imports	*Of All Oil Used*	*Of Primary Energy Used*
United States	38.2 (.77 mbd)	205.7 (4.23 mbd)	18.6	5.4	2.2
Western Europe	229.8 (4.63 mbd)	418.2 (8.39 mbd)	55	38.2	18.9
Japan	137 (2.76 mbd)	205.8 (4.14 mbd)	66.6	66.2	40.3
Australasia	8 (.16 mbd)	14.7 (.30 mbd)	54.4	22.5	8.9
Total[a]	413 (8.32 mbd)	844.4 (17.06 mbd)	48.9	26.7	12.2

Source: BP Statistical Review of World Energy 1982, British Petroleum Company, 1983, pp. 12, 14. Some percentages may vary because of rounding.

[a]This excludes Canada, which is a net exporter.

Notes

Works frequently cited in the notes are identified by the following abbreviations:

CSM	*Christian Science Monitor*
FBIS	*Foreign Broadcast Information Service, Middle East and Africa*
FT	*Financial Times*
JPRS	*Joint Publication Research Service, North East/ North Africa*
MECS	*The Middle East Contemporary Survey* (eds. Colin Legum et al.)
MEED	*The Middle East Economic Digest*
MERIP	*Middle East Research and Information Project*
NYT	*The New York Times*
QER, BQOY	*Quarterly Economic Review of Bahrain, Qatar, Oman, the Yemens*
QER, E	*Quarterly Economic Review of Egypt*
QER, IN	*Quarterly Economic Review of Iran*
QER, IQ	*Quarterly Economic Review of Iraq*
QER, K	*Quarterly Economic Review of Kuwait*
QER, SA	*Quarterly Economic Review of Saudi Arabia*
QER, UAE	*Quarterly Economic Review of the UAE*
WSJ	*The Wall Street Journal*

Chapter 1

1. The reference simply to the "Gulf" is not only as a convenience. It also avoids the controversy over the usage of the term "Persian Gulf" versus "Arabian Gulf." Hermann F. Eilts traces the controversy to Nasser's promotion of Arab nationalism in the 1950s and 1960s, and notes the official preference of the United States for "Persian Gulf"

on the basis of long-standing international usage (Eilts, "Security Considerations in the Persian Gulf," *International Security* 5 (Fall 1980): 79, n. 1).

2. *NYT,* October 7, 1983, p. D5.

3. *NYT,* October 25, 1982, pp. 1, A14; *Time,* October 25, 1982, pp. 47, 49.

Chapter 2

1. This approach is derived from the more rigorous approach of Morton A. Kaplan, *System and Process in International Politics* (New York: John Wiley and Sons, 1957) as well as Kaplan's subsequent works, including *Macropolitics* (Chicago: Aldine, 1969), pp. 49–76; "The Systems Approach to International Politics" in Kaplan, ed., *New Approaches to International Relations* (New York: St. Martin Press, 1968), pp. 381–404; "Some Problems of International Systems Research", in *International Political Communities* (Garden City, N.Y.: Doubleday Anchor, 1966), pp. 469–501.

2. For more complex systems models that include other variables such as "essential rules" that prescribe the norms of international political behavior in each system, see Kaplan, *System and Process,* pp. 9–12.

3. See Leonard Binder, *The Ideological Revolution in the Middle East* (New York: John Wiley and Sons, 1964), pp. 254–278, and Tareq Y. Ismael, "The Middle East: A Subordinate System in Global Politics," in *The Middle East in World Politics,* ed. Ismael (Syracuse, N.Y.: Syracuse Univ. Press, 1974), pp. 240–56.

4. The sources for the historical accounts related in the balance of this chapter include the following titles in the Area Handbook Series of the Foreign Area Studies (Washington, D.C.: The American University), Richard F. Nyrop, ed.: *Iran: A Country Study,* 1978; *Iraq: A Country Study, 1979; Area Handbook for Saudi Arabia,* 1977; *Area Handbook for the Persian Gulf States,* 1977; *Area Handbook for the Yemens,* 1977 (hereafter citation will be made to individual volumes as Nyrop, *Iran,* etc.). Other general historical sources for international and regional affairs include J.C. Hurewitz, *Diplomacy in the Near and Middle East* (Princeton, N.J.: D. Van Nostrand, 1956); G.P. Gooch and Harold Temperly, eds, *British Documents on the Origins of the War 1898–1914* (London: His Majesty's Stationery Office, 1938); G.P. Gooch, *Before the War: Studies in Diplomacy,* 2 vols. (London: Longmans, Green, 1938); William L. Langer, *The Diplomacy of Imperialism 1890–1902,* vol. 2 (New York: Alfred A. Knopf, 1935); Aran

J.Hall, *The Great Illusion 1900–1914* (New York: Harper & Row, 1971); Lord Kinross, *The Ottoman Centuries* (New York: William Morrow, 1977); Bradford G. Martin, *German–Persian Diplomatic Relations 1873–1912* ('S-Gravenhage, The Netherlands: Mouton, 1959); Malcolm H. Kerr, *The Arab Cold War,* 3d ed. (London: Oxford University Press, 1971); Donald Hawley, *The Trucial States* (London: George Allen and Unwin, 1970); M. Burrell, *The Persian Gulf,* The Washington Papers, vol. 1, no. 1 (New York: Sage, 1972); John Marlowe, *The Persian Gulf in the Twentieth Century* (London: The Cresset Press, 1962). Historical sources for specific countries include Robin Bidwell, ed., *The Affairs of Kuwait* (London: Frank Cass, 1971); H.R.P. Dickson, *Kuwait and Her Neighbours* (London: George Allen and Unwin, 1956); Robert G. Landen, *Oman since 1856* (Princeton, N.J.: Princeton Univ. Press, 1967); K.S. Twitchell, *Saudi Arabia* (Princeton, N.J.: Princeton Univ. Press, 1958); H. St. John Philby, *Sa'udi Arabia* (London: Ernest Benn, 1955); Robin Bidwell, *The Affairs of Arabia 1905–1906* (London: Frank Cass, 1971); J.B. Kelley, *Eastern Arabian Frontiers* (New York: Frederick A. Praeger, 1964); Stephen Helmsley Longrigg, *Iraq, 1900 to 1950: A Political, Social and Economic History* (London: Oxford University Press, 1953); R.J. Gavin, *Aden under British Rule, 1839–1967* (London: C. Hurst, 1975); Rouhallah K. Ramazani, *The Foreign Policy of Iran 1500–1941* (Charlottesville, Va.: Univ. Press of Virginia, 1966); Ervand Abrahamian, *Iran between Two Revolutions* (Princeton, N.J.: Princeton Univ. Press, 1982); Major Clarence Mann, *Abu Dhabi: Birth of an Oil Sheikhdom* (Beirut: Khayats, 1964).

5. The Baghdad Railway was never fully completed. See Edward M. Earle, *Turkey, the Great Powers, and the Bagdad Railway* (New York: MacMillan, 1923).

6. See section on "Iran and the UAE" in chapter 3.

7. *WSJ,* November 10, 1983, p. 33.

8. *QER,BQOY* (4th Quarter, 1979): 20–21.

9. Ibid. (3d Quarter, 1981): 5–6; *QER,SA,* (1st Quarter, 1981): 6.

10. *QER,K,* (2nd Quarter, 1981): 3; *MECS,*1980–81, p. 31.

11. *QER,BQOY,* (4th Quarter, 1981): 15–16.

12. *QER,UAE,* (1st Quarter): 7.

13. Ibid. (4th Quarter, 1982): 8; *QER,SA,* (4th Quarter, 1982): 7.

14. *QER,UAE,* (1st Quarter, 1983): 7–8; *MEED,* March 25, 1983, p. 59; *MEED,* May 20, 1983, p. 2.

15. *NYT,* October 16, 1983, p. 17; *The Middle East,* November, 1983, pp. 16–17.

16. *NYT,* March 6, 1983, p. 20.

17. *QER,BQOY*, (3rd Quarter, 1982): 16; *QER,BQOY*, (2nd Quarter, 1980): 24; see also *QER,BQOY*, (4th Quarter, 1982): 62.

18. *QER,BQOY*, (Annual Supplement), 1980, p. 47.

19. Ibid. (4th Quarter, 1982): 22; *Middle East,* April, 1982, p. 6.

Chapter 3

1. See Evan Luard, ed., *The International Regulation of Frontier Disputes* (New York: Praeger, 1970), pp. 14–17.

2. Anthony H. Cordesman, "Lessons of the Iran–Iraq War: The First Round," *Armed Forces Journal International* (April 1982): 44.

3. Ibid., p. 32; *NYT,* September 18, 1980, p. A8; Stephen R. Grummon, *The Iran–Iraq War,* The Washington Papers, vol. 92 (New York: Praeger, 1982), p. 10; Robert Litwak, *Security in the Persian Gulf, Vol. 2: Sources of Inter-State Conflict* (Montclair, N.J.: Allanheld Osmun, for the International Institute of Strategic Studies, 1981), p. 11.

4. Litwak, *Security in the Persian Gulf,* p. 7; Robert D. Tomasek, "The Resolution of Major Controversies between Iran and Iraq," *World Affairs* 139 (Winter 1976–77): 211.

5. Tomasek, "Major Controversies between Iran and Iraq," p. 224.

6. Litwak, *Security in the Persian Gulf,* p. 13.

7. Grummon, *The Iran–Iraq War,* pp. 10, 12; Edgar O'Ballance, "Khuzistan: Another Casus Belli?", *The Army Quarterly and Defense Journal* 110 (April 1980): 139–40.

8. Michael Vlahos and Geoffrey Kemp, "The Changing Strategic Tapestry in the Middle East," *MECS,* vol. 4, 1979–80, p. 40; Cordesman, "Lessons of the Iran–Iraq War," pp. 34, 44–47; Grummon, *Iran–Iraq War,* pp. 16–18

9. *WSJ,* December 9, 1983, p. 18.

10. *NYT,* November 24, 1983, p. D4.

11. J.B. Kelly, *Arabia, the Gulf and The West* (New York: Basic Books, 1980), p. 276.

12. Richard Nyrop, *Area Handbook for Saudi Arabia,* (Washington, D.C.: The American University), pp. 208–209.

13. Litwak, *Security in the Persian Gulf,* p. 34; Lenore G. Martin, "A Systematic Study of Boundary Disputes in the Persian Gulf, 1900 to Present," unpublished Ph.D. dissertation, Univ. of Chicago, 1979, p. 103; see Kelly, *Arabia,* p. 288.

14. *NYT,* December 28, 1981, p. A9; *FBIS,* February 25, 1982, vol. 5, p. C7; Litwak, *Security in the Persian Gulf,* p. 35.

15. Will D. Swearingen, "Sources of Conflict over Oil in the Persian/Arabian Gulf," *Middle East Journal* 35 (1981): 320–21, 328–29: Litwak, *Security in the Persian Gulf,* p. 39.

16. Kelly, *Arabia,* p. 276.

17. Martin, "Boundary Disputes in the Persian Gulf," p. 92.

18. Ibid.; Litwak, *Security in the Persian Gulf,* pp. 27–28, 30–31; Kelly, *Arabia,* p. 277.

19. *QER, K* (3rd Quarter, 1981) p. 4; *FBIS,* January 18, 1983, vol. 5, p. C12; *FBIS,* April 8, 1981, vol. 5, p. C6; *Economist,* March 27, 1982, p. 35; *MEED,* March 25, 1983, p. 33; *FBIS,* January 18, 1983, vol. 5, p. C2; see also Litwak, *Security in the Persian Gulf,* pp. 28–29.

20. Kelly, *Arabia,* p. 55; Burrell, *The Persian Gulf,* The Washington Papers, vol. 1, no. 1 (New York: Sage Publications, 1972), pp. 41–42; Martin, "Boundary Disputes in the Persian Gulf," pp. 97–98; Litwak, *Security in the Persian Gulf,* pp. 43–44.

21. Litwak, *Security in the Persian Gulf,* pp. 45–46; *Time,* October 25, 1982, p. 49.

22. Kelly, *Arabia,* pp. 92–93.

23. Swearingen, *Sources of Conflict Over Oil,* p. 327; Kelly, *Arabia,* pp. 88–89.

24. Nyrop, *Persian Gulf States,* p. 342; Litwak, *Security in the Persian Gulf,* p. 68. See Anthony H. Cordesman, "Oman: The Guardian of the Eastern Gulf," *Armed Forces Journal International* (June 1983): 29.

25. Kelly, *Arabia,* pp. 61–62.

26. Martin, "Boundary Disputes in the Persian Gulf," p. 87; Litwak, *Security in the Persian Gulf,* pp. 51, 54; Kelly, *Arabia,* pp. 69, 210–11; Nyrop, *Saudi Arabia,* p. 210.

27. Litwak, *Security in the Persian Gulf,* p. 40; Swearingen, *Sources of Conflict over Oil,* pp. 323–25.

28. Aryeh Shmuelevitz, "Gulf States," *MECS,* vol. 1, 1976–1977, pp. 343–344; Litwak, *Security in the Persian Gulf,* p. 40; Kelly, *Arabia,* p. 172.

29. Swearingen, *Sources of Conflict over Oil,* p. 328; Litwak, *Security in the Persian Gulf,* p. 66; Nyrop, *Persian Gulf States,* p. 2; Kelly, *Arabia,* p. 182.

30. See J.E. Peterson, *Yemen: The Search for a Modern State* (Baltimore: The Johns Hopkins Univ. Press, 1982), pp. 89–93; Kelly, *Arabia,* pp. 24, 26; Litwak, *Security in the Persian Gulf,* pp. 87–88.

31. Nyrop, *Yemens,* pp. 210–11.

32. Warren Richey, "North Yemen," pt. 1, *CSM,* January 12, 1983, pp. 12–13; *The Economist,* January 16, 1982, p. 45.

33. Litwak, *Security in the Persian Gulf,* pp. 91–92. *Mideast File* 1, no. 4 (December 1982): 567.

34. Litwak, *Security in the Persian Gulf,* pp. 74, 88, n. 3. Nyrop, *Saudi Arabia,* p. 210; *QER,BQOY,* (2d Quarter, 1980) 20.

35. Bard E. O'Neill and William Brundage, "Revolutionary Warfare in Oman: A Strategic Appraisal," *Middle East Review* 10 (Summer 1978): 53; Litwak, *Security in the Persian Gulf,* p. 77.

36. Litwak, ibid., pp. 89, 92.

37. Martin, "Boundary Disputes in the Persian Gulf," pp. 94–95.

38. *MEED,* June 17, 1983, p. 84; *QER,BQOY,* (1st Quarter 1983): 16; ibid., (4th Quarter, 1982): 19.

39. *QER,BQOY,* (2d Quarter, 1982): 22; *The Guardian,* June 27, 1982, p. 12.

40. Richey, "North Yemen," p. 12.

41. Litwak, *Security in the Persian Gulf,* p. 73, n. 1; *MEED,* April 1, 1983, p. 35; Kelly, *Arabia,* pp. 65, 73.

42. Cordesman, "Oman," p. 27; Litwak, *Security in the Persian Gulf,* pp. 72–77; Liesl Graz, *The Omanis: Sentinels of the Gulf* (London: Longman, 1982), pp. 36–37; John Duke Anthony, "Insurrection and Intervention: the War in Dhofar," in *The Persian Gulf and Indian Ocean in International Politics* ed. Abbas Amirie (Teheran: Institute for International Political and Economic Studies, 1975), pp. 297–300.

43. Cordesman, "Oman," p. 27; Esther Webman, "The Gulf States," *MECS,* vol. 5, 1980–81, pp. 492–493; *The Middle East and North Africa 1981–82,* 28th ed. (London: Europa Publications 1981), p. 638.

44. Cordesman, "Oman," p. 30.

45. *Keesings* (March 1983) p. 32048; *FBIS,* vol. 5, January 14, 1983, p. C1.

46. Kelly, *Arabia,* p. 158; Litwak, *Security in the Persian Gulf,* pp. 53–55.

47. Litwak, ibid., pp. 59–60, 71; Aryeh Shmuelevitz, "The Gulf States," *MECS,* vol. 2, 1977–78, pp. 414–15; Cordesman "Oman," p. 26.

48. Gerald Blake, *Maritime Aspects of Arabian Geopolitics,* Arab Papers no. 11 (London: The Arab Research Centre, 1982), p. 21; *QER,UAE,* Annual Supplement, 1982, p. 39; Webman, "Gulf States," p. 505.

49. Nyrop, *Persian Gulf States,* p. 354.

50. Kelly, *Arabia,* p. 186; Litwak, *Security in the Persian Gulf,* pp. 48–49.

51. *QER,BQOY,* (3rd Quarter, 1982): 12; Litwak, *Security in the Persian Gulf,* pp. 49–50, 69.

52. Litwak, ibid., p. 67; Swearingen, *Sources of Conflict over Oil,* p. 329.

53. Litwak, ibid., pp. 62–63, 70; *QER,BQOY,* (1st Quarter, 1980): 16.

54. Martin, "Boundary Disputes in the Persian Gulf," p. 96; Kelly, *Arabia,* p. 200.

55. Nyrop, *Persian Gulf States,* p. 276; Litwak, *Security in the Persian Gulf,* p. 49; Kelly, *Arabia,* pp. 200–207.

56. *BP Statistical Review of World Energy 1982,* British Petroleum Company, 1983, p. 2. See "How Much Oil and Gas?", Exxon Background Series, Exxon Corporation, New York, May 1982, pp. 3–8.

57. Walter J. Levy, "If OPEC's Pact Fails, We Lose," *NYT,* April 6, 1983, p. A23.

58. W.B. Fisher, *The Middle East: A Physical, Social and Regional Geography* (London: Methuen, 1978), pp. 258–60. See David A. Deese and Joseph S. Nye, eds., *Energy and Security* (Cambridge, Mass.: Ballinger, 1981), p. 10; Douglas J. Feith, "The Oil Weapon De-Mystified," *Policy Review* 15 (Winter 1981): 22–23; John Gault, "Middle Eastern Oil Producers: New Strength or New Vulnerability?" *Middle East Annual,* vol. 1, ed. David H. Partington, (Boston: G.K. Hall, 1981), pp. 174–78; Arlon R. Tussing, "An OPEC Obituary," *The Public Interest,* 70 (Winter, 1983): 7–8.

59. Gault, "Middle Eastern Oil Producers," p. 173.

60. See Dankwart A. Rostow, "Middle East Oil: International and Regional Developments," *MECS,* vol. 5, 1980–81, pp. 366–67; William B. Quandt, *Saudi Arabia's Oil Policy* (Washington, D.C.: The Brookings Institution, 1982), p. 30; Sheikh Ahmad Zaki Yamani, "Petroleum: A Look into the Future," speech of January 31, 1981 reprinted in an edited version in William B. Quandt, *Saudi Arabia in the 1980s: Foreign Policy; Security, and Oil* (Washington, D.C.: The Brookings Institution, 1981), pp. 164–74.

61. See *WSJ,* October 27, 1983, p. 34; ibid., November 9, 1983, p. 2.

62. See Conoco, *World Energy Outlook through 2000* (Stamford, Conn: Conoco Corporation, April 1983, pp. 1–5; *Wall Street Journal,* July 25, 1983, p. 4 (a World Bank report); Robert Stobaugh, "World

Energy to the Year 2000," in *Global Insecurity,* eds. Daniel Yergin and Martin Hillenbrand (Boston: Houghton Mifflin, 1982), pp. 29–57; S. Fred Singer, "Oil Pricing Blunders Now Have Saudis in a Jam," *WSJ,* May 28, 1981, p. 33; Eliyahu Kanovsky, "The Diminishing Importance of Middle East Oil: A Harbinger of the Future?" *MECS,* vol. 5, 1980–81, p. 396.

63. Swearingen, *Sources of Conflict over Oil,* p. 327.

64. *MEED,* January 28, 1983, p. 22.

65. Martin, "Boundary Disputes in the Persian Gulf," pp. 45–46; Litwak, *Security in the Persian Gulf,* pp. 51–55.

66. Cordesman, "Oman," p. 27.

67. Swearingen, *Sources of Conflict over Oil,* pp. 316–19; Blake, *Maritime Aspects of Arabian Geopolitics,* pp. 15–16.

68. Swearingen, ibid., pp. 328–29; Litwak, *Security in the Persian Gulf,* p. 39.

69. *QER,UAE,* Annual Supplement, 1982, p. 37.

70. Litwak, *Security in the Persian Gulf,* p. 40; Swearingen, *Sources of Conflict over Oil,* pp. 323–24.

Chapter 4

1. H.A.R. Gibb, *Mohammedanism* (New York: Oxford Univ. Press, A Galaxy Book, 1962), pp. 120–26; Charles F. Gallagher, "Contemporary Islam: The Plateau of Particularism Problems of Religion and Nationalism in Iran" (New York: American University Field Staff, Southwest Asia Series, vol. 15, no. 2, 1966), pp. 4–15; Leonard Binder, *The Ideological Revolution in the Middle East* (New York: John Wiley and Sons, 1964), pp. 32–38.

2. Gibb, *Mohammedanism,* pp. 124–25; Gallagher, "Contemporary Islam," p. 24; see James A. Brill, "Power and Religion in Revolutionary Iran," *Middle East Journal* 36 (Winter 1982): 22–23.

3. Gibb, *Mohammedanism,* p. 166; Binder, *Ideological Revolution in the Middle East,* pp. 41–42.

4. Liesl Graz, *The Omanis: Sentinels of the Gulf* (London: Longman, 1982), pp. 64–69.

5. Cordesman, "Lessons of the Iran–Iraq War: The First Round," *Armed Forces Journal International* (April 1982): 32.

6. Grummon, *The Iran–Iraq War,* The Washington Papers, vol. 92 (New York: Praeger, 1982), p. 9; Cordesman, "Lessons of the Iran–Iraq War," p. 34; John W. Amos II, "The Iraq–Iran War: Calculus of Regional Conflict," *Middle East Annual,* vol. 1, ed. David H. Par-

tington (Boston: G.K. Hall, 1981), p. 142; *NYT,* March 3, 1982, p. A17.

7. Marvin Zonis, "Gulf Arabs Are Wary," *NYT,* August 2, 1982, p. A34; Barry Rubin, "Iran, the Ayatollah, and U.S. Options," *Washington Quarterly* 6 (Summer 1983): 152.

8. Amos, *Iran–Iraq War,* p. 143; Cordesman, "Lessons of the Iran–Iraq War," p. 32.

9. Phebe Marr, "Iraq: Sociopolitical Developments," *American Enterprise Institute Foreign Policy and Defense Review* 2 (August 1980): 33.

10. Hanna Batatu, "Iraq's Underground Shi'a Movements: Characteristics, Causes and Prospects," *The Middle East Journal* 35 (Autumn 1981): 578–80.

11. Ibid., p. 593.

12. David Menashri, "Iran," *MECS,* vol. 3, 1978–79, p. 531; Ofra Bengio, "Iraq," *MECS,* vol. 4, 1979–80, p. 514.

13. *NYT,* June 26, 1980, p. 24.

14. Batatu, "Iraq's Underground," p. 591; Ami Ayalon, "The Iraqi–Iranian War," *MECS,* vol. 4., 1979–80, p. 15; *NYT,* January 11, 1981, p. E5; ibid., May 19, 1982, p. A2; *Weekly Media Abstract,* Report no. 68, December 3, 1980.

15. Bengio, "Iraq," p. 514.

16. *NYT,* July 5, 1980, p. 2; ibid., May 19, 1982, p. A2.

17. *NYT,* July 25, 1982, p. 3; *WSJ,* February 10, 1982, p. 31; *QER,BQOY,* (3rd Quarter, 1979): 5.

18. *FT,* November 4, 1980, p. XII; *NYT,* March 6, 1983, p. 20.

19. *WSJ,* February 10, 1982, p. 31; *FBIS,* January 8, 1982, p. C6; Adeed Dawisha, "Iran's Mullahs and the Arab Masses," *Washington Quarterly* 6 (Summer 1983): 164; Litwak, *Security in the Persian Gulf,* p. 45.

20. *QER,BQOY,* (4th Quarter, 1979): 4.

21. Michael C. Hudson, *Arab Politics: The Search for Legitimacy* (New Haven, Conn.: Yale Univ. Press, 1977) p. 193.

22. *NYT,* July 25, 1982, p. 3; *WSJ,* February 10, 1982, p. 31; *Keesings,* February 26, 1982, pp. 3153–54; *FBIS,* January 7, 1982, vol. 5. p. C2.

23. *Keesings,* February 26, 1982, p. 3154.

24. *QER,BQOY,* (4th Quarter, 1979): 4.

25. *NYT,* April 27,1983, p. A6.

26. Bayley Winder, "Saudi Arabia: Sociopolitical Developments," *American Enterprise Institute Foreign Policy and Defense Review* 2 (August 1980): 17; Ghassane Salameh, "Political Power and the Saudi State," *MERIP Reports* 91 (October 1980): 20.

27. Jacob Goldberg, "The Saudi Arabian Kingdom," *MECS,* vol. 5, 1980–81, p. 734; Winder, "Saudi Arabia," p. 15.

28. James Buchan, "Secular and Religious Opposition in Saudi Arabia," in *State, Society and Economy in Saudi Arabia,* ed. Tim Niblock (New York: St. Martin's Press, 1982), p. 118.

29. Jacob Goldberg, "The Saudi Arabian Kingdom," *MECS,* vol. 4, 1979–80, pp. 689–90; Buchan, "Secular and Religious Opposition in Saudi Arabia," p. 119.

30. Goldberg, "Saudi Arabia," 1979–80, pp. 688–89; *CSM,* February 20, 1980, p. 23.

31. "The Shi'is of Saudi Arabia," *MERIP Reports,* 91 (October 1980): 21; *FT,* December 5, 1979, p. XII; Goldberg, "Saudi Arabia," p. 688.

32. Buchan, "Secular and Religious Opposition in Saudi Arabia," p. 120; Goldberg, "Saudi Arabia," 1979–80, p. 688; *NYT,* January 30, 1980; *FT,* March 12, 1980.

33. *FT,* May 5, 1981, p. X; Goldberg, "Saudi Arabia," 1980–81, p. 734.

34. *FT,* April 28, 1980, p. XXVI; Buchan, "Secular and Religious Opposition in Saudi Arabia," p. 117; Nyrop, *Saudi Arabia,* p. viii.

35. Buchan, "Secular and Religious Opposition in Saudi Arabia," p. 122; *NYT,* November 30, 1979, p. A23.

36. Buchan, ibid., p. 122.

37. Goldberg, "Saudi Arabia," 1979–80, p. 683; *FT,* April 28, 1980, p. XXVI; Buchan, "Secular and Religious Opposition in Saudi Arabia," p. 122.

38. Goldberg, "Saudi Arabia," pp. 683, 686–87; Jim Paul, "Insurrection at Mecca," *MERIP Reports* 91 (October 1980): 3.

39. Michael Collins, "Riyadh: The Saudi Balance," *Washington Quarterly* 4 (Winter 1981): 204; *Newsweek,* March 30, 1980, p. 29.

40. *WSJ,* January 21, 1980, p. 27; Goldberg, "Saudi Arabia," 1980–81, p. 732.

41. James Buxton, "Challenge to Internal Stability," *FT,* April 28, 1980, p. II; Buchan, "Secular and Religious Opposition in Saudi Arabia," p. 123.

42. *QER,K,* (2nd Quarter, 1979): 16; *QER,K,* (4th Quarter, 1979): p. 17; Eli Flint, "The Gulf States,"; *MECS,* vol. 3, 1978–79, p. 450; *NYT,* March 6, 1983, p. A14; Ari Plascov, *Security in the Persian Gulf, vol. 3: Modernization, Political Development, and Stability* (Montclair, N.J.: Allanheld, Osmun: 1982), p. 36.

43. Flint, "The Gulf States," p. 450; Esther Webman, "The Gulf States," *MECS,* 4, 1979–80, p. 403.

44. Webman, "The Gulf States," p. 404.

45. Nyrop, *The Yemens,* p. 68.

46. Peterson, *Yemen*, pp. 38–39.

47. Robert W. Stookey, *Yemen* (Boulder: Colo.: Westview Press, 1978), p. 182.

48. Peterson, *Yemen*, p. 79.

49. Ibid., p. 91.

50. Ibid., pp. 91, 134 n. 48; Stookey, *Yemen*, p. 233.

51. *QER,BQOY,* (2d Quarter, 1981), 14. *The Middle East,* April 1982, p. 7; Michael Dunn, "The Yemens Two Years Later," *Defense and Foreign Affairs Daily,* February 2, 1981, p. 1.

52. Peterson, *Yemen*, p. 81; Stookey, *Yemen*, pp. 205–206.

53. Edmund Ghareeb, *The Kurdish Question in Iraq* (Syracuse, N.Y.: Syracuse Univ. Press, 1981), p. 4; Nyrop, *Iraq*, pp. 80–81.

54. Ghareeb, ibid., p. 87. Majid Khadduri, *Socialist Iraq: A Study in Iraqi Politics since 1968* (Washington, D.C.: The Middle East Institute, 1978), pp. 231–40 reprints the entire Manifesto.

55. Martin Short and Anthony McDermott, *The Kurds* (London: Expedite Graphic, 1977), p. 12; *Annals of American Political and Social Sciences* 433 (1975): 112–24.

56. Ghareeb, *The Kurdish Question in Iraq*, p. 189; Marr, p. 34.

57. Ghareeb, ibid., pp. 181–85; *FBIS*, January 19, 1979, p. C4; *The Middle East,* August 1983, p. 24.

58. *NYT,* October 2, 1980, p. A16; *QER,IQ,* (1st Quarter, 1983) p. 9; *MEED,* June 24, 1983, p. 29. *Keesings,* November 9, 1979, p. 29923.

59. Lois Beck, "Revolutionary Iran and Its Tribal Peoples," *MERIP Reports,* 87 (May 1980): 16; Nyrop, *Iran*, pp. 144–45.

60. Ghareeb, *The Kurdish Question in Iraq*, pp. 12–14.

61. Ibid., pp. 14–27; David Menashri, "Iran," *MECS,* vol. 4, 1979–80, p. 467; *The Middle East* (August, 1983), p. 25; *MEED,* May 27, 1983, p. 81.

62. *The Middle East,* August 1983, p. 25; *QER,IN,* (2d Quarter, 1983): 12.

63. *NYT,* February 3, 1981, p. A8; *FBIS,* September 23, 1981, p. C6; *CSM,* January 31, 1983, p. 12.

64. Akbar Aghajanian, "Ethnic Inequality in Iran: An Overview," *International Journal of Middle East Studies,* 15 (1983): 220–21; Nyrop, *Iran,* p. 171.

65. *NYT,* December 7, 1979, p. 1; Ervand Abrahamian, "Iran's Turbaned Revolution," *Middle East Annual,* vol. 1, ed. David H. Partington (Boston: G.K. Hall, 1981), p. 97.

66. *NYT,* January 13, 1980, p. 9; William F. Hickman, *Ravaged and Reborn: The Iranian Army, 1982* (Washington, D.C.: The Brookings Institution, 1982), p. 11.

67. Menashri, "Iran," 1978–79, p. 529; Leonard M. Helfgott, "The

Structural Foundations of the National Minority Problem in Revolutionary Iran," *Iranian Studies* 13 (1980): 210; John C. Campbell, "The United States and the Middle East, 1979–80," *MECS*, vol. 4, 1979–80, p. 46.

68. Menashri, "Iran," 1978–79, p. 529; Nyrop, *Iran*, p. 147; Beck, "Revolutionary Iran," p. 16; *NYT*, April 11, 1979, p. A8.

69. Beck, "Revolutionary Iran," p. 18; Menashri, "Iran," 1978–79, p. 469; David Menashri, "Iran," *MECS*, vol. 5, 1980–81, p. 556.

70. Lois Beck, "Tribe and State in Revolutionary Iran: The Return of the Qashqa'i Khans," *Iranian Studies* 13 (1980): 248.

71. *WSJ*, April 26, 1982, p. 1; *Mideast File* 2 (March 1983): 68.

72. Nyrop, *Iran*, p. 151; Beck, "Revolutionary Iran," p. 16, n. 5; Cordesman, "Lessons of the Iran–Iraq War," p. 34; Menashri, "Iran" 1979–80, p. 528; Beck estimates that only one-half of Iran's Arab population is Sunni ("Revolutionary Iran," p. 16).

73. Cordesman, "Lessons of the Iran–Iraq War," p. 34; Menashri, "Iran," 1978–79, p. 529. *NYT*, May 6, 1980, p. 20.

74. O'Ballance, "Khuzistan," p. 140; Cordesman, "Lessons of the Iran–Iraq War," p. 34; Menashri, "Iran," 1980–81, p. 557; Nader Entessar, "Arab Factions in Post-Revolutionary Iranian Politics," *Middle East Review* 12 (Spring 1980): 53.

75. Beck, "Revolutionary Iran," p. 16; Nyrop, *Iran*, pp. 145–47.

76. Menashri, "Iran," 1979–80, pp. 469–70; *NYT*, April 11, 1979.

77. Beck, "Revolutionary Iran," p. 16; Nyrop, *Iran*, pp. 144, 148, 151–54.

78. Rubin, "Iran, the Ayatollah, and U.S. Options" *Washington Quarterly* 6 (Summer 1983) p. 148.

79. *MEED*, June 3, 1983, p. 38; *FBIS*, August 19, 1982, pp. C1–C2.

80. *MEED*, February 18, 1983, p. 58; *The Economist*, February 19, 1983, p. 26; *FBIS*, August 19, 1982, pp. C1–C2.

81. Ibid.; *FT*, April 28, 1980, p. XVI; *MEED*, March 25, 1983, p. 25; *FT*, April 28, 1980, p. XVI; see also, *NYT*, October 15, 1983, p. 4.

82. *The Middle East*, February 1983, p. 32; *FT*, April 28, 1980, p. XVI.

83. *FBIS*, July 10, 1980, p. A11; *FT*, April 28, 1980, p. XVI.

84. John A. Shaw and David E. Long, *Saudi Arabian Modernization: The Impact of Change on Stability*, Washington Papers no. 89 (New York: Praeger, and the Center for Strategic and International Studies, Washington, D.C., 1982), p. 68.

85. James Buchan, p. 112.

86. *MEED,* June 3, 1983, p. 38 (giving 1982 figures); Webman, "Gulf States," 1980–81, p. 478; *Mideast File,* March 1983, p. 7.

87. *QER,K,* (3rd Quarter 1982): 24; Alan G. Hill, "Population, Migration and Development in the Gulf States," in *Security in the Persian Gulf 1: Domestic Political Factors,* ed. Shahram Chubin (Montclair, N.J.: Allenheld, Osmun, 1981), p. 61. *MEED,* March 25, 1983, p. 25.

88. Nyrop, *Persian Gulf States,* p. 193; Alvin J. Cottrell, Robert J. Hanks, and Frank T. Bray, "Military Affairs in the Persian Gulf, " *The Persian Gulf States: A General Survey,* ed. Alvin J. Cottrell et al. (Baltimore: The Johns Hopkins Univ. Press, 1980), pp. 166–67.

89. Nyrop, *Persian Gulf States,* p. 171; Shmuelevitz, "Gulf States," *MECS,* vol. 2, 1977–78, p. 429.

90. Shmuelevitz, "Gulf States," *MECS,* vol. 2, 1977–78, p. 429; Webman, "Gulf States," 1980–81, pp. 478–79; *MEED,* May 6, 1983, p. 35; *The Middle East,* February 1983, p. 31.

91. Webman, "Gulf States," 1980–81, p. 478; *MEED,* March 25, 1983; ibid., April 22, 1983, p. 26.

92. *FBIS,* August 19, 1982, C1–C2; *MEED,* June 3, 1983, p. 38; *JPRS,* 80603, no. 2527, April 19, 1982, pp. 96–98; *Mideast File,* March 1982, p. 129.

93. *FBIS,* August 19, 1982, pp. C1–C2; *MEED,* March 25, 1983; *FBIS,* July 10, 1980, p. A11.

94. Nyrop, *Persian Gulf States,* p. 324; Cottrell, *A General Survey,* p. 164.

95. *Mideast File,* December 1982, pp. 564–65; ibid., March 1983, p. 144; *MEED,* May 27, 1983, p. 22; Hill, "Population, Migration and Development," p. 69.

96. *FBIS,* August 19, 1982, pp. C1–C2; *The Economist,* February 19, 1983, p. 26; *MEED,* June 3, 1983, p. 28; Cordesman, "Oman," pp. 22–23, p. 30; Cottrell, *A General Survey,* p. 159.

97. See also Binder, *The Ideological Revolution,* p. 154; Daniel Pipes, " 'This World Is Political!!' The Islamic Revival of the Seventies," *Orbis* 24 (Spring 1980): 10–17; Nabeel Khoury, "The Pragmatic Trend in Inter-Arab Politics," *Middle East Journal* 36 (Summer 1982): 374–86.

98. Hudson, *Arab Politics,* p. 246.

99. Pipes, "Islamic Revival," p. 33; James A. Bill, "Power and Religion in Revolutionary Iran," *Middle East Journal* 36 (Winter 1982): 24–27; Kambiz Afrachteh, "Iran," *The Politics of Islamic Reassertion,* ed. Mohammed Ayoob (London: Croom Helm, 1981), pp. 101–103.

100. Rubin, "Iran," pp. 148–150; Bill, "Power and Religion in Revolutionary Iran," pp. 35–41.

101. Rubin, "Iran," p. 152; *Mideast File,* vol. 4, December 1982, p. 544.

102. See Bill, "Power and Religion in Revolutionary Iran," p. 47; Afrachteh, "Iran," pp. 111–117.

103. Rubin, "Iran," pp. 147–48; Afrachteh, "Iran," p. 114; Ervand Abrahamian, *Iran between Two Revolutions* (Princeton, N.J.: Princeton Univ. Press, 1982), pp. 483–95.

104. *NYT,* May 5, 1983, pp. 1, A6; *MEED,* May 13, 1983, p. 27; Rubin, "Iran," p. 148; *MEED,* February 11, 1983, p. 22.

105. *NYT,* January 10, 1983, p. A4; *QER,IN,* (1st Quarter 1983), p. 8; Rubin, "Iran," p. 148; Afrachteh, "Iran," p. 114; *JPRS,* 82594, no. 2688. January 5, 1983, pp. 5–8.

106. Gordon H. Torrey, "The Ba'th—Ideology and Practice," *Middle East Journal* 23 (Autumn 1969): 445; Hanna Batatu, *The Old Social Classes and the Revolutionary Movements of Iraq* (Princeton, N.J.: Princeton Univ. Press, 1978), p. 1077; see also Kamel S. Abu Jaber, *The Arab Ba'th Socialist Party* (Syracuse, N.Y.: Syracuse Univ. Press, 1966), pp. 97–138; Binder, pp. 160–92.

107. Jaber, "Ba'th Socialist Party," pp. 9–15, 52–54.

108. Batatu, *Old Social Classes,* pp. 1085–94; *NYT,* January 11, 1981, E5; Marr, "Iraq," p. 35.

109. Batatu, *Old Social Classes,* p. 1098; Marr, "Iraq," pp. 34–35; *Mideast File,* December 1982, p. 495; Claudia Wright, "Behind Iraq's Bold Bid," *New York Times Magazine,* October 26, 1980, p. 114.

110. Ronald MacIntyre, "Saudi Arabia," *The Politics of Islamic Reassertion,* ed. Mohammed Ayoob (London: Croom Helm, 1981), pp. 12–15.

111. Pipes, "Islamic Revival," pp. 26–29; MacIntyre, "Saudi Arabia," pp. 22–27.

112. Fisher, *The Middle East,* p. 523; MacIntyre, "Saudi Arabia," pp. 16–17.

113. Hudson, *Arab Politics,* pp. 6, 244, 247–51, 354.

114. Peterson, *Yemen,* p. 133 n. 38; *QER,BQOY,* (2d Quarter, 1981), p. 15.

115. Hudson, *Arab Politics,* pp. 354–56.

116. Haim Shaked and Tamar Yegnes, "The People's Democratic Republic of Yemen," *MECS,* vol. 2, 1977–78, pp. 655–56; "South Yemen: The Heart of Darkness," *Armed Forces Journal International* (November 1980), p. 82.

117. *QER,BQOY,* Annual Supplement, 1981, pp. 60–61.

118. Jacob Goldberg, "People's Democratic Republic of Yemen,"

MECS, vol. 4, 1979–80, pp. 660–61; "South Yemen," *Armed Forces Journal International, p. 82.*

119. Hudson, *Arab Politics,* pp. 356–59; *FBIS,* January 22, 1980, p. C4–C5.

120. Goldberg, "Yemen," 1979–80, p. 722; Jacob Goldberg, "The People's Democratic Republic of Yemen," *MECS,* vol. 3, 1978–79, p. 724; Jacob Goldberg, "People's Democratic Republic of Yemen," *MECS,* vol. 5, 1980–81, pp. 720, 723.

121. J.E. Peterson, *Oman in the Twentieth Century Political Foundations of an Emerging State* (London: Croom Helm, 1978), pp. 187–88. The population of the Dhofar province is accounted by Peterson at anywhere from 60,000 to 130,000. See also Grax, *The Omanis,* p. 35.

122. Peterson, *Oman,* pp. 188–89; Graz, *The Omanis,* p. 40.

123. Peterson, *Oman,* pp. 191–93; Hudson, *Arab Politics,* p. 363; Anthony, "Dhofar," p. 294.

124. Graz, *The Omanis,* p. 41; Cordesman, "Oman," p. 27.

125. Flint, "The Gulf States," *MECS,* vol. 3, p. 461; Esther Webman, "The Gulf States," *MECS,* vol. 4, 1979–80, pp. 413–414.

126. Webman, "Gulf States," *MECS,* vol. 5, 1980–81, pp. 491–492; Webman, "Gulf States," *MECS,* vol. 4, 1979–80, p. 414.

127. Hudson, *Arab Politics,* pp. 97–98, 190, 193, 199, 202.

128. Plascov, *Modernization, Political Development,* pp. 93–94; Webman, "Gulf States," 1979–80, p. 398; Webman, "Gulf States," 1980–81, p. 468.

129. Webman, "Gulf States," 1980–81, p. 474; Plascov, *Modernization, Political Development,* pp. 93–94.

130. Webman, "Gulf States," 1979–80, p. 423.

131. Plascov, *Modernization, Political Development,* p. 95; Webman, "Gulf States," 1980–81, pp. 503–504.

132. Nyrop, *Iran,* pp. 59–65; Abrahamian, *Iran between Revolutions,* pp. 424–26.

133. Nyrop, *Saudi Arabia,* pp. 36–37; George Lenczowski, *The Middle East in World Affairs,* 4th. ed. (Ithaca, N.Y.: Cornell Univ. Press, 1980), pp. 588–89, 593–98.

134. Hudson, *Arab Politics,* pp. 190, 198.

135. Abrahamian, *Iran between Revolutions,* pp. 233–237.

Chapter 5

1. See W. Scott Thompson, "The Persian Gulf and the Correlation of Forces," *International Security* 7 (Summer 1982): 159; Albert Wohl-

stetter, "Meeting the Threat in the Persian Gulf," *Survey* 25 (Spring 1980): 140; J.B. Kelly, *Arabia, The Gulf and the West* (New York: Basic Books, 1980), pp. 459–77.

2. See Hermann F. Eilts, "Security Considerations in the Persian Gulf," *International Security* 5 (Fall 1980): 80–81; Keith A. Dunn, "Constraints on the USSR in Southwest Asia: A Military Analysis," *Orbis* 25 (Fall 1981): 610–11, 627; see also David D. Newsom, "America Engulfed," *Foreign Policy* 43 (Summer 1981): 19.

3. See James H. Noyes, *The Clouded Lens* (Stanford, Calif.: Hoover Institution Press, 1979), p. 47, citing The Central Intelligence Agency report of April 1977 (CIA, *The International Energy Situation: Outlook to 1985*, ER 77-10240 U, April 1977; Gordon B. Smith, "C.I.A. Views on Soviet Oil: Risky," *NYT*, July 13, 1981, p. A15. Marshall I. Goldman, *The Enigma of Soviet Petroleum Half-Full or Half-Empty?* (London: George Allen and Unwin, 1980, p. 173), and William B. Quandt, *Saudi Arabia in the 1980s* (Washington, D.C.: Brookings, 1982), p. 166.

4. Thompson, "Gulf and Correlation of Forces," p. 166; Wohlstetter, "Meeting the Threat in the Gulf," pp. 161–62; Richard F. Nyrop, *Iran: A Country Study* (Washington, D.C.: American Univ., 1978), pp. 52, 55–58; Barry Rubin, *Paved with Good Intentions: The American Experience and Iran* (Harmondsworth, England: Penguin Books, 1981), pp. 29–36.

5. Dunn, "Constraints on the USSR in Southwest Asia," pp. 617–625; Newsom, "America Engulfed," pp. 18–19. Geoffrey Kemp, "Military Force and Middle East Oil," in David A. Deese and Joseph S. Nye, eds. *Energy and Security* (Cambridge, Mass.: Ballinger, 1981), p. 379.

6. See Roberta Wohlstetter, *Pearl Harbor: Warning and Decision* (Stanford, Calif.: Stanford Univ. Press, 1962), pp. 364–67.

7. Robert O. Freedman, *Soviet Policy toward the Middle East since 1970,* 3d. ed. (New York: Praeger, 1982), pp. 78–83.

8. Francis Fukuyama, "The Soviet Union and Iraq since 1968," Rand Note N-1524-AF, Rand Corporation, July 1980, pp. vi–vii.

9. Karen Dawisha, "The U.S.S.R. in the Middle East: Superpower in Eclipse?" *Foreign Affairs* 61 (Winter 1982–83): 446. Stephen R. Grummon, *The Iran–Iraq War,* The Washington Papers, vol. 92 (New York: Praeger, 1982) p. 67.

10. Shahram Chubin, *Security in the Persian Gulf, vol 4: The Role of Outside Powers* (Montclair, N.J.: Allenheld Osmun, 1982), p. 29.

11. Tamar Yenges, "The Yemeni Arab Republic," *MECS*, vol. 1,

1976–77, p. 662; Haim Shaked and Tamar Yenges, "The Yemeni Arab Republic," *MECS,* vol. 2, 1977–78, p. 804; Jacob Goldberg, "The Yemeni Arab Republic," *MECS,* vol. 3, 1978–79, p. 898.

12. Christopher Van Hollen, "North Yemen: A Dangerous Pentagonal Game," *Washington Quarterly* 15 (Summer 1982): 138–40; "North Yemen: The Shadow Game," *Armed Forces Journal International* (November 1980): 82; Freedman, *Soviet Policy toward the Middle East,* pp. 352–53.

13. Jacob Goldberg, "People's Democratic Republic of Yemen," *MECS,* vol. 5, 1980–81, p. 720; see also, "South Yemen: A Slow Move towards the West," *The Middle East* (August 1982): 20–21.

14. Blake, "Maritime Aspects of Arabian Geopolitics," Arab Papers no. 11 (London: Arab Research Centre, 1982), pp. 26, 29; Anthony H. Cordesman, "Oman: The Guardian of the Eastern Gulf," *Armed Forces Journal International* (June 1983), p. 27; *WSJ,* October 11, 1983, p. 2.

15. Blake, "Maritime Aspects," pp. 29–31.

16. L. Thomas Walsh, "Bab-el-Mandeb: The Gateway of Tears for the US?" *Armed Forces Journal International* (September 1980): 74; Blake, "Maritime Aspects," p. 26.

17. *QER,E,* (2d Quarter, 1982), p. 14.

18. *QER,E,* (1st Quarter, 1982), p. 12.

19. Blake, "Maritime Aspects," p. 29.

20. A. Wohlstetter, "Meeting the Threat in the Persian Gulf," pp. 143, 145; Blake, "Maritime Aspects," p. 31.

21. *QER, BQOY* (4th Quarter, 1980), p. 18.

22. Walsh, "Bab-el-Mendeb," p. 76.

23. Jeffrey Record, *The Rapid Deployment Force and U.S. Military Intervention in the Persian Gulf* (Cambridge, Mass.: Institute for Foreign Policy Analysis, 1981), pp. 58–60

24. *NYT,* October 25, 1982, p. A14; ibid., May 20, 1983, p. A8; ibid., June 24, 1983, p. A9; *Strategic Survey 1982–1983* (London: International Institute for Strategic Studies, 1983), p. 136.

25. John M. Collins, *U.S.–Soviet Military Balance: Concepts and Capabilities 1960–1980* (New York: McGraw-Hill, 1980), p. 375.

26. Thompson, "Gulf and the Correlation of Forces," p. 174; A. Wohlstetter, "Meeting the Threat in the Persian Gulf," pp. 180–81; *NYT,* October 25, 1982, p. A14; *Strategic Survey 1982–83,* p. 136.

27. Cordesman, "Oman," pp. 22, 26–27, 30; *QER,BQOY,* (2d Quarter, 1980), p. 16.

28. *FT,* November 4, 1980, p. II; *Time,* October 25, 1982, p. 49.

29. See Anthony H. Cordesman, "The Changing Military Balance in the Gulf and Middle East," *Armed Forces Journal International* (September 1981): 52, 54–56, 58, 60; *Newsweek,* October 13, 1980, p. 60; *NYT,* April 2, 1981, pp. 1, A5; *NYT,* February 10, 1982, p. A14.

30. *Strategic Survey 1982–1983,* p. 136; *NYT,* April 4, 1983, p. A3; Cordesman, "Military Balance," p. 56.

31. *Strategic Survey 1982–83,* p. 136.

32. *The Economist,* December 11, 1982, p. 62; Record, *Rapid Deployment Force,* p. 55.

33. See Thompson, "Gulf and the Correlation of Forces," pp. 173–76.

34. *The Economist,* December 11, 1982, p. 63; *NYT,* October 25, 1982, p. A14.

35. *QER,BQOY,* (3rd Quarter, 1982): 16; Webman, "Gulf States," *MECS* vol. 5, 1980–81, pp. 493–94.

Chapter 6

1. John M. Collins, *U.S.–Soviet Military Balance, Concepts and Capabilities 1960–1980* (New York: McGraw-Hill, 1980), p. 382; Kenneth N. Waltz, "A Strategy for the Rapid Deployment Force," *International Security* 15 (September 1981): 62–63. Waltz cites a secret Defense Department study of 1979 (known as The Wolfowitz Report) summarized in Richard Burt, "U.S. Sees Need for Nuclear Arms to Repel a Soviet Attack on Iran," *NYT,* February 2, 1980, p. 1 (p. 59, n. 13). See also Christopher Van Hollen, "Don't Engulf the Gulf," *Foreign Affairs* 59 (Summer 1981): 1067; also Joseph S. Nye, David A. Deese, Alvin L. Alm, "Conclusion: A U.S. Strategy for Energy Security," in David A. Deese and Joseph A. Nye, *Energy and Security* (Cambridge, Mass.: Ballinger, 1981) p. 411.

2. William B. Quandt, *Saudi Arabia's Oil Policy* (Washington, D.C.: Brookings, 1982), p. 34. Collins, "U.S.–Soviet Military Balance," p. 392.

3. Collins, "U.S.–Soviet Military Balance," pp. 379, 382; G. Henry M. Schuler, "Coping with Oil Dependence," *Washington Quarterly* 6 (Winter 1983): 55.

4. *QER,UAE,* (1st Quarter, 1981): 6

5. *QER,UAE,* (3rd Quarter, 1982): 14–15; John M. Gault, "Middle Eastern Oil Producers: New Strength or New Vulnerability," in David A. Partington, *The Middle East Annual: Issues and Events,* vol. 1 (Boston: G.K. Hall, 1982), p. 174.

6. Quandt, *Oil,* p. 34; Collins, "U.S.–Soviet Military Balance," pp. 383–84.

7. See also *WSJ,* October 11, 1983, p. 2.

8. See Schuler, "Coping with Oil Dependence," p. 54; Arlon R. Tussing, "An OPEC Obituary," *Public Interest* (Winter 1983): 3; Joseph S. Nye, "Energy and Security," in Deese and Nye, *Energy and Security,* p. 11; *Newsweek,* September 12, 1983, pp. 57–58; *WSJ,* October 5, 1983, p. D24.

9. Quandt, *Saudi Arabia,* p. 165; see also Tussing, "OPEC Obituary," p. 17.

10. See note 3 of chapter 5.

11. *WSJ,* August 29, 1983, p. 13; ibid., September 14, 1983, p. 14.

12. *NYT,* October 5, 1983, p. D24.

13. Alvin L. Alm, William Colglazier, Barbara Kates-Garnick, "Coping with Interruptions," in Deese and Nye, *Energy and Security,* pp. 325, 329–32.

14. *NYT,* August 2, 1983, p. A18; ibid., September 25, 1983, p. 52; *WSJ,* September 30, 1983, p. 2; *Newsweek,* September 12, 1983, p. 60; James L. Plummer, "United States Oil Stockpiling Policy," *Journal of Contemporary Studies* 4 (Spring 1981): 8–9.

15. *Newsweek,* January 24, 1983, p. 55; ibid., September 12, 1983, p. 58; *WSJ,* September 23, 1983, pp. 1, 22; *NYT,* November 9, 1983, p. A15; see also Henry S. Rowen and John P. Weyant, "Oil and National Security: An Integrated Program for Surviving an Oil Crisis," *Annual Review of Energy* 6 (1981): 185.

16. *NYT,* September 25, 1983, p. 52; *Newsweek,* November 12, 1983, p. 58.

17. *WSJ,* September 26, 1983, p. 33.

18. *NYT,* August 7, 1983, p. 1; see also Peter R. Odell, "Towards a Geographically Reshaped World Oil Industry," *World Today* 37 (December 1981): 448, 452–453.

19. Alm et al., "Coping," p. 324; *WSJ,* July 8, 1983, pp. 1, 9; *BP Statistical Review of World Energy 1982,* British Petroleum Company, 1983, pp. 4, 6, 14; *Exxon Background Series,* Exxon Corporation, New York, May 1982, p. 11; *WSJ,* September 14, 1983, p. 14; *Newsweek,* September 12, 1983, p. 58.

20. *WSJ,* September 14, 1983, p. 14.

21. See Walter J. Levy, "Oil: An Agenda for the 1980s," *Foreign Affairs* 59 (Summer 1981): 1089–94; Nye, "Energy and Security," pp. 18–20.

22. Nye et al., "Conclusion," p. 394.

23. *WSJ,* September 14, 1983, p. 14; ibid., September 26, 1983, p. 33.

24. Alm et al, "Coping," pp. 329–44.

25. The Library of Congress Congressional Research Service, *Western Vulnerability to a Disruption Of Persian Gulf Oil Supplies: U.S. Interests And Options,* Report 83-24F, March 24, 1983, p. 80.

26. See ibid., pp. 53–61 for explication of the IEA allocation formula and activation methods; Nye et al., "Conclusion," pp. 427–430; Alm et al., "Coping," pp. 317–322. Melvin A. Conant, *The Oil Factor in U.S. Foreign Policy, 1980–1990* (Lexington, Mass.: Lexington Books, 1982), pp. 74–76.

27. Rowen and Weyant, "Oil and National Security," p. 194; Alm et al., "Coping," p. 323.

28. Kelly, *Arabia,* pp. 388–423, 494–495; Quandt, *Oil,* pp. 9–21; Gault, "Middle Eastern Oil Producers," pp. 174–178; Nye, "Energy and Security," p. 10.

29. Kelly, *Arabia,* pp. 400–401.

30. Ibid.

31. Ibid., p. 495.

32. See Feith, "The Oil Weapon," pp. 27–31; Schuler, "Coping with Oil Dependence," pp. 57–58; Quandt, *Oil,* pp. 28–29; S. Fred Singer and Stephen Stamas, "An End to OPEC?" *Foreign Policy* (Winter 1981–82): 116; Kelly, *Arabia,* p. 456–57; Conant, *The Oil Factor,* p. 74; William R. Brown, "The Oil Weapon," *Middle East Journal* 36 (Summer 1982): 310–18; Noyes, pp. 93–94.

33. Schuler, "Coping with Oil Dependence," p. 58.

34. See notes 10 and 13 of chapter 2.

35. Haim Shaked, "The Nuclearization of the Middle East: The Israeli Raid of Osirak," *MECS,* vol. 5, 1980–81, p. 195. Shai Feldman, *Israeli Nuclear Deterrence: A Strategy for the 1980s* (New York: Columbia Univ. Press, 1982), pp. 77–78.

36. Ibid., pp. 71–83.

Appendix B

1. All information is from *The Military Balance 1983–84* (London: International Institute for Strategic Studies, 1983), pp. 52–65. The *Military Balance* provides its data as of July 1983. All dollar figures are in billions of U.S. dollars.

2. GNP is gross national product.

3. GDP is gross domestic product, which is GNP less net income from abroad (*Military Balance,* p. vi).

4. Oil exports in 1983 are subject to an OPEC quota for each member. Iran's quota was 2.4 mbd; Iraq's 1.2 mbd. There are varying reports as to Iran's oil exports not meeting or exceeding that quota in

1983. (See *NYT,* November 24, 1983, p. D1; *WSJ,* November 8, 1983, p. 38.) Iraq's exports were limited by the unavailability of its Gulf ports and pipeline through Syria to the Mediterranean because of the Iraq–Iran war. The capacity of the one available pipeline through Turkey was increased during 1983 from 650,000 bd to 800,000 bd (*NYT,* November 25, 1983, p. A14).

5. These figures exclude wartime expenditures for reconstruction of destroyed and damaged facilities.

6. Iraq received approximately $13 billion in aid from Saudi Arabia, Kuwait, and the UAE in 1983 (*NYT,* December 11, 1983, p. A21). About the same amount was provided in 1982 (*Newsweek,* August 15, 1983, p. 34). Some of these funds are from sales of approximately 300,000 bd of oil by Saudi Arabia and Kuwait on behalf of Iraq (*WSJ,* August 19, 1983. p. 9).

7. These are subject to wartime losses. Losses during the first three years of the Iraq–Iran war have been estimated as 150,000 dead, 400,000 wounded, and 45,000 captured of Iran's forces; 150,000 in all categories for Iraq (*WSJ,* December 9, 1983, p. 18; ibid., August 19, 1983, p. 9).

8. Of these 400,000 are regular reserves; 150,000 are Revolutionary Guards.

9. These include the Iranian *Hezbollahi* ('Home Guard'); see William F. Hickman, *Ravaged and Reborn: The Iranian Army, 1982* (Washington, D.C.: Brookings, 1982), pp. 13–14. Other Iranian militia forces, not numbered by *Military Balance,* include youth volunteers, Gendarmerie, and Border Tribal Militia. Iraq also has 4,800 security troops and 10,000 volunteers from Arab countries.

10. Combat vehicles refers to tanks, armored personnel carriers, and similar armored fighting vehicles; it excludes self-propelled, towed, or other artillery.

11. Delivery dates have not been provided for weaponry on order.

12. Wartime losses to ships have been reported as 11–12 for Iran; 16–19 for Iraq.

13. Combat aircraft refers to bombers and fighters; it excludes reconnaissance, trainers, and transport aircraft. Iran possesses more aircraft but only 70 are considered serviceable. (*NYT,* November 25, 1983, p. A14). See also Anthony H. Cordesman, "Lessons of the Iran–Iraq War: The First Round," *Armed Forces Journal International* (April 1980), pp. 40, 43.

14. Iran is also scheduled to receive an unspecified number of North Korean MIG-19 and MIG-21 fighters. Iraq has also received 5 French Super Etandard bombers and Exocet missiles, previously reported as on order. (*NYT,* November 9, 1983, p. A3).

15. Air defense refers to missile defense systems and not antiair-

craft artillery. The Hawk and Improved Hawk are U.S. systems. The SA-2, etc., are Soviet made.

16. See the discussion of aliens in chapter 4 for the numbers of aliens that may be included in these population figures.

17. Only three of the seven constituents of the UAE export oil, the mainstay of the UAE's GNP: Abu Dhabi, Dubai, and Sharjah.

18. Oil revenues contribute to approximately two-thirds of Saudi Arabia's GNP, and its foreign reserves have been estimated at from $150–$200 billion. *MEED,* April 15, 1983, p. 52; *WSJ,* April 14, 1983, p. 2; G. Henry M. Schuler, "Coping with Oil Dependence," *Washington Quarterly* 6 (Winter 1983): 58. Kuwait's foreign investments have been estimated between $70–$100 billion, much of the income of which is dedicated to Kuwait's Fund for Future Generations (for revenues after depletion of its oil reserves) (*WSJ,* August 10, 1983, p. 29; *NYT,* February 15, 1983, pp. 1, A14).

19. Saudi Arabia has an implied quota limitation imposed on exports of oil by OPEC of 5 mbd. In 1983 Saudi production varied over the year and was reported as averaging 3.2 mbd in the first quarter. (*MEED,* April 15, 1983, p. 52; *WSJ,* July 7, 1983, p. 26; ibid., December 28, 1983, p. 2, reports 3.5 mbd as the lowest production in 1983.) OPEC's quota for Kuwait was 1.2 mbd (*NYT,* January 18, 1984, p. 33).

20. These estimates are for different years: Saudi Arabia, 1983–84; Kuwait, 1981–82; and the UAE, 1982.

21. Of these 25,000 constitute the National Guard; 10,000, foreign contract military personnel.

22. The Saudi forces are the Frontier Force and Coastguard; the Kuwaiti forces are police.

23. The Saudis have also ordered upgrading kits for their 150 U.S. made battle tanks.

24. Kuwait's navy is composed of coastal patrol craft only.

25. The Saudi air defense system also includes the use of American AWACS. The Shahine missile is French made and is apparently designed to protect tank forces.

26. Orders for approximately $4.5 billion have been placed for Shahine systems in January, 1984 by Saudi Arabia, and for $140 million by Kuwait (*NYT,* January 17, 1984, pp. 1, A14; *WSJ,* January 17, 1984, p. 35).

27. The United States also supplies military assistance to Oman (*MEED,* April 1, 1983, pp. 34–35). Bahrain no longer exports oil. It is reported as receiving subsidies from Saudi Arabia, Kuwait, and the UAE (*NYT,* March 6, 1983, p. 20). Qatar has estimated foreign reserves of $9 billion (*MEED,* February 18, 1983, p. 35).

28. *BP Statistical Review of World Energy* 1982, British Petroleum Company, 1983, p. 4.

29. The Omani forces are the *Firqat* ('Home Guard').

30. The Bahraini forces are its Coastguard.

31. Bahrain presently has only a helicopter force.

32. Foreign aid estimates for North Yemen include approximately $350–450 million from Saudi Arabia annually, and approximately $1–1.5 billion in military assistance from the Soviet Union (*CSM*, January 12, 1983, p. 13).

33. The North Yemeni force is composed of 20,000 tribal levies and 5,000 National Security Forces.

34. See chapter 4 for a description of alien components of GCC state populations included in this figure.

35. This includes the UAE's GNP figure.

36. This includes figures from different years.

37. The GCC has reportedly discussed the formation of a 100,000 troop joint military force (*WSJ*, November 7, 1983, p. 38).

Appendix C

1. All information is from *The Military Balance 1983–84* (London: International Institute for Strategic Studies, 1983), pp. 11–18, except as noted.

2. *NYT*, December 26, 1983, p. A8.

3. See Keith A. Dunn, "Constraints on the USSR in Southwest Asia: A Military Analysis," *Orbis* 25 (Fall 1981): 613–14.

4. Ibid., p. 614.

Appendix D

1. Information has been obtained primarily from *The Military Balance 1983–84* (London: International Institute for Strategic Studies, 1983), pp. 3–10, as well as *Strategic Survey 1982–1983* (London: International Institute for Strategic Studies, 1983), pp. 133–38; "Rapid Deployment Force: Will Europe Help American Help Europe?," *Economist,* December 11, 1982, pp. 62–64; Jeffrey Record, *The Rapid Deployment Force and U.S. Military Intervention in the Persian Gulf* (Cambridge, Mass.: Institute for Foreign Policy Analysis, 1981); "Special U.S. Force for Persian Gulf is Growing Swiftly," *NYT,* October 25, 1982, pp. 1, A14.

2. Record estimates from 2 days for the delivery of the first elements of any unit to 6 days to 50 days for "closure" (delivery of the last elements of the units involved) (*Rapid Deployment Force,* p. 21).

Bibliography

Books and Pamphlets

Abrahamian, Ervand. *Iran between Two Revolutions.* Princeton, N.J.: Princeton Univ. Press, 1982.

Abu Jaber, Kamel S. *The Arab Ba'th Socialist Party.* Syracuse, N.Y.: Syracuse Univ. Press, 1966.

Alessa, S.Y. *The Manpower Problem in Kuwait.* Boston: Kegan Paul International, 1981.

Arab Ba'th Socialist Party, The. *Political Report: Tenth National Congress.* Iraq: The National Bureau of Culture, 1976.

Ayoob, Mohammed, ed. *The Politics of Islamic Reassertion.* London: Croom Helm, 1981.

Bakhash, Shaul. *The Politics of Oil and Revolution in Iran.* Washington, D.C.: The Brookings Institution, 1982.

Batatu, Hanna. *The Old Social Classes and the Revolutionary Movements of Iraq.* Princeton, N.J.: Princeton Univ. Press, 1978.

Bidwell, Robin, ed. *The Affairs of Kuwait 1896–1905.* 2 vols. London: Frank Cass, 1971.

Binder, Leonard. *The Ideological Revolution in the Middle East.* New York: John Wiley and Sons, 1964.

British Petroleum Company, The. *BP Statistical Review of World Energy.* England: Dix Motive Press, 1982.

Burrell, R.M. *The Persian Gulf.* The Washington Papers, vol. 1, no. 1. Beverly Hills, Calif.: Sage Publications, 1972.

Chubin, Shahram. *Soviet Policy Towards Iran and the Gulf.* Adelphi Papers, no. 157. London: International Institute for Strategic Studies, 1980.

Chubin, Shahram. *Security in the Persian Gulf: Domestic Political Factors.* vol. 1. Montclair, N.J.: Allanheld and Osmun, 1981.

Chubin, Shahram. *Security in the Persian Gulf: The Role of Outside Powers.* vol. 4. Montclair, N.J.: Allanheld and Osmum, 1982.

Clements, F.A. *Oman: The Reborn Land.* London: Longman, 1980.

Collins, John M. *U.S.–Soviet Military Balance, Concepts and Capabilities 1960–1980.* New York: McGraw-Hill, 1980.

Conant, Melvin A. *The Oil Factor in U.S. Foreign Policy, 1980–1990.* Lexington, Mass.: Lexington Books, 1982.

Congressional Research Service. *Western Vulnerability to a Disruption of Persian Gulf Oil Supplies: U.S. Interest and Options.* Report 83-24F. Washington, D.C.: The Library of Congress, 1983.

Conoco. *World Energy Outlook through 2000.* Coordinating and Planning Department of Conoco, Inc., Stamford, Conn., 1983.

Cottrell, Alvin J., and Associates. *Sea Power and Strategy in the Indian Ocean.* Beverly Hills, Calif.: Sage Publications, 1981.

Cottrell, Alvin J., ed. *The Persian Gulf States.* Baltimore: The Johns Hopkins Univ. Press, 1980.

Cottrell, Alvin J., and Frank Bray. *Military Forces in the Persian Gulf.* Washington Papers, vol. 6, no. 60. Beverly Hills, Calif.: Sage Publications, 1978.

Dann, Uriel. *Iraq under Qassem.* New York: Praeger, 1969.

Deese, David A., and Joseph S. Nye, eds. *Energy and Security.* Cambridge, Mass.: Ballinger, 1981.

Dickson, H.R.P. *Kuwait and Her Neighbors.* London: George Allen and Unwin, 1956.

Donaldson, Robert H. *The Soviet Union in the Third World: Successes and Failures.* Boulder, Colo.: Westview Press, 1981.

Earle, Edward Mead. *Turkey, the Great Powers and the Bagdad Railway.* New York: MacMillan, 1923.

Exxon Corporation. *How Much Oil and Gas?* Public Affairs Department of Exxon Corporation, New York, 1982.

Farid, Abdel Majid, ed. *Oil and Security in the Arabian Gulf.* London: Croom Helm, 1981.

Feldman, Shai. *Israeli Nuclear Deterrence.* New York: Columbia Univ. Press, 1982.

Fischer, Michael M.J. *Iran: From Religious Dispute to Revolution.* Cambridge, Mass.: Harvard Univ. Press, 1980.

Fisher, W.B. *The Middle East: A Physical, Social and Regional Geography.* London: Methuen, 1978.

Forbis, William H. *Fall of the Peacock Throne.* New York: McGraw-Hill, 1981.

Freedman, Robert O. *Soviet Policy toward the Middle East since 1970.* New York: Praeger, 1982.

Fukayama, Francis. *The Soviet Union and Iraq since 1968.* Rand Note N-1524-AF. Rand Corporation, Santa Monica, Calif., 1980.

Gallagher, Charles F. *Contemporary Islam: The Plateau of Particularism, Problems of Religion and Nationalism in Iran.* Asia Series, vol. 15, no. 2. New York: American Universities Field Staff, 1966.

Gavin, R.J. *Aden under British Rule, 1839–1967.* London: C. Hurst, 1975.

Ghareeb, Edmund. *The Kurdish Question in Iraq.* Syracuse, N.Y.: Syracuse Univ. Press, 1981.

Gibb, H.A.R. *Mohammedanism.* New York: Oxford Univ. Press, 1972.

Goldman, Marshall I. *The Enigma of Soviet Petroleum: Half-Full or Half-Empty?* London: George Allen and Unwin, 1980.

Gooch, G.P. *Before the War, Studies in Diplomacy,* 2 vols. London: Longmans, Green, 1936 (vol. 1) and 1938 (vol. 2).

Gooch, G.P., and Harold Temperly, eds. *British Documents on the Origins of the War, 1898–1914,* vol. 1: *The Near and Middle East on the Eve of the War.* London: His Majesty's Stationery Office, 1936.

Gooch, G.P. and Harold Temperly, eds. *British Documents on the Origins of the War, 1898–1914,* vol. 10: *The Last Years of Peace.* London: His Majesty's Stationery Office, 1938.

Graves, Philip. *The Life of Sir Percy Cox.* London: Hutchinson, 1941.

Graz, Liesl. *The Omanis: Sentinels of the Gulf.* London: Longman, 1982.

Grummon, Stephen R. *The Iran–Iraq War.* New York: Praeger, 1982.

Hale, Oran J. *The Great Illusion, 1900–1914.* New York: Harper & Row, 1971.

Harwich, George, and Edward J. Mitchell, eds. *Policies for Coping with Oil Supply Disruptions.* Washington, D.C.: American Enterprise Institute for Public Policy Research, 1982.

Hawley, Donald. *The Trucial States.* London: George Allen and Unwin, 1970.

Hickman, William F. *Ravaged and Reborn: The Iranian Army, 1982.* Washington, D.C.: The Brookings Institution, 1982.

Hudson, Michael C. *Arab Politics.* New Haven, Conn.: Yale Univ. Press, 1977.

Hurewitz, J.C. *Diplomacy in the Near and Middle East,* 2 vols. Princeton, N.J.: D. Van Nostrand, 1956.

Hussein, Saddam. *Social and Foreign Affairs in Iraq,* trans. Khalid Kishtainy. London: Croom Helm, 1979.

International Institute for Strategic Studies, The. *Strategic Survey, 1982–1983.* London: IISS, 1983.

International Institute for Strategic Studies, The. *The Military Balance, 1982–1983.* London: IISS, 1982.

Ismael, Tareq Y. *Iraq and Iran.* Syracuse, N.Y.: Syracuse Univ. Press, 1982.

Jane's All the World's Aircraft, 1980–81.

Jane's Fighting Ships, 1982–83.

Jane's Weapon Systems, 1980–81.

Kaplan, Morton A. *System and Process in International Politics.* New York: John Wiley and Sons, 1957.

Kaplan, Morton A. "Some Problems of International Systems Research." *In International Political Communities*. Garden City, N.Y.: Doubleday Anchor, 1966.

Kaplan, Morton A. *New Approaches to International Politics*. New York: St. Martin's Press, 1968.

Kaplan, Morton A. "The Systems Approach to International Politics." *In New Approaches to International Relations*. New York: St. Martin's Press, 1968.

Kaplan, Morton A. *Macro Politics*. Chicago: Aldine, 1969.

Kedourie, Elie. *Islam in the Modern World*. New York: Holt, Rinehart and Winston, 1980.

Kelly, J.B. *Arabia, the Gulf and the West*. New York: Basic Books, 1980.

Kelly, J.B. *Eastern Arabian Frontiers*. New York: Praeger, 1964.

Kerr, Malcolm H. *The Arab Cold War*. London: Oxford Univ. Press, 1971.

Khadduri, Majid. *Socialist Iraq: A Study in Iraqi Politics since 1968*. Washington, D.C.: The Middle East Institute, 1978.

Khalifa, Ali Mohammed. *The United Arab Emirates: Unity in Fragmentation*. Boulder, Colo.: Westview Press, 1979.

Kinross, Lord. *The Ottoman Centuries*. New York: William Morrow, 1977.

Koury, Enver M. *The Arabian Peninsula, Red Sea and Gulf: Strategic Considerations*. Hyattsville, Md.: The Institute of Middle Eastern and North African Affairs, 1979.

Kramer, Martin. *Political Islam*. The Washington Papers, vol. 8, no. 73. Beverly Hills, Calif.: Sage Publications, 1980.

Landen, Robert Geran. *Oman since 1856*. Princeton, N.J.: Princeton Univ. Press, 1967.

Langer, William L. *The Diplomacy of Imperialism, 1890–1902*, vol. 2. New York: Alfred A. Knopf, 1935.

Legum, Colin, and Haim Shaked, eds. *Middle East Contemporary Survey*, vol. 1, 1976–1977. New York: Holmes and Meier, 1978.

Legum, Colin; Haim Shaked and Daniel Dishon, eds. *Middle East Contemporary Survey*, vol. 2., 1977–78. New York: Holmes and Meier, 1979.

Legum, Colin; Haim Shaked and Daniel Dishon, eds. *Middle East Contemporary Survey*, vol. 3, 1978–79. New York: Holmes and Meier, 1980.

Legum, Colin; Haim Shaked and Daniel Dishon, eds. *Middle East Contemporary Survey*, vol. 4, 1979–80. New York: Holmes and Meier, 1981.

Legum, Colin; Haim Shaked and Daniel Dishon, eds. *Middle East Contemporary Survey,* vol. 5, 1980–81. New York: Holmes and Meier, 1982.

Lenczowski, George. *The Middle East in World Affairs,* 4th ed. Ithaca, N.Y.: Cornell Univ. Press, 1980.

Lenczowski, George. *Russia and the West in Iran, 1918–1948.* Ithaca, N.Y.: Cornell Univ. Press, 1949.

Litwak, Robert. *Security in the Persian Gulf 2: Sources of Inter-State Conflict.* The International Institute for Strategic Studies. Montclair, N.J.: Allanheld and Osmun, 1981.

Longrigg, Stephen Hemsley. *Four Centuries of Modern Iraq.* Oxford: Clarendon Press, 1925.

Longrigg, Stephen Hemsley. *Iraq, 1900 to 1950: A Political, Social and Economic History.* London: Oxford Univ. Press, 1953.

Luard, Evan, ed. *The International Regulation of Frontier Disputes.* New York: Praeger, 1970.

Maclean, Sir Fitzroy. *Current Soviet Trends.* A Lecture Presented on December 5, 1978. Middlebury, Vt.: Middlebury College Press, 1979.

McLaurin, R.D.; Mohammed Mughisuddin and Abraham R. Wagner. *Foreign Policy Making in the Middle East.* New York: Praeger, 1977.

McLaurin, R.D.; Don Peretz and Lewis W. Snider. *Middle East Foreign Policy.* New York: Praeger, 1982.

Mann, Major Clarence. *Abu Dhabi: Birth of an Oil Sheikdom.* Beirut: Khayats, 1964.

Marlowe, John. *The Persian Gulf in the Twentieth Century.* London: Cresset Press, 1962.

Martin, Bradford G. *German-Persian Diplomatic Relations, 1873–1912.* 'S-Gravenhage, The Netherlands: Mouton, 1959.

Martin, Lenore G. "A Systematic Study of Boundary Disputes in the Persian Gulf, 1900 to Present." Unpublished Ph.D. dissertation, University of Chicago, 1979.

Middle East and North Africa, The. 28th ed. London: Europa Publications, 1981.

The Military Balance 1983–84. London: International Institute for Strategic Studies, 1983.

Mughisuddin, Mohammed, ed. *Conflict and Cooperation in the Persian Gulf.* Praeger Special Studies. New York: Praeger, 1977.

Niblock, Tim, ed. *Social and Economic Development in the Arab Gulf.* London: Croom Helm, 1980.

Niblock, Tim, ed. *State, Society and Economy in Saudi Arabia*. New York: St. Martin's Press, 1982.

Novik, Nimrod. *On the Shores of Bab Al-Mandab*. Philadelphia: Foreign Policy Research Institute, 1979.

Noyes, James H. *The Clouded Lens*. Stanford, Calif.: Hoover Institution Press, 1979.

Nyrop, Richard F.; B.L. Benderly; L.N. Carter; D.R. Eglin; and R.A. Kirchner. *Area Handbook for Saudi Arabia*. Washington, D.C.: U.S. Government Printing Office, 1977.

Nyrop, Richard F.; B.L. Benderly; L.N. Carter; D.R. Eglin; R.A. Kirchner; and A.G. Wing. *Area Handbook for the Yemens*. Washington, D.C.: U.S. Government Printing Office, 1977.

Nyrop, Richard F., ed. *Iran: A Country Study*. Washington, D.C.: The American University, 1978.

Nyrop, Richard F., ed. *Iraq: A Country Study*. Foreign Area Studies. Washington, D.C.: U.S. Government Printing Office, 1979.

Nyrop, Richard F., and Foreign Area Studies of the American University. *Area Handbook for the Persian Gulf States*. Washington, D.C.: U.S. Government Printing Office, 1977.

Nyrop, Richard F., and Foreign Area Studies of the American University. *Area Handbook for Saudi Arabia*. Washington, D.C.: U.S. Government Printing Office, 1977.

Nyrop, Richard F., and Foreign Area Studies of the American University. *Area Handbook for the Yemens*. Washington, D.C.: U.S. Government Printing Office, 1977.

Peterson, J.E. *Oman in the Twentieth Century*. London: Croom Helm, 1978.

Peterson, J.E. *Yemen, the Search for a Modern State*. Baltimore: The Johns Hopkins Univ. Press, 1982.

Philby, H. St. John. *Saudi Arabia*. London: Ernest Benn, 1955.

Plascov, Avi. *Security in the Persian Gulf.: Modernization, Political Development and Stability*. vol. 3. The Institute for Strategic Studies. Montclair, N.J.: Allanheld and Osmun, 1982.

Price, David Lynn. *Oil and Middle East Security*. The Washington Papers, vol. 7, no. 41. Beverly Hills, Calif.: Sage Publications, 1976.

Quandt, William B. *Saudi Arabia in the 1980's*. Washington, D.C.: The Brookings Institution, 1981.

Quandt, William B. *Saudi Arabia's Oil Policy*. Washington, D.C.: The Brookings Institution, 1982.

Ramazani, Rouhollah V. *The Foreign Policy of Iran 1500–1941*. Charlottesville, Va.: Univ. Press of Virginia, 1966.

Record, Jeffrey. *The Rapid Deployment Force and U.S. Military In-*

tervention in the Persian Gulf. Cambridge, Mass.: Institute for Foreign Policy Analysis, Special Report, 1981.

Rubin, Barry. *Paved with Good Intentions.* New York: Oxford Univ. Press, 1980.

Searle, Pauline. *Dawn over Oman.* London: George Allen and Unwin, 1979.

Shaw, John A., and David E. Long. *Saudi Arabian Modernization.* New York: Praeger, 1982.

Short, Martin, and Anthony McDermott. *The Kurds.* London: Expedite Graphic, 1977.

Stempel, John D. *Inside the Iranian Revolution.* Indiana Univ. Press, 1981.

Strategic Survey 1982–1983. London: International Institute for Strategic Studies, 1983.

Stookey, Robert W. *Yemen.* Boulder, Colo.: Westview Press, 1978.

Tahtinen, Dale R. *National Security Challenges to Saudi Arabia.* Washington, D.C.: American Enterprise Institute for Public Policy Research, 1978.

Townsend, John. *Oman: The Making of a Modern State.* London: Croom Helm, 1977.

Twitchell, K.S. *Saudi Arabia,* 3d ed. Princeton, N.J.: Princeton Univ. Press, 1958.

U.S. Department of State. *U.S. Policy Toward the Persian Gulf.* Current Policy no. 390. May 10, 1982.

Wenner, Manfred W. *Modern Yemen 1918–1966.* Baltimore: Johns Hopkins Univ. Press, 1967.

Wohlstetter, Roberta. *Pearl Harbor: Warning and Decision.* Stanford, Calif.: Stanford Univ. Press, 1962.

Yergin, Daniel, and Martin Hillenbrand, eds. *Global Insecurity.* Boston: Houghton Mifflin, 1982.

Yodfat A., and M. Abir. *In the Direction of the Persian Gulf.* London: Frank Cass, 1977.

Yorke, Valerie. *The Gulf in the 1980's.* Chatham House Papers. England: Royal Institute of International Affairs, 1980.

Articles in Journals and Collections

Afrachteh, Kambiz. "Iran." In Mohammed Ayoob, ed., *The Politics of Islamic Reassertion.* London: Croom Helm, 1981, pp. 90–199.

Al-Bustany, Basil. "Iraq: Economic Developments." *American Enterprise Institute Foreign Policy and Defense Review* 2 (August 1980): 38–43.

Alm, Alvin L.; William Colglazier; and Barbara Kates-Garnick. "Coping with Interruptions." In David A. Deese and Joseph S. Nye, eds., *Energy and Security*. Cambridge, Mass.: Ballinger, 1981, pp. 303–46.

Amos, John W., II. "The Iraq–Iran War: Calculus of Regional Conflict." In David H. Partington, ed., *The Middle East Annual: Issues and Events,* vol. 1-1981. Boston: G.K. Hall, 1982, pp. 133–58.

Anthony, John Duke. "Insurrection and Intervention: The War in Dhofar." Abbas Amirie Institute for International Political and Economic Studies. Teheran, 1975.

Armed Forces Journal International. "North Yemen: The Shadow Game," "South Yemen: The Heart of Darkness," "The Key Message: Military Forces Can Do Little to Help Reduce the Risks of Western Dependence on Oil Imports." (November 1980): 75–86.

Batatu, Hanna. "Iraq's Underground Shi'a Movements: Characteristics, Causes and Prospects." *The Middle East Journal* 35 (Autumn 1981): 578–94.

Batatu, Hanna. "Iraq's Underground Shi'a Movements." *MERIP Reports* 12 (January 1982): 3–9.

Bazarian, Carl. "Bahrain and Qatar: Economic Developments." *American Enterprise Institute Foreign Policy and Defense Review* 2 (August 1980): 68–69.

Bazarian, Carl. "Kuwait: Economic Developments." *American Enterprise Institute Foreign Policy and Defense Review* 2 (August 1980): 50–55.

Bazarian, Carl. "United Arab Emirates: Economic Developments." *American Enterprise Institute Foreign Policy and Defense Review* 2 (August 1980): 61–64.

Beck, Lois. "Revolutionary Iran and Its Tribal Peoples." *MERIP Reports* 87 (1980): 14–20.

Blake, Gerald. "Maritime Aspects of Arabian Geopolitics." Arab Papers, no. 11. London: Arab Research Centre, 1982.

Bligh, Alexander, and Steven E. Plaut, "Saudi Moderation in Oil and Foreign Policies in the Post-AWACS-Sale Period." *Middle East Review* 14 (Spring-Summer 1982): 24–32.

Brown, William R. "The Oil Weapon." *The Middle East Journal* 36 (Summer 1982): 301–18.

Burrell, R.M. "Policies of the Arab Littoral States in the Persian Gulf Region," ed. Abbas Amirie. *The Persian Gulf and Indian Ocean in International Politics*. Teheran: Institute for Political and Economic Studies, 1975, pp. 227–55.

Chubin, Shahram. "U.S. Security Interests in the Persian Gulf in the 1980's." *Daedalus* (Fall 1980): 31–66.

Chubin, Shahram. "The Soviet Union and Iran." *Foreign Affairs* 61 (Spring 1983): 921–49.

Collins, Michael. "Riyadh: The Saud Balance." *Washington Quarterly* 4 (Winter 1981): 200–208.

Cordesman, Anthony H. "Lessons of the Iran–Iraq War: The First Round." *Armed Forces Journal International* (April 1982): 32–47.

Cordesman, Anthony H. "The Iraq–Iran War: Attrition Now, Chaos Later." *Armed Forces Journal International* (May 1983): 36–117.

Cordesman, Anthony H. "Oman: The Guardian of the Eastern Gulf." *Armed Forces Journal International* (June 1983): 22–31.

Dawisha, Adeed. "Iraq: The West's Opportunity." *Foreign Policy* (Winter 1980–81): 134–53.

Dawisha, Adeed. "Iran's Mullahs and the Arab Masses." *Washington Quarterly* 6 (Summer 1983): 162–168.

Dawisha, Karen. "The U.S.S.R. and the Middle East: Superpower in Eclipse?" *Foreign Affairs* 61 (Winter 1982–83): 438–52.

Deese, David A. "Oil, War, and Grand Strategy." *Orbis* 25 (Fall 1981): 525–56.

Dunn, Keith A. "Constraints on the USSR in Southwest Asia: A Military Analysis." *Orbis* 25 (Fall 1981): 607–630.

Ebinger, Charles K. "Oil Glut Psychology." *Vital Speeches of the Day* 49 (August 15, 1983): 642–45.

Eilts, Hermann F. "Security Considerations in the Persian Gulf." *International Security* 5 (Fall 1980): 79–113.

Entessar, Nadar. "Arab Factions in Post-Revolutionary Iranian Politics." *Middle East Review* 12 (Spring 1980): 52–54.

Erb, Richard D. "The Gulf Oil Producers: Overview and Oil Policy Implications." *American Enterprise Institute Foreign Policy and Defense Review* 2 (August 1980): 5–13.

Erb, Richard D. "Saudi Arabia: Economic Developments." *American Enterprise Institute Foreign Policy and Defense Review* 2 (August 1980): 21–29.

Erb, Richard D., and Nebin N. Al-Shawaf. "Economic Intergration: Nascent Linkages." *American Enterprise Institute Foreign Policy and Defense Review* 2 (August 1980): 70–76.

Feer, Frederic S. "Problems of Oil Supply Disruptions in the Persian Gulf." In George Horwich and Edward Mitchell, eds., *Policies for Coping with Oil Supply Disruptions*. Washington, D.C.: American Enterprise Institute for Public Policy Research, 1982, pp. 11–30.

Feith, Douglas J. "Love and Oil." *The New Republic* (November 22, 1980): 20–23.

Feith, Douglas J. "The Oil Weapon De-Mystified." *Policy Review* 15 (Winter 1981): 19–39.

Foster, Joe B. "What We Learned from Oil's Boom and Bust: The Market Works." *Vital Speeches of the Day* 49 (August 15, 1983): 645–48.

Freedman, Robert O. "Soviet Policy toward Ba'athist Iraq 1968–1979." In Robert H. Donaldson, ed., *The Soviet Union in the Third World: Successes and Failures.* Boulder, Colo.: Westview Press, 1981, pp. 161–91.

Gail, Bridget (pseud.). "The World Oil Crisis and U.S. Power Projection Policy: The Threat Becomes a Reality." *Armed Forces Journal International* (January 1980): 25–30.

Gault, John. "Middle Eastern Oil Producers: New Strength or New Vulnerability?" In David H. Partington, ed., *The Middle East Annual: Issues and Events,* vol. 1-1981. Boston: G.K. Hall, 1982, pp. 159–91.

Goldmuntz, Lawrence. "Lower Oil Prices Are Needed." *Middle East Insight* 3 (1983): 19–22.

Gottesman, Lois. "Saudi Arabia: OPEC Giant with Feet of Clay." *Middle East Review* 15 (Spring-Summer 1983): 68–72.

Halliday, Fred. "Current Soviet Policy and the Middle East." *MERIP Reports* 13 (January 1983): 18–22.

Hanks, Robert J. "Oil and Security in U.S. Policy toward the Arabian Gulf–Indian Ocean Area." *Oil and Security in the Arab Gulf.* Arab Papers no. 5. London: Arab Research Centre, 1980.

Harrison, Selig. "Baluch National and Superpower Rivalry." *International Security* 5 (Winter 1980–81): 152–63.

Hill, Alan G. "Population, Migration and Development in the Gulf States," *Security in the Persian Gulf 1: Domestic Political Factors,* ed. Shahram Chubin (Montclair, N.J.: Allanheld Osmun, 1981): 58–83.

Hirschfeld, Yair, P. "Moscow and Khomeini: Soviet–Iranian Relations in Historical Perspective." *Orbis* 24 (Summer 1980): 219–40.

Hollingsworth, James F., and Allan T. Wood. "The Light Armored Corps—A Strategic Necessity." *Armed Forces Journal International* (January 1980): 20–24.

Honigman, Gerald A. "British Petroleum Politics, Arab Nationalism and the Kurds." *Middle East Review* 15 (Fall-Winter 1982–83): 33–39.

Hooglund, Eric. "Rural Participation in the Revolution." *MERIP Reports* 87 (1980): 3–6.

Irani, Robert G. "Changes in Soviet Policy toward Iran." In Robert H. Donaldson, ed., *The Soviet Union in the Third World: Successes and Failures.* Boulder, Colo.: Westview Press, 1981, pp. 192–207.

Ismael, Tareq Y. "The Middle East: A Subordinate System in Global Politics." In Ismael, ed., *The Middle East in World Politics.* Syracuse, N.Y.: Syracuse Univ. Press, 1974, pp. 240–56.

Janka, Les. "Security Risks and Reactions." *American Enterprise Institute Foreign Policy and Defense Review* 2 (August 1980): 82–88.

Kelly, J. B. "A Response to Hermann Eilts' 'Security Considerations in the Persian Gulf'." *International Security* 5 (Spring 1981): 186–203 (includes Eilts' "A Rejoinder to J.B. Kelly" pp. 195–203).

Kemp, Geoffrey. "Military Force and Middle East Oil." In David A. Deese and Joseph S. Nye, eds., *Energy and Security*. Cambridge, Mass.: Ballinger, 1981, pp. 365–87.

Khoury, Nabeel A. "The Pragmatic Trend in Inter-Arab Politics." *Middle East Journal* 36 (Summer 1982): 374–87.

Khuri, Fuad I. *Tribe and State in Bahrain*. Chicago: Univ. of Chicago Press, 1980.

Klinghoffer, Arthur Jay. "U.S. Foreign Policy and the Soviet Energy Predicament." *Orbis* 25 (Fall 1981): 557–78.

Knauerhase, Ramon. "Saudi Arabia: Fifty Years of Economic Change." *Current History* (January 1983): 19–23.

Koury, Enver M. "The Impact of the Geopolitical Situation of Iraq upon the Gulf Cooperation Council." *Middle East Insight* 2 (1983): 28–35.

Kroft, Joseph. "Letter from Baghdad." *The New Yorker,* October 20, 1980, pp. 140–65.

Lantzke, Ulf. "Toward A Coherant Energy Strategy." *Washington Quarterly* 6 (Winter 1983): 66–70.

Levy, Walter J. "Oil: An Agenda for the 1980's." *Foreign Affairs* 59 (Summer 1981): 1079–1101.

MacIntyre, Ronald R. "Saudi Arabia." In Mohammed Ayoob, ed., *The Politics of Islamic Reassertion*. London: Croom Helm, 1981, pp. 9–29.

Mansur, Abdul Karim (pseud.). "The American Threat to Saudi Arabia." *Armed Forces Journal International* (September 1980): 47–60.

Marr, Phebe. "Iraq: Sociopolitical Developments." *American Enterprise Institute Foreign Policy and Defense Review* 2 (August 1980): 30–37.

Melamid, Alexander. "The Shatt al'Arab Boundary." *Middle East Journal* 22 (1968): 350–57.

Menon, P.K. "Settlement of International Boundary Disputes." *Anglo-American Law Review* 24, no. 8 (1979).

MERIP Reports. "Our Strategy for the Persian Gulf." *MERIP Reports* 12 (May 1982): 16–21.

Middle East International. "Military Linkage." *Middle East International,* no. 200 (May 13, 1983), pp. 8, 9.

Nakhleh, Emile. "Political Relations among the Arab Gulf States: Developments and Prospects." *American Enterprise Institute Foreign Policy and Defense Review* 2 (August 1980): 77–81.

Newsom, David D. "America Engulfed." *Foreign Policy* (Summer 1981): 17–32.

Nye, Joseph S. "Energy and Security." In David A. Deese and Joseph S. Nye, eds., *Energy and Security*. Cambridge, Mass.: Ballinger, 1981, pp. 3–22.

Nye, Joseph S.; David A. Deese; and Alvin L. Alm. "A U.S. Strategy for Energy Security," In David A. Deese and Joseph S. Nye, eds., *Energy and Security*. Cambridge, Mass.: Ballinger, 1981, pp. 391–424.

O'Ballance, Edgar. "Khuzistan: Another Casus Belli?" *Army Quarterly and Defense Journal* 110 (April 1980): 139–144.

Olson, William J. "The Successor Crisis in Iran." *Washington Quarterly* 6 (Summer 1983): 156–61.

O'Neill, Bard E., and William Brundage. "Revolutionary Warfare in Oman: A Strategic Appraisal." *Middle East Review* 10 (Summer 1978): 48–56.

Pipes, Daniel. " 'This World is Political!!' The Islamic Revival of the Seventies." *Orbis* 24 (Spring 1980): 9–42.

Pipes, Daniel. "Increasing Security in the Persian Gulf." *Orbis* 26 (Spring 1982): 30–34.

Plummer, James L. "United States Oil Stockpiling Policy." *Journal of Contemporary Studies* 4 (Spring 1981): 5–22.

Rouleau, Eric. "Khomeini's Iran." *Foreign Affairs* 59 (Fall 1980): 1–20.

Rowen, Henry S., and John P. Weyant. "Oil and National Security: An Integrated Program for Surviving an Oil Crisis." In Jack M. Hollander, Melvin K. Simmons, and David O. Wood, eds.: *Annual Review of Energy*, vol. 6, Palo Alto, Calif.: Annual Reviews, 1981, pp. 171–98.

Rubin, Barry. "Iran, the Ayotollah, and U.S. Options." *Washington Quarterly* 6 (Summer 1983): 142–55.

Rubinstein, Alvin Z. "The Evolution of Soviet Strategy in the Middle East." *Orbis* 24 (Summer 1980): 323–338.

Rubinstein, Alvin Z. "The Soviet Union's Imperial Policy in the Middle East." *Middle East Review* 15 (Fall-Winter 1982–83): 19–24.

Ruskiewicz, John J. "How the U.S. Lost Its Footing in the Shifting Sands of the Persian Gulf—A Case History in the Yemen Arab Republic." *Armed Forces Journal International* (September 1980): 62–72.

Salameh, Ghassane. "Political Power and the Saudi State." *MERIP Reports* 91 (October 1980): 5–23.

Schechterman, Bernard. "Political Instability in Saudi Arabia and Its Implications." *Middle East Review* 14 (Fall-Winter 1981–82): 15–23.

Schuler, G. Henry M. "Coping with Oil Dependence." *Washington Quarterly* 6 (Winter 1983): 53–59.

Sciolino, Elaine. "Iran's Durable Revolution." *Foreign Affairs* 61 (Spring 1983): 893–920.

Sevian, Vahe. "The Evolution of the Boundary between Iraq and Iran." In Charles Fischer, ed., *Essays in Political Geography*. London: Methuen, 1968, pp. 211–223.

Singer, S. Fred, and Stephen Stamas. "An End to OPEC?" *Foreign Policy* (Winter 1981–82): 115–25.

Smart, Ian. "Energy and the Powers of Nations." In Daniel Yergin and Martin Hillenbrand, eds., *Global Insecurity*. Boston: Houghton Mifflin, 1982, pp. 349–76.

Smolansky, Oles M. "The Kremlin and the Iraqi Ba'th, 1968–1982: An Influence Relationship." *Middle East Review* 15 (Spring-Summer 1983): 62–67.

Springborg, Robert. "Egypt, Syria and Iraq." In Mohammed Ayoob, ed., *The Politics of Islamic Reassertion*. London: Croom Helm, 1981, pp. 30–54.

Stobaugh, Robert. "World Energy in the Year 2000." In Daniel Yergin and Martin Hillenbrand, eds., *Global Insecurity*. Boston: Houghton Mifflin, 1982, pp. 29–59.

Stookey, Robert W. "Red Sea Gate-Keepers: The Yemen Arab Republic and the People's Democratic Republic of Yemen." *Middle East Review* 10 (Summer 1978): 39–47.

Stork, Joe. "Saudi Oil and the U.S.: Special Relationship under Stress." *MERIP Reports* 91 (October 1980) pp. 24–29.

Stork, Joe, and Jim Paul. "Arms Sales and the Militarization of the Middle East." *MERIP Reports* 13 (February 1983): 5–15.

Swearingen, Will D. "Sources of Conflict over Oil in the Persian/Arabian Gulf." *Middle East Journal* 35 (1981): 314–30.

Tahir-Kheli, Shirin, and William O. Staudenmaier. "The Saudi-Pakistani Military Relationship: Implications for U.S. Policy." *Orbis* 26 (Spring 1982): 155–71.

Thompson, W. Scott. "The Persian Gulf and the Correlation of Forces." *International Security* 7 (Summer 1982): 157–80.

Tomasek, Robert D. "The Resolution of Major Controversies between Iran and Iraq." *World Affairs* 139 (1976–77): 206–30.

Torrey, Gordon H. "The Ba'th Ideology and Practice." *Middle East Journal* 23 (Autumn 1969): 445–70.

Tussing, Arlon R. "An OPEC Obituary." *Public Interest* (Winter 1983):
    3–21.
Van Hollen, Christopher. "Don't Engulf the Gulf." *Foreign Affairs* 59
    (Summer 1981): 1064–78.
Van Hollen, Christopher. "North Yemen: A Dangerous Pentagonal
    Game." *Washington Quarterly* 15 (Summer 1982): 137–42.
Walsh, L. Thomas. "Bab-el-Mandeb: The Gateway of Tears for the
    U.S.?" *Armed Forces Journal International* (September 1980): 74–
    76.
Waltz, Kenneth N. "A Strategy for the Rapid Deployment Force."
    International Security 5 (Spring 1981): 49–73.
Winder, Bayly. "Saudi Arabia: Sociopolitical Developments." *Amer-
    ican Enterprise Institute Foreign Policy and Defense Review* 2 (Au-
    gust 1980): 14–26.
Wohlstetter, Albert. "Meeting the Threat in the Persian Gulf." *Survey*
    25 (Spring 1980): 128–188.
Wright, Claudia. "Iraq: New Power in the Middle East." *Foreign Af-
    fairs* 58 (Winter 1979): 257–77.

Newspapers and Periodicals

Businessweek

Christian Science Monitor

Defense and Foreign Affairs Daily

Economist (London)

Economist Intelligence Unit (London)
    Quarterly Economic Review of:
    Bahrain, Qatar, Oman, The Yemens
    Egypt
    Kuwait
    Iran
    Iraq
    Saudi Arabia
    United Arab Emirates

Financial Times (London)

Foreign Broadcast Information Service
Middle East and North Africa

The Guardian (London)

Joint Publication Research Service
Middle East and North Africa

Keesings Contemporary Archives

Middle East (London)

Middle East Annual

Middle East Economic Digest (London)

Mideast File

Newsweek

New York Times

Time

Wall Street Journal

Washington Post

Weekly Media Abstract (Jerusalem)

Index

Abadan Island, 36, 38, 41, 66
'Abbās Mutrī, 85
'Abd al-'Azīz ibn 'Abd al-Rahmān Āl Sa'ūd. *See* Ibn Saud
'Abd Allāh al-Qahstānī, Muhammad ibn, 84
Abu Arish, Yemen, 55
Abu Dhabi: and Iran, 50; and Qatar, 63, 72–73; and Saudi Arabia, 19, 51, 52, 61, 63, 71; as member of UAE, 63–64
Abu Musa (island), 23, 24, 39, 48, 49, 73
Abu Nuayr (island), 50
Abu Safah, 54, 72
Aden, 15–21 *passim,* 51–60 *passim,* 86, 102, 125. *See also* South Yemen
Afars (Djibouti), 126
Afghanistan, 20, 91; and USSR, 27, 41, 112, 118, 119, 122
'Aflaq, Michel, 99
Afshars (Iran), 93
Akr, Muhammad ad, 81
Al-Ahwaz (formerly called Hawiza) (Iran), 35, 41
Al-Ahwaz Liberation Front, 40, 93
Al-Arabiyah (island), 45
Al-Ayn, Abu Dhabi, 61
Āl Bū Sa'id dynasty (Oman), 50
Al-Da'wah al-Islāmīyah (the "Islamic call"), 79, 80
Al-Ghaydah (South Yemen), 61
Al-Hasa (Ottoman Empire), 14, 15, 17, 19, 36
Āl Khalīfaha (Bahrain), 47, 62, 81
Āl Makhtūm sheikhs (Dubai), 64
Al Niyahan sheikhs, 64
Āl Nu'aym tribe (Qatar), 62
Āl Sabāh family (Kuwait), 14
Āl Thāni sheikhs (Qatar), 62
Alaskan oil, 145, 147
Algeria, 69
Algiers Agreement (1975), 24, 33, 36, 39–40, 41, 42, 43, 47, 66, 89, 110, 122, 123
'Ali, 77, 78
'Alī Nasser Muhammad, 103, 105

'Alī, Sālim Rabī, 102
Alien populations, 87, 88, 93–96, 113
Aminoil, 73
Anglo-Iranian Agreement (1919), 18
Anglo-Iranian Treaty (1929), 18, 47
Anglo-Iraqi Treaty (1922), 18
Anglo-Iraqi Treaty (1930), 18
Arab-Israeli wars. *See* October War; Six Day War
Arab League, 22, 46, 47, 59
Arab nationalism, 96, 99, 102, 103, 105, 106, 113, 114, 115
Arab Nationalist Movement (ANM) (renamed Popular Front for the Liberation of Palestine), 102, 104, 105
Arabestan. *See* Khuzestan
Arabic Peninsula Peoples Union, 101
Arabs, 47, 95; in Iran, 40, 41, 82, 90, 92–93, 112, 163
Aramco (Arabian American Oil Company), 52, 143
'Ārif, 'Abd al-Sālam, 100
Armenia, 88
Aseb, Ethiopia, 126
Ashura, defined, 83
Asian population, 95
Asir, Yemen, 17, 54, 55, 57
Association of Arabs of the Gulf (1936), 43
AWACS, 26, 129, 132
Ayatollah, defined, 77
Azerbaijan/Azerbaijanis, 18, 22, 35, 90, 91, 93, 109, 111–112, 119, 120, 130
'Aziz, Tariq, 80

Bab al-Mandab, 2, 5, 19, 58, 65, 119, 124, 125, 126, 128
Badrah, Iraq, 39
Baghdad, 15, 20, 34, 80
Baghdad Pact (1955), 21, 22, 38, 127. *See also* CENTO
Baghdad Railway, 15, 16, 36
Bahais, 82
Bahrain, 6, 15, 23, 27, 52, 96; and Iran, 33, 47–48, 65, 66, 67, 71,

219

About the Author

Lenore G. Martin is an associate professor and chairperson of the Department of Political Science at Emmanuel College in Boston. She received her Ph.D. from the University of Chicago in 1979 and is a faculty associate of the Center for Middle Eastern Studies at Harvard University.